# Shopping List of Non-Tools to Keep Around for Repairs

- **All-purpose utility knife:** A myriad of uses and handy when you're doing a fix-it project.

- **Bin or Klitz sealer:** The only two primer/sealers that seal water-stained drywall or cover crayon, ink, and felt-pen marks on walls. Nothing else can match them.

- **Bleach:** Not just for laundry, it works great on grout, mildew, stains, and minor drain blockages. Never mix it with ammonia; the two make a toxic gas that's dangerous to inhale.

- **Brushes:** Get soft-bristle brushes to remove dust and small particles.

- **Clamps:** Ratchet straps, a variety of plastic or metal clip-type clamps, and one or two C-clamps of different sizes come in handy for a variety of fix-it projects. Ratchet straps are also great for securing mattresses on the roof of a car and maneuvering large appliances.

- **Duct tape:** Okay, you can laugh, but once you have it around you'll find ingenious ways to use it — and probably never for wrapping air ducts!

- **Dum Dum toy putty:** We're serious! This putty never hardens and although developed for puttying windows, it's great for keeping pictures and mirrors level and temporarily securing photos and posters. It doesn't damage paint or paper.

- **Masking tape:** Don't settle for one width; you'll inevitably wish you had the other as well.

- **Old toothbrushes:** Use them to clean the gaskets sealing refrigerators, freezers, and ovens, scour around faucets, and get paint and dirt out of crevices.

- **Plunger:** Use it to unblock drains and toilets.

- **Putty knife:** Use this non-tool tool for fix-its, scraping wallpaper, stripping furniture, getting under surfaces. You'll use it a lot.

- **Rulers and yardsticks:** These are an absolute necessity if you want to cut wood, drywall, or anything else. If you splurge just a little, you can get metal rulers that won't snap or break.

- **Sandpaper:** Buy an assortment from very fine grit to coarse grit and you'll have them available when you're working on a project.

- **Single-edge razor blades:** One small package will last a long time because they're reusable, especially after scraping paint splatters off glass.

- **Steel wool:** You don't need a lot, just fine, medium, and coarse grades.

- **Stud finder:** Stop guessing where to drive a nail into the wall. It locates nails under your drywall, and thus, the stud.

- **Two-way tape:** Also called carpet tape, this holds down throw rugs and, temporarily, loose carpeting and vinyl. You'll find other uses as well.

- **WD-40:** Use one or two drops on hinges, locks, and anything else needing lubrication.

- **White vinegar:** Use it on rugs and tablecloths when someone spills red wine.

# How to Fix Everything For Dummies®

Cheat Sheet

## Things to Ask a Contractor or Repair Specialist

When you have to work with a professional, you need to know exactly what the job entails, especially if you're asking for bids. If you don't get the answers you want, then move on to someone else. Also, before you sign a contract, take time to call the Better Business Bureau to find out whether there are any complaints against this contractor or specialist. If the contractor works on your home, you also can call to verify that he or she is a member of the local professional organization as claimed.

- ✔ **Do you have a list of referrals?** Ask for names and phone numbers of people that had similar work that the contractor or specialist completed.

- ✔ **How long have you been in business?** Sometimes contractors want to retire and sell an established business with a good reputation, but there's no guarantee that the new owner will know as much or be as good.

- ✔ **Can I see your certificates of insurance?** You want to know that the contractor is licensed and bonded, and that he or she carries workman's compensation insurance.

- ✔ **Who will do the actual work, the contractor, an employee, or an independent contractor retained by the company?** If the contractor outsources the job, that might entail potential risk on your part if that person is injured.

- ✔ **Can I have a detailed contract?** It should describe the project in detail and what materials and products will be used, as well as labor costs, and the contractor's name, address, phone number, and license numbers with the city and state.

- ✔ **Can I buy the materials myself and get them delivered to my home?** You can save money that way.

- ✔ **How long will the project take?** Get a specific date for starting and ending the project.

- ✔ **Who is responsible for cleaning up after the project is completed?** If it's the contractor, make sure you have it in writing.

- ✔ **Is a building permit needed for the work?** Make sure the contractor will get it.

- ✔ **Can I have a warranty on work and materials?** Is it a full warranty on repair or replacement of the product and for how long — 90 days or a year?

- ✔ **Can I establish a payment schedule for work that will take some time to complete?** Never agree to pay all costs up front because if you're dissatisfied with the work, you'll never be able to get the contractor back to your home.

Wiley, the Wiley Publishing logo, For Dummies, the Dummies Man logo, the For Dummies Bestselling Book Series logo and all related trade dress are trademarks or registered trademarks of John Wiley & Sons, Inc. and/or its affiliates. All other trademarks are property of their respective owners.

Copyright © 2005 Wiley Publishing, Inc. All rights reserved.
Item 7209-1.
For more information about Wiley Publishing, call 1-800-762-2974.

*For Dummies: Bestselling Book Series for Beginners*

# How to Fix Everything

## FOR DUMMIES®

**by Gary and Peg Hedstrom**
Home Repair Experts

**&**

**Judy Ondrla Tremore**

**WILEY**

Wiley Publishing, Inc.

MAY 1 8 2005

2394486

**How to Fix Everything For Dummies®**

Published by
**Wiley Publishing, Inc.**
111 River St.
Hoboken, NJ 07030-5774
www.wiley.com

Copyright © 2005 by Wiley Publishing, Inc., Indianapolis, Indiana

Published by Wiley Publishing, Inc., Indianapolis, Indiana

Published simultaneously in Canada

No part of this publication may be reproduced, stored in a retrieval system, or transmitted in any form or by any means, electronic, mechanical, photocopying, recording, scanning, or otherwise, except as permitted under Sections 107 or 108 of the 1976 United States Copyright Act, without either the prior written permission of the Publisher, or authorization through payment of the appropriate per-copy fee to the Copyright Clearance Center, 222 Rosewood Drive, Danvers, MA 01923, 978-750-8400, fax 978-646-8600. Requests to the Publisher for permission should be addressed to the Legal Department, Wiley Publishing, Inc., 10475 Crosspoint Blvd., Indianapolis, IN 46256, (317) 572-3447, fax (317) 572-4355, or online at http://www.wiley.com/go/permissions.

**Trademarks:** Wiley, the Wiley Publishing logo, For Dummies, the Dummies Man logo, A Reference for the Rest of Us!, The Dummies Way, Dummies Daily, The Fun and Easy Way, Dummies.com, and related trade dress are trademarks or registered trademarks of John Wiley & Sons, Inc., and/or its affiliates in the United States and other countries, and may not be used without written permission. All other trademarks are the property of their respective owners. Wiley Publishing, Inc., is not associated with any product or vendor mentioned in this book.

LIMIT OF LIABILITY/DISCLAIMER OF WARRANTY: THE PUBLISHER AND THE AUTHOR MAKE NO REPRESENTATIONS OR WARRANTIES WITH RESPECT TO THE ACCURACY OR COMPLETENESS OF THE CONTENTS OF THIS WORK AND SPECIFICALLY DISCLAIM ALL WARRANTIES, INCLUDING WITHOUT LIMITATION WARRANTIES OF FITNESS FOR A PARTICULAR PURPOSE. NO WARRANTY MAY BE CREATED OR EXTENDED BY SALES OR PROMOTIONAL MATERIALS. THE ADVICE AND STRATEGIES CONTAINED HEREIN MAY NOT BE SUITABLE FOR EVERY SITUATION. THIS WORK IS SOLD WITH THE UNDERSTANDING THAT THE PUBLISHER IS NOT ENGAGED IN RENDERING LEGAL, ACCOUNTING, OR OTHER PROFESSIONAL SERVICES. IF PROFESSIONAL ASSISTANCE IS REQUIRED, THE SERVICES OF A COMPETENT PROFESSIONAL PERSON SHOULD BE SOUGHT. NEITHER THE PUBLISHER NOR THE AUTHOR SHALL BE LIABLE FOR DAMAGES ARISING HEREFROM. THE FACT THAT AN ORGANIZATION OR WEBSITE IS REFERRED TO IN THIS WORK AS A CITATION AND/OR A POTENTIAL SOURCE OF FURTHER INFORMATION DOES NOT MEAN THAT THE AUTHOR OR THE PUBLISHER ENDORSES THE INFORMATION THE ORGANIZATION OR WEBSITE MAY PROVIDE OR RECOMMENDATIONS IT MAY MAKE. FURTHER, READERS SHOULD BE AWARE THAT INTERNET WEBSITES LISTED IN THIS WORK MAY HAVE CHANGED OR DISAPPEARED BETWEEN WHEN THIS WORK WAS WRITTEN AND WHEN IT IS READ.

For general information on our other products and services, please contact our Customer Care Department within the U.S. at 800-762-2974, outside the U.S. at 317-572-3993, or fax 317-572-4002.

For technical support, please visit www.wiley.com/techsupport.

Wiley also publishes its books in a variety of electronic formats. Some content that appears in print may not be available in electronic books.

Library of Congress Control Number: 2005923207

ISBN: 0-7645-7209-1

Manufactured in the United States of America

10 9 8 7 6 5 4 3 2 1

1O/RR/QU/QV/IN

WILEY

# About the Authors

Do-it-yourself experts **Gary and Peg Hedstrom** extensively remodeled six houses and built two from scratch, doing all the work themselves. A retired diesel mechanic, Gary describes himself as a jack-of-all-trades who's happiest taking things apart to see how they're built and putting them back together. He hates sitting still and willingly shares his knowledge with others so they can fix things themselves. Peg liked to get her hands "dirty," as she puts it, fixing appliances and discarded televisions long before she met Gary. So she willingly tackled everything else once she and Gary started working on homes. Her favorite pastime, however, is restoring wood and old, damaged furniture, as well as doing the finishing touches in a home. Lifelong Michigan residents, the couple has homes in Grand Rapids and Florida.

**Judy Ondrla Tremore,** a veteran reporter and business writer, wrote two books and co-authored another before writing *How to Fix Everything For Dummies*. Her articles and stories have appeared in *The Grand Rapids Press, Cadence* (where she was managing editor), *Legal Assistant Today, Grand Rapids Business Journal, Grand Rapids Magazine, Cosmopolitan Home, Our Children, Applause,* and several other Michigan and Illinois publications. She was the Grand Rapids editor of *Metropolitan Woman*. Among her favorite articles were those pertaining to home improvement and design and restoration projects, because they dovetail with her deep interest in architecture and homes. She grew up in the Chicago area and has lived in Michigan for more than 30 years.

# Dedication

We dedicate this book to you, the readers, in hopes that you will find it a useful resource for a number of years and that you will progress from a new do-it-yourselfer to one who is willing and able to tackle just about any project in your home.

# Authors' Acknowledgments

Many thanks Jane Haradine, who was instrumental in bringing together home repair experts Gary and Peg Hedstrom and Judy Tremore. We've enjoyed working as a team to write this book. Thank you Frank J. Varada and Ray Simpson for sharing your extensive knowledge about communication and entertainment equipment in Chapter 12.

Thanks Shane Hedstrom for contributing to Chapter 8.

Thanks to the cheerful, helpful, and patient editors at Wiley, Natalie Harris, project editor; Jennifer Bingham, copy editor; John Zerbo, technical editor; Tracy Boggier, acquisitions editor; and the art department. Thanks also to Jessica Faust at Bookends, LLC.

And thanks John Tremore — proofreader, commentator, and contributor.

## Publisher's Acknowledgments

We're proud of this book; please send us your comments through our Dummies online registration form located at www.dummies.com/register/.

Some of the people who helped bring this book to market include the following:

*Acquisitions, Editorial, and Media Development*

**Project Editor:** Natalie Faye Harris

**Acquisitions Editor:** Tracy Boggier

**Copy Editor:** Jennifer Bingham

**Editorial Program Assistant:** Courtney Allen

**Technical Reviewer:** John Zerbo

**Senior Permissions Editor:** Carmen Krikorian

**Editorial Managers:** Christine Beck, Michelle Hacker

**Editorial Assistants:** Nadine Bell, Melissa Bennett

**Cartoons:** Rich Tennant, www.the5thwave.com

*Production*

**Project Coordinator:** Adrienne Martinez

**Layout and Graphics:** Karl Brandt, Carl Byers, Andrea Dahl, Kelly Emkow, Denny Hager, Joyce Haughey, Barry Offringa, Rashell Smith, Mary Gillot Virgin

**Proofreaders:** Laura Albert, Leeann Harney, Joe Niesen, TECHBOOKS Production Services

**Indexer:** TECHBOOKS Production Services

**Publishing and Editorial for Consumer Dummies**

    **Diane Graves Steele,** Vice President and Publisher, Consumer Dummies

    **Joyce Pepple,** Acquisitions Director, Consumer Dummies

    **Kristin A. Cocks,** Product Development Director, Consumer Dummies

    **Michael Spring,** Vice President and Publisher, Travel

    **Kelly Regan,** Editorial Director, Travel

**Publishing for Technology Dummies**

    **Andy Cummings,** Vice President and Publisher, Dummies Technology/General User

**Composition Services**

    **Gerry Fahey,** Vice President of Production Services

    **Debbie Stailey,** Director of Composition Services

# Contents at a Glance

# Table of Contents

# Introduction

*I*n a perfect world, after we finish fixing up our homes and then decorating them, everything would stay the same until we decided to change colors, replace furniture, or do some extensive remodeling. In the real world, we know that doesn't happen. Even if you never break or bump anything yourself, faucets start dripping, an appliance stops working, stairs start to creak, chair legs wobble, the roof leaks, doors won't lock, and nails pop out of drywall. We can all add to the annoying list of things that perpetually seem to need fixing. Most breakdowns in a home are caused by normal wear and tear on all of the components. But fix-its are also necessary when an errant baseball flies through a window, someone scratches or stains a table, or a toy punctures a hole in the drywall.

Most frustrating of all, breakdowns inevitably occur at the least convenient moment. If we want to tip towards paranoia, we'd say the washer detects we have a mountain of laundry to do and is saying, "Gotcha!" The furnace reminds us how much we need it on the coldest, windiest weekends. And of course, it's always sultry outdoors when the air conditioner goes out.

*How to Fix Everything For Dummies* is full of step-by-step instructions designed to help do-it-yourselfers — novices or those with some experience — to repair and fix many of the things that go wrong in their homes. Because this fix-it book also delves into fixing personal household items, small appliances, and furniture, it's a book that both homeowners and apartment dwellers can use.

We include tips about what typically goes wrong and give you a sequence of repairs from very easy to more difficult when we can. If your first attempt isn't successful, you can progress to another that may be slightly more complicated or time-consuming.

*How to Fix Everything For Dummies* will be a lifelong friend to keep in your home, long after you become a skilled do-it-yourselfer. If you consult it frequently, you'll rarely have to wait for a service call or pay for service on a simple repair that you could have handled yourself. Best of all, it will keep you grounded — those frustrating, but laughable gaffes happen to everyone. It's not just you!

# Foolish Assumptions

In this book we assume that up until now you've been interested in fixing things around the house but aren't sure how to proceed, or you have some experience but need some guidance on tackling more repairs. We assume your home is slowly accumulating things that sometimes need to be repaired. And we assume you may be afraid to tackle some repairs because they may take more time than you have to spare. Or you may be more worried that a project will be too complicated for you to finish. We also assume that you may be frustrated about throwing things away because you don't know where to go to repair them, or you get irritated when you have to pay for service calls when all that was wrong was a minor adjustment. If you fall into any of these categories, this book is for you.

# How to Use This Book

Every breakdown in your home occurs randomly. One day it may be a leaky faucet, weeks later, a broken window. That's why the format of *How to Fix Everything For Dummies* is perfect for do-it-yourselfers. You don't have to read a whole chapter about fixing plumbing or working on windows to get exactly what you need at the moment you most need it. The detailed Table of Contents leads you right to the spots designed to give you step-by-step instructions for repairing almost everything. And it gives you alternatives, too. You can start out with the easiest fix-it, and then progress to a repair that's a little more difficult if the first one doesn't work. This book also provides information about safety, tools, tips, and warnings, as well as about when it's best to call in a skilled professional or to replace an appliance, for instance.

This book is organized so that each chapter focuses on logical components of a home: doors and windows, floors and stairs, walls and ceilings, and plumbing, for instance. Throughout the book, new words are *italicized,* followed up by an explanation of what they mean. Each part explains what typically goes wrong and what to look for. You'll find out how to recognize what's causing the problem and the tools and equipment you need to repair it. And you'll find the steps highlighted in **bold**. Additional details and information are included in regular text.

# What You're Not to Read

You don't have to read a whole chapter about floors and stairs — unless you really want to — if all you're concerned about is silencing a squeak. You don't have to read the basic information about tools and how to use them if you're well acquainted with your father's workshop. You don't have to read the introduction to each chapter (but thanks if you do!). And you don't have to read the beginning text in each section. If you do, however, we think you'll have a better understanding of what you're dealing with. In other words, you can concentrate only on the steps that explain *How to Fix Everything* in your home and find the book a valuable text.

# How This Book Is Organized

Like all books in the *For Dummies* series, *How to Fix Everything For Dummies* is divided into parts, and each part has chapters that start with an overview of the content that follows. Headlines enumerate specific problems you'll encounter, and when there are several different causes, they are highlighted individually as subtopics. Two other ways to find the specific information you need quickly are to refer to the detailed Table of Contents and the Index.

## Part 1: Gearing Up to Fix Everything

Whether you want to fix a leaky faucet or repair the legs on a favorite piece of furniture, you need the tools and equipment necessary to perform the task. Part I introduces you to the ins and outs of repairs and explains the common tools needed. It also has a few tips about how not to go broke getting them. If your father wasn't handy, or even if he was and you rarely paid attention, you'll find out what each tool does, why some tools are better than others, and how you can get a quality product that will last most people a lifetime. (That is, if it doesn't grow a pair of legs and "walk away" from your home on its own initiative.)

## Part II: Repairing Your Home's Interior

Part II concentrates on working inside the house on the structural components: floors and stairs; windows and doors; walls and ceilings; and such things as cabinets, closets, and countertops. These chapters deal with what goes wrong with items due to constant use. You'll find out how easy most of these problems are to correct and how to bring hardware such as hinges and locks back into good working order.

# Part III: Conquering Simple Electrical, Air, and Plumbing Repairs

Major structural components develop problems over the course of time. In Part III, we concentrate on the essentials, things we take for granted that make all homes livable — electricity, heating, air conditioning, and plumbing. You'll find many simple repairs you can do yourself with confidence. There's also advice about when it's best to call for the services of a trained technician.

# Part IV: Keeping Your Stuff in Good Shape

Almost everyone takes pride in the "stuff" they've acquired: home furnishings, small and large appliances, and communication and entertainment equipment. So it's frustrating when these items stop working. And some people resent having to spend hundreds of dollars to replace items simply because they can't find service or parts.

This part is designed to lengthen the life of some of your favorites and to save on your pocketbook as well. It may be great for the economy when everyone throws out the old and spends money on the new, but planned obsolescence wreaks havoc on most household budgets. So turn to this part in self-defense.

# Part V: Working Outside Your House

Home repair and maintenance are just as necessary outdoors as they are inside, perhaps even more so when you think of roof leaks, damaged siding, rotted soffits, and structural damage caused by termites, carpenter ants, large and small rodents, and other pests. Part V will help you get your house in shape so it can withstand the assaults of weather and critters. It will show you how you can keep it in the best condition with periodic maintenance. It also includes ways to prolong the life of concrete and asphalt driveways and swimming pools, which are costly to replace.

# Part VI: The Part of Tens

Every *For Dummies* book ends with The Part of Tens. The Tens in *How to Fix Everything For Dummies* include ten repairs that you shouldn't attempt yourself — along with the reasons why — and tips for finding the best repair specialists and what to ask and look for when you have to call one in.

# Icons Used in This Book

We use the good ol' *For Dummies* icons to help guide you through the contents throughout this book. Here is what each icon means:

When you see this icon, you'll find additional information, pointers, and shortcuts to help you complete the repair.

This icon points out important bits of information to keep in mind as you proceed with your home repair projects.

When you see this icon, stop and read it. *Please*. In some instances, fixing things yourself can be dangerous. Within these warnings you will also find some safety pointers.

Sad to say, some repairs involve major headaches you should watch for and perhaps leave to a professional. This icon alerts you to those trouble-prone projects, and points out when you should seriously consider hiring someone else to deal with them before they get worse.

Some people just have to know how innards of the doorbell or the toilet really work. This book doesn't bombard you with this kind of information, because we assume you probably just want to fix the darn thing. But if you're thrilled at the prospect of knowing something about air conditioners that your neighbor doesn't know, look for this icon and have fun digesting the details!

# Where to Go from Here

Now that you have an overview of what you'll find in *How to Fix Everything For Dummies,* you're ready to make a list of items that need attention. Start with the easiest tasks, small jobs that don't take much time or skill, and then work your way through progressively more involved repairs. Then just flip through the Table of Contents and find out how to start your new tasks.

# Part I

# Gearing Up to Fix Everything

The 5th Wave — By Rich Tennant

"I think I've fixed the intercom. Just remember to speak into the ceiling fan when the doorbell rings."

# In this part . . .

First things first, as the saying goes. Before you can start fixing up your home and prized possessions, you need to know what you're getting into. In this section, we give you an overview of repairing. Then we let you in on which basic tools are necessary to your future as a fix-it person, what kind to get, and where to find them.

# Chapter 1

# If Your Broken Stuff Needs Repair...

- - - - - - - - - - - - - - - - - - - - - - - - - - - - - - - - - - - - - - - - - -

- - - - - - - - - - - - - - - - - - - - - - - - - - - - - - - - - - - - - - - - - -

Throughout the ages, people have used whatever materials were handy to build homes. They cut wood, logs, and twigs from nearby trees, moved rocks, and quarried stone to make a structural frame strong enough to support a roof. They enclosed the frame, placing layers of leaves, twigs, straw, clay, slate — whatever they had — on the roof structure and fashioned walls to keep their homes warm, dry, and safe from the elements, wild animals, and other people. From Greek temples to simple huts with mud-plastered walls and thatched roofs, to utilitarian stone fortresses, homes evolved. We've had homes made of animal skins and logs, clapboard siding, bricks, stones, concrete, cement blocks, various metals, and now even glass.

Instead of a single wall shelter we now have interior and exterior walls with the space in between stuffed with insulation and the components necessary for providing utilities throughout the house. And walls now are decorative so that they appeal to us inside and out.

Buildings, however, can only fulfill that dual function — safety and pleasure — when they're maintained and repaired as needed. To that end, owning a home is a never-ending job. Faucets start leaking and pipes get clogged. The circuit breakers keep tripping. It's too late to wish you'd paid more attention when dad or your next-door neighbor tore things apart to fix them. But even if you think you're all thumbs, you can still do a lot of repairs yourself.

## When not to "leaf" things for professionals

It's frustrating to have a minor repair and not know who to call or to hesitate about calling a repair service because of the standard minimum "walk-in" fee — generally no less than $50.

To illustrate that point, we only have to mention a blustery autumn day some years back. Our furnace wasn't kicking in and the house was getting very cold. Novices that we were, we naturally called for service: We wanted heat

immediately. Imagine our chagrin when we had to pay $60 to have a large leaf removed from the mouth of the furnace's air intake pipe. It was located on the back of the house in a corner that collected huge piles of leaves!

Not all fix-jobs are as simple as removing a leaf, but you'll be surprised at how much you can accomplish even if you concentrate on do-it-yourself tasks for beginners.

In *How to Fix Everything For Dummies* we concentrate on simple repairs, things a novice can tackle with confidence. When possible, we give you steps that are reversible, and then options to try another fix that might be a little more complicated or require more time and tools. But these alternate fix-its are still within reason for beginners. And finally, we tell you when to call for repairs or give up and buy a replacement.

If saving money on easy fix-its isn't enough incentive to do it yourself, think of this: When you delay doing anything around the house, it quickly evolves into a much larger project that will cost even more. An untended roof leak is a good example because it doesn't take long before you have a damp ceiling or wall, and if the insulation and drywall or plaster get soggy, you not only have the leak to fix, but insulation that has to be replaced and drywall or plaster that have to be redone — along with priming and painting the damaged area.

As you become proficient at simple repairs, you may want to do more complicated work. In that case, we recommend the most recent editions of some of the other *For Dummies* books such as *Plumbing For Dummies* by Gene and Katie Hamilton, *Carpentry For Dummies* by Gene Hamilton, Katie Hamilton, and Roy Barnhart, *Bathroom Remodeling For Dummies* by Gene and Katie Hamilton, *Home Maintenance For Dummies* by James and Morris Carey, *Home Improvement For Dummies* by Gene and Katie Hamilton, *Upgrading and Fixing PCs For Dummies* by Andy Rathbone, or one of the dozens of other *For Dummies* titles (all published by Wiley). They go into topics covered in this book in more depth.

# Following Basic Safety Tips (Before You Do Anything Else!)

 When getting ready to repair something, you need to think about safety for yourself and your family. We'll call your attention to important safety issues throughout the book, but here are some basic practical safety tips that are good to know up front:

- ✔ Keep safety goggles handy and use them when there's a risk of something flying up into your face or when you're painting or fixing plasterboard ceilings.

- ✔ Keep your free hand away from the cutting edges of a bit or saw.

- ✔ Follow manufacturer directions whenever you use a power tool.

- ✔ Don't wear loose clothing or jewelry that may catch on something and result in an accident.

- ✔ Keep cords of power tools grounded in a three-prong receptacle.

- ✔ Don't use power tools if they have frayed wires.

- ✔ Use gloves when you're handling caustic or acid materials such as cleaning products, paint thinners, and some types of glue.

- ✔ Read directions that come with packages — the manufacturer has tips on how to use products and how to ensure safety.

- ✔ Don't mix ingredients. For instance, when ammonia and bleach are mixed together, they produce a dangerous gas that gets into your lungs and can cause death in a poorly ventilated area.

- ✔ If the label says work in a well-ventilated area, do just that. Open doors or windows even if it's cold outside. This is especially true if you're susceptible to asthma and other lung problems.

- ✔ If you use a pesticide, wear gloves to handle it. If the manufacturer recommends that the house or room be vacated for a period of time, go out to dinner and a movie or visit your mother-in-law.

- ✔ In most cases, more isn't helpful or healthy. For instance, if the directions say ¼ cup of ammonia in a gallon of water does the job, don't add 2 cups of ammonia.

- ✔ If you're on a ladder, never, ever lean out to the side or climb up to the top rung or step. The top rungs are meant for handholds, not feet. And have a buddy hold the ladder steady for you.

- ✔ Never step on the drop-down shelf on step ladders; the shelf is designed for holding paint buckets and tools, not people.

When you're ready to make repairs, one useful place to refer to for safety information is the Web site for the U.S. Department of Labor's Occupational Safety and Health Administration (OSHA): www.osha.gov. The site is for professionals, but it contains valuable information on all topics of safety.

# Preparing for Repairing

In order to become a successful do-it-yourselfer, you need certain tools. That doesn't mean you need a fully equipped shop or have to buy every hammer stocked in stores. But removing a screw with a kitchen knife or using plain white glue for everything is not only frustrating, but it usually won't work. So it's important to start with what you need as a novice do-it-yourselfer.

In Chapter 2 we cover tools — many of the different kinds available and what we consider absolutely essential to have on hand. We tell you why these tools are important, what to consider when you're in the store, how to judge quality, and where you'll find good bargains on tools that will last a long time. And we promise you won't break the bank to get them. We even let you know when and why it's best to rent rather than purchase tools.

Many people are often astonished to find out how many things can be fixed by simply cleaning them. Cleaning goes a long way toward repairing things, considering how hard it is (for example) for machinery to work properly when it's choked up with dust and gunk. However, you need to make sure that when you do clean something, you do it properly. Have no fear — this book explains how to clean (and subsequently fix) things correctly.

# Tackling Repairs Inside Your Home

In Part II we go over some of the simplest — and most essential — repairs. In Chapter 3, we talk about what causes floors to squeak, creak, and sag. We explain how easily you can fix wood floors and stairs with as little as a couple nails or screws, a hammer, scrap lumber, or a few *shims* — those wood wedges that can be stuffed between two surfaces. We also tell you how to easily secure loose banisters to prevent accidents, using glue and wood screws, or reinforce them with scraps of wood. Going beyond wood, you can replace or refasten ceramic and clay tiles, mend vinyl flooring, and restore carpets. And it's also possible to patch and seal concrete floors; we promise you won't need a jackhammer or a truckload of concrete. Our easy-to-follow steps will show you the way to do these repairs with confidence.

## Getting clues to what needs fixing

All it takes is one fussy baby — like our first — for a parent to quickly realize that creaky stairs and squeaky floors make it awfully difficult to back out of a room silently. Why do you need silence? Because after it took so long to get baby to sleep, the last thing you want to do is wake him (or her).

In Chapter 4, we open your eyes to the wonderful world of fixing windows and doors. When doors sag, stick, and warp, you don't have to replace them; nor do you need to strain your back trying to push a window up (and then prop it with a stick so that it stays open). Getting old windows and doors back into working order takes a little time, but you can do it by following the steps in Chapter 4. And you won't need a locksmith or new locks to make your home secure again. You can realign latch plates, and lubricate and clean moving parts. That, too, is easier than you think. Forget about lifting sliding patio doors to get them open or closed. They're heavy, but fixing them costs little compared to the cost of buying a replacement. We tell you how to put in or fix cracked thresholds and give you tips for adjusting cranky casements, caulking and weather stripping openings, replacing torn screens, and maintaining automatic garage doors.

If you're tired of cracked plaster or popped nails in drywall, Chapter 5 shows you the way to get walls looking good again. We show you how easy it is to repair holes, dents, and gouges, and to lift sagging drywall. We tell you what to do when taped drywall edges come loose or droop. We also explain how to banish water stains on drywall, repair holes in ceilings, replace broken tiles, patch torn wallpaper, and restore paneling so that it looks as good as new.

Chapter 6 gives you tips that will keep your cabinets on track. Cabinets, countertops, and closets frequently need attention because of accidents, constant use, and overloaded shelves and drawers. Along with repairing warped doors, we let you know how much depends on hinges and other hardware, and screws that stay tightly fastened. Even those marred countertops — laminate and tile — can look as good as new. And if you're tired of yanking drawers open or struggling to close them, you'll be thrilled at how quickly they can be restored to working order.

# *From Drains to Wires: Repairing Plumbing, Wiring, and More*

Part III concentrates on structural components in every home: the electrical system, heating, air conditioning, and plumbing. You can light up your life without worrying about getting zapped if you follow the steps in Chapter 7. And you won't have to blow a fuse to do the work. To take some of the mystique out of electricity, we explain shorts, opens, fuses, circuit breakers, and service panels. We also show you how to test and replace switches, dimmers, thermostats, humidistats, and wall outlets. And then we let you in on some easy repairs for light fixtures, table lamps, fluorescent lights, doorbells, and garage door openers.

Chapter 8 is all about heating, ventilation, and air conditioning — commonly called *HVAC* by professional engineers, architects, and builders. Whether you can repair a furnace often depends on its age; the latest models very likely have electronic parts, and you need to be professionally trained to do much with them, but countless numbers of the older models are still around. We explain how to adjust and maintain furnaces, as well as furnace humidifiers on forced air systems.

Air conditioners use a lot of electricity, and if they're laboring hard because they need repairs or maintenance, it's just about the same as trying to air-condition the outdoors — expensive!

Common-sense maintenance tips include such things as cleaning out heat registers and cold air returns, and getting fans, humidifiers, and dehumidifiers to work. Chapter 8 is about improving your comfort and saving your money, even before anything breaks down.

What one problem occurs most frequently in everybody's home? "Mom, Dad! The toilet's plugged!" (Or it might be the sink, the tub, or the shower that's backed up.) You can't call a plumber every time a drain or line gets plugged. Not when a plunger costs a couple bucks and a plumbing snake just a few dollars more. Unblocking drains is grunt work; it takes a little muscle, but is well worth your time to get rid of the inconvenience right away. Chapter 9 is full of tips on what you can do. We also tell you how to unclog aerators — those strainers at the ends of faucets — and let you in on how easy it is to get rid of leaks in faucets and toilets. It's better to fix them than lose sleep wishing that nonstop drip would just disappear. This chapter also shows you how to work on hot water tanks and repair or replace sump pumps.

# Knowing What to Chuck and What to Fix

Part IV is all about keeping prized possessions functioning smoothly. We discuss large and small appliances, describe ways to fine-tune expensive electronic and communication equipment, and tell you how to refurbish your favorite furnishings so that you can pass them on to your children or grandchildren.

## Was Grandma's stuff made better?

Your mother or grandmother may still have the stove, fridge, or washer and dryer that she got when she first set up house. Back then, large appliances didn't have all the bells and whistles found on today's models, but they did last just about forever. That's because when they were made, manufacturers also made replacement parts so you could easily fix whatever went wrong. Jump into the 21st century and it's a whole different game. Today you're lucky to get 20 years of service out of most appliances and if something goes wrong, you'll be even luckier to find a replacement part. They simply aren't made.

Chapter 10 is full of tips on what you can actually do for most major appliances. And the good news is that while longevity isn't prized today, most large appliances are relatively trouble free throughout their somewhat truncated lifetime. So check out what you can actually do and concentrate on providing basic maintenance to keep appliances trouble free.

If a faulty component in an appliance is electronic, forget about repairing it. Nowadays, you need a 2-year certificate to tackle most electronic repairs, so you're better off buying a replacement.

Small appliances, discussed in Chapter 11, have the same problem as do large appliances. The latest models have circuit boards and all-in-one components that a technician has to replace — if the part is available. But we explain common sources of trouble for most small appliances, what you need to test them, and how to determine when to head for the appliance store. We also describe how to check out cords and plugs. No need to throw out the toaster if all you have to do is put in a new power cord. But if you do have to replace a small appliance, take comfort in the fact that most are not big-ticket items. A new coffeepot costs little when you compare it to a new refrigerator.

If you're like most people today, you probably have thousands of dollars of electronic equipment in a super-sophisticated, surround-sound entertainment center that seems part of your house itself. You also have shelves full of DVDs, CDs, the latest video games, and powerful computer equipment and peripherals. Probably half of us want to "fix" things when one of these devices gets touchy: If you fall into this category, Chapter 12 is for you. It can help you maintain and preserve most of your communication equipment. In this chapter, we help you readjust and clean printers and copiers, work on fax machines and scanners, and clean components. We also include information about improving your satellite system, and adjusting CD, DVD, and VCR players.

Chapter 13 is all about keeping prized furniture looking good (unless you really prefer extremely distressed furniture). You put a lot of thought and care into buying furniture for your home, so it's frustrating when a piece gets scratched or nicked, a leg wobbles, or the veneer pulls loose. Instead of throwing it out or picking up the phone, fix it yourself. You may be amazed at how simple repairing furniture is and wonder why you ever considered asking someone else to do it. Getting rid of scratches takes little more than a melted crayon or colored wax. Split caning on chairs can be replaced. With the right glue, clamps, and toothpicks, you can stop legs from wobbling.

Bringing a fine chest or table back to life is an extremely rewarding task, so don't be surprised if you want to do more and start combing antique shops and estate and garage sales to find pieces with potential.

# Making Repairs in the Great Outdoors

When you purchase a home, you've committed yourself to maintaining it inside and out. And it can be expensive to hire someone to do small jobs that you can handle yourself for a fraction of the cost. In Chapter 14, we tell you what to do to recondition the exterior of your home — replacing missing or melted vinyl siding, getting dents out of aluminum, repairing wood siding, filling holes and cracks in stucco, and patching the mortar between bricks. You get tips on why paint peels, blisters, and cracks, and what to do to get rid of mildew. We talk about sealing cracks that interfere with heating and cooling efficiency. And we explain how to replace and refasten roofing materials, find water leaks, and add flashing. Chapter 14 also includes information about how to repair flat roofs, revive gutters and downspouts, and replace rotted soffits.

Leisure areas and accessories need attention periodically. Decks, fences, patios, porches, grills, fountains and sprinklers, and outdoor furniture are covered in Chapter 15. We show you how to replace rotted floorboards, add joists under sagging floors, spot-treat dry rot, get rid of mildew on porch and deck floors, repair decorative columns, and replace and stabilize wood posts and bottom fence rails. We also provide information about lifting sagging gates and repairing hinges. Chain link fences last a long time before they show signs of wear, but when they do, you don't have to replace them. You can clean off rust and repaint worn spots or put in new pipes or links. We also explain how to replace burners on your gas grill and rejuvenate lawn and porch furniture.

In Chapter 16, we talk about more grunt work: repairing and patching concrete and asphalt driveways, sidewalks, stairs, and patios. We also give you information about sealing cracked concrete blocks and replacing broken blocks. You may think there's no need to worry about paving stones and blocks, but they're susceptible to weather extremes. And after a number of years, they can crack and heave. We show you how to level and replace them. Swimming pools develop small cracks that should be patched; if you delay and water gets behind the concrete, you may end up with a much larger and more expensive repair to tackle.

The Part of Tens Chapters 17 and 18, in Part VI, are devoted to giving you tips on dealing with professionals when you don't have a choice but to hire them. So, when you have a project that you suspect needs a pro, or if you aren't sure what you ask the pros when you need them, turn to these chapters for help.

# Chapter 2

# Tackling Basic Tools and Equipment

*In This Chapter*

▶ Getting the right tools and equipment

▶ Renting more expensive tools

*W*andering through the tool section in a hardware store can be overwhelming experience when you're a novice do-it-yourselfer. Not only are there many different tools, from familiar to strange, but everything's available in a multitude of shapes, sizes, and prices. But don't let that first impression linger. When you want to tackle home repairs, you need some basic tools. The good news is that the ones you need won't cost a fortune or take up a lot of storage space.

So how do you decide which tools you need? Are all tools the same? Is it necessary to buy the most expensive tools? And what features should they have? This chapter gives you a good start on what to look for when you shop for equipment and tools. We also tell you which basic tools you should buy.

## Tools and Equipment to Keep Handy

You can spend a fortune on tools, but it's really not necessary for do-it-yourselfers. A few choice selections can handle most tasks. Expensive top-of-the-line tools are for professionals or serious hobbyists who use them every day. Most do-it-yourselfers use tools occasionally (although you may use some more than others); therefore, good-quality tools that are moderately priced are sufficient for most of their needs.

That being said, we also don't recommend that you buy the cheapest tools you can find. Always spend as much as you can afford when it comes to mid-range and midpriced tools because you get what you pay for. The least expensive tools tend to be made of inferior steel that's either much more brittle or softer than better-grade steel. That means the steel on hammers and screw-drivers can crack or chip or the handles can break. Wrenches and pliers won't retain a grip and you may round off or strip the screws.

You can buy tools many places: hardware stores, variety stores, home improvement centers, and budget shops featuring items costing a dollar or less. Our first choice for good quality tools in a budget-conscious range of prices is one of the national home improvement centers.

When shopping for tools, if you still aren't sure what you need for your project, don't be shy about getting advice from the hardware store clerk. There's an old saying about how any job is easy with the right tools, and one of the main jobs of the hardware store clerk is to know what those tools are!

## Looking for drills

There are three kinds of drills: electric, battery operated, and hand operated antiques. They use exchangeable bits (the cutting edge) that come in different sizes and snap into the drill. You can drill anything from a fine pilot path for screws to large holes in masonry, wood, plastic, metal, and other materials. With a screwdriver bit, you can insert or remove screws.

Some people prefer portable electric drills for working around the house. We have a portable electric drill that has an electric cord dangling off the end, but our drill of choice is a cordless battery operated model. It's convenient and fits into tight spaces. You can take a cordless drill anywhere without worrying about hauling a power cord or finding a nearby outlet. We believe battery operated drills have caught up with electric drills in quality and power.

Battery drills come in sizes by volts: 6 to 12 volts, 14 to 14.4 volts, and 18 to 24 volts. Generally, with higher voltage, you get larger chuck size, longer-lasting batteries, and more power. Although a 12-volt is the least expensive, it doesn't have enough power to finish most jobs. We recommend that you get a 14- to 14.4-volt drill with these features:

- ✔ Variable speeds.
- ✔ Chuck capacity of ⅜ inch. (That's the maximum diameter or largest bit it can handle.)
- ✔ Reversible, so you can *back out* (remove) screws.

Also compare brands to see whether any extras are included. One manufacturer may include two battery packs (instead of one) and a carrying case along with the drill. With an extra battery, you never have to stop working; if one dies, snap in the other and recharge the first while you finish the job.

Some drill packages may also include a few bits, but as a rule, you have to purchase them separately. Look for a variety pack with an assortment of sizes and types. Then you're set for most projects.

Later, if you need other accessories for a special project, you can also buy polishing, grinding, or sanding attachments.

## Tap, tap, tapping with hammers

A *curved claw (carpenter's)* hammer handles a multitude of tasks when you're driving or pulling nails. It's a must for your toolbox. But when you shop, you'll also find *straight claw* hammers (carpenters use them like a pickax to rip out things), *ball peen* hammers (mechanics use them when working on engines and metal), and various mallets and *mauls* (baby sledgehammers) used for heavy-duty pounding. You probably won't need these special-duty hammers.

Claw hammers should be made of quality steel that won't crack or chip. It doesn't matter whether you choose one with a wood, fiberglass, or steel handle. Wood has long been a favorite, but it actually is breakable — although breakage isn't likely with ordinary use.

Hammer sizes and weights vary, but for most purposes, a 16-ounce hammer is your best choice. Don't get one that weighs less than 13 ounces and stay away from 20-ounce hammers. Carpenters use them to tear down old construction, but like most householders, you'll probably think a 20-ounce hammer feels heavy and if you try to use it, your arm will quickly tire.

As you shop, compare brands by handling each claw hammer and selecting one that feels best in terms of weight and balance. Any of the midpriced hammers sold at your home improvement center will be made from quality steel and do a good job for 75 percent of your projects. You can find a good, inexpensive claw hammer in stores, and if you shop garage or estate sales, don't hesitate to buy any that you happen to find. It's always good to have several hammers, particularly several different types, around the house.

## Selecting pliers

Don't be stymied by the pliers displays at hardware stores. You can find all kinds and sizes, but three handle most tasks: slip joint pliers, lineman's pliers, and locking pliers. (See Figure 2-1.) You don't have to purchase all three types right away; wait until you need them for a specific project.

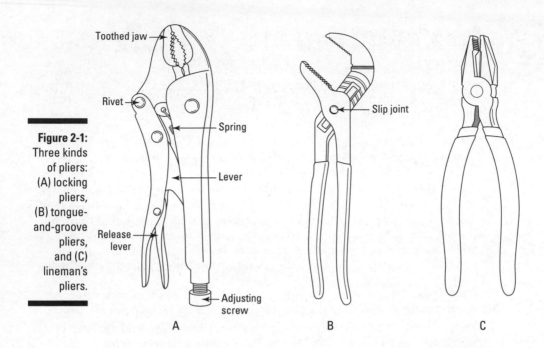

**Figure 2-1:** Three kinds of pliers: (A) locking pliers, (B) tongue-and-groove pliers, and (C) lineman's pliers.

*Locking pliers* have a screw in the base of one handle. (See Figure 2-1A.) You can roughly adjust the screw, and then squeeze the handle for maximum grip and holding power. After it's tightened, the exceptionally strong grip won't slip even if you take your hands off the tool. A 10-inch size is the most versatile and inexpensive too.

*Tongue and groove pliers* have angled, adjustable jaws and are used primarily for plumbing. (See Figure 2-1B.) The jaws open wide enough to grasp pipes and packing nuts. A good size to get is 12 inches.

*Lineman's pliers,* with two ridged jaws that open parallel, are all-around pliers that have a good grip. (See Figure 2-1C.) They won't slip or round off the edges on screws, especially if they're made of good quality steel. They can also be used to splice, cut, and bend heavy wires. Look for a U.S.-made product that's 9 inches long. Although cheaper brands are available, they're definitely inferior and can be frustrating to use.

Some day, you may want to get needle-nose pliers as well. They have an exceptionally long, tapered, straight or bent nose that fits into tight places and grips small screws or nails. There is no locking action on either style.

# *I saw what I saw!*

Different saws have different purposes, as well as different "teeth." But you needn't worry about keeping them straight or buying any of them until needed for a specific project. Most well known are two flexible blade handsaws that cut wood and plastic:

- ✔ The *crosscut saw* has 7 to 12 points or teeth per inch (tpi) and cuts wood efficiently — without much sawdust — across the grain. The teeth are set so that the cut will be wider than the blade. If you need a crosscut saw, look for sharp beveled points that will give you a finer cut than one with flatter teeth on the blade.
- ✔ A *ripsaw*, somewhat longer than a crosscut saw, has seven or fewer points per inch and is designed to make coarser cuts along the grain of the wood.

You need a *hacksaw* to cut metal. From the side, hacksaws have a rectangular outline with a handle attached.

A *miter saw is* also called a *back saw*. Rectangular solid blade with a metal cap on the top, it is used with a miter box to cut angles in molding. You also can use a miter box with a hacksaw to cut angles on metal or pipe.

 Power saws are obviously a bit different from hand saws (see Figure 2-2). Power saws are good investments if you have a job that requires a great deal of cutting. For more information on the different types of power saws and other tools commonly used in woodworking, please visit the tool glossary at the Amateur Woodworker Web site: www.am-wood.com.

Another specialty saw you'll see is the *drywall saw* used to punch starter holes in drywall and other surfaces or to do ornamental work. It has a slender 6- to 8-inch blade attached to a handle.

---

## Do you really need power tools?

Many hand tools, including saws and screwdrivers, come in power or battery-operated versions. They're great for carpenters and builders because these folks need them every day for their speed and precision. But power tools cost more than hand tools and aren't essential unless you're tackling a major project, such as adding onto the house, completely renovating it, or putting up a deck or fence.

We know some people love all the newest bells, whistles, and gadgets and that's fine. Others want to save money for other things, so they won't need power tools unless they already have a carpal tunnel injury.

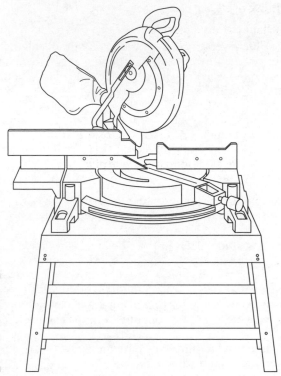

**Figure 2-2:**
Many types
of power
saws come
with stands.

# Buying screwdrivers

Every home should have an assortment of screwdrivers even if fixing things isn't a priority. Screws are one of the most common fasteners on furniture, appliances, entertainment equipment, and the house itself. Over time, many of these screws work loose and need to be tightened.

Screws vary in size and type. And because the tip of a screwdriver should be just as large as — and no larger than — the slot, cross, or star on the screw head, you need an assortment of screwdrivers. If the screwdriver you're using has the wrong size or shape, it will likely slip and you'll damage the screw. So for starting out, you need to keep at least six screwdrivers handy. Figure 2-3 illustrates five of them:

- Medium flat-blade
- Small flat-blade
- #2 Phillips screwdriver (with an x-shaped pointed blade)

✔ #1 Phillips screwdriver

✔ Short, stubby flat-blade screwdriver

✔ Short, stubby #2 Phillips screwdriver

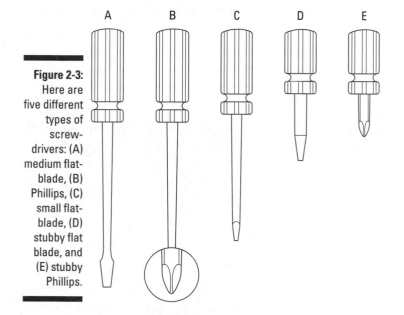

**Figure 2-3:**
Here are five different types of screw-drivers: (A) medium flat-blade, (B) Phillips, (C) small flat-blade, (D) stubby flat blade, and (E) stubby Phillips.

We also recommend getting a *torx* screwdriver set; it has star-shaped tips for those tiny screws manufacturers use on small appliances. Introduced in the mid-1990s, a torx screw has exceptional holding power. In fact, the only reason you'll need to remove one is when you want to repair a small appliance and have to take it apart.

Square screwdrivers are used on RVs, motor homes, and manufactured housing.

You can save a bundle of money if you purchase a screwdriver set. The package usually includes a case, a universal handle, and an assortment of interchangeable bits to insert into the magnetized handle. Because they're magnetized, they won't slip out. We recommend getting one of the larger sets, at least as big as a half sheet of typing paper. It will contain all the sizes and shapes you need — flat, Phillips, torx, and square — plus you probably won't have to buy a small socket set separately because screwdriver sets usually include a good assortment of sockets as well. Many kits also come with an assortment of Allen wrenches — an additional saving. A good screwdriver kit costs much less than you'd spend purchasing these tools individually.

# Getting a grip with adjustable wrenches

Whether you're working in the house or on your car, a wrench comes in handy to turn large nuts and bolts. Designed to give you a tight grip, a wrench has more locking power than pliers so that you can turn even the most rusted bolts in the least accessible places. You need a good tight fit; otherwise your wrench will round off or strip nuts and bolts.

The most useful wrench for your toolbox is the *crescent* or adjustable *wrench*. It has a screw wheel that moves one of the jaws and when you tighten the jaw around large nuts and bolts, the wrench locks into place. Crescent wrenches can handle most jobs.

Combination wrenches — one end is open and the other is closed — are popular too. The most useful sizes are ⅜, ⁷⁄₁₆, ½, and ⁹⁄₁₆ inches. You'll rarely need anything larger. If you do, get out your adjustable wrench.

Allen wrenches are different and we discuss them in the next section. Figure 2-4 shows an adjustable wrench and Allen wrenches.

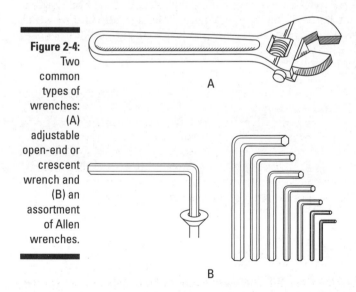

**Figure 2-4:** Two common types of wrenches: (A) adjustable open-end or crescent wrench and (B) an assortment of Allen wrenches.

A

B

When you're shopping for wrenches, get the best you can afford. Cheap brands may slip as you try to turn them and round off the nut and bolt. And the jaws tend to catch as you try to tighten them.

Always use the box (closed end) of a combination wrench whenever possible because it will hold better than the open end.

## Building furniture: Allen wrenches

If you've built furniture from a *knockdown kit* (a kit that's ready to assemble), you probably used an Allen wrench to tighten some of the screws. Remember that tiny steel implement included in the box? An Allen wrench looks like an "L" made out of octagonal steel. The tip of the short arm fits into tiny screw heads so you can remove or adjust them. If you kept that tool, you've already started your Allen wrench collection.

Manufacturers use Allen screws because they're extremely hard and have higher tensile strength as a fastener than a typical screw. That makes them ideal for moving parts that get stressed from typical use: chair and furniture legs, fans, pulleys, and many small motors. So keep your Allen wrenches handy.

## Utilizing utility and putty knives

These tools don't vary much in quality or price: You can find a utility knife for under $5 and a putty knife for less than that. *Utility knives* have very sharp blades that can be changed or reversed when they're dull. You'll find they're useful throughout the house for stripping wire and slicing wallpaper or wood. When you're shopping for utility knives, keep safety in mind. Look for a knife with a retractable blade so you won't inadvertently cut yourself when you carry it around in your pocket.

Versatile *putty knives* are useful for scraping paint, refinishing furniture, spreading goop on drywall, and getting gum off a shoe. A 1-inch-wide putty knife can be used to fill small holes and nicks in furniture; the 4-inch blades come in handy if you're spackling a wall or doing any other kind of wall repairs. You can select rigid or flexible blades. Use flexible blades when you have to follow the contours of shaped pieces or to give a smoother finish. It doesn't matter how much you spend either. At less than $5, you can always replace the putty knife if the blade gets chipped or the handle cracks.

## Using sockets

If you purchased a screwdriver set, as we recommend in the section on screwdrivers, you'll have a set of the most useful sockets. Otherwise, get a set of small sockets. They can be used to tighten or loosen bolts, especially in those rusted gummed-up ones in your car.

Just be sure your sockets have both metric and Standard Automotive Engineer (SAE) sizing. Like it or not, the U.S. sizing system is on its way out. Most appliance manufacturers have already adapted their fittings into the metric system, which is used by most of the rest of the world. If you don't remember metrics, better pull out the books and bone up on it.

# Holding things together with clamps

Keep an assortment of clamps handy for projects that have to be glued. The last few steps of a project usually require you to apply pressure until the glue dries and sets. A stack of books will do if you've glued a flat surface, but there's no way they'll do the job on anything else. Figure 2-5 shows three different types of clamps that everyone should own.

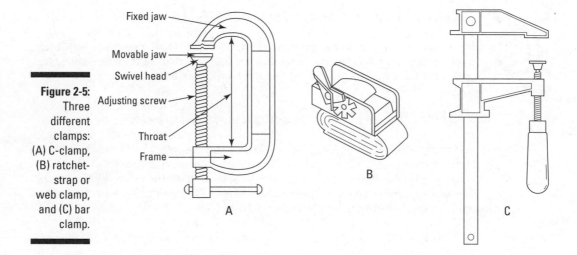

**Figure 2-5:** Three different clamps: (A) C-clamp, (B) ratchet-strap or web clamp, and (C) bar clamp.

Labels in figure: Fixed jaw, Movable jaw, Swivel head, Adjusting screw, Throat, Frame, A, B, C

*C-clamps*, named for their shape, are limited in usefulness only by how wide the threaded shaft on the clamp opens. (See Figure 2-5A.) You'll find metal and plastic C-clamps with openings ranging in size from 1 inch to 12 inches. Metal clamps have a threaded shaft turned by a T-shaped handle. The most useful is a midsize C-clamp with a 4- to 6-inch opening.

*Ratchet strap clamps* have exceptional holding power — they exert 300- to 1,000-pound pressure. (See Figure 2-5B.) You can wrap one around a refrigerator or another appliance and move it onto a two-wheel dolly. And these straps are versatile as well; you can apply pressure to a picture frame or mirror until the glue dries. The strap has a metal ratchet wheel (with metal teeth) and lever or handle that you pump to apply pressure. (Some straps may need pliers or a wrench to turn a nut.) You needn't worry about price; a cheap ratchet strap will do just as good a job as one that costs ten times as much.

Get a couple of ratchet-strap clamps and keep one in your home and another in the car. Then you won't have to worry if you impulsively purchase a large mattress or piece of furniture. You can haul it home on the roof of your car and shut the car doors without harming your ratchet strap.

*Bar clamps* have an adjustable metal jaw and a round wooden handle. As you turn the handle, the jaw clamps the bar to your project. (See Figure 2-5C.) A bar clamp is used when you need to exert pressure on a large object. Bar clamps are available in various lengths. You need a very long bar if you want to put pressure on a very large object. But all you need to get for most home projects is a midsized bar, 12 to 18 inches long. If you ever need a larger bar clamp, rent or borrow one because you probably won't use it again.

## Leveling and measuring tools

Say thanks to the person who invented flexible steel tape measures. Very likely every architect, engineer, builder, contractor, decorator, interior designer, and real estate salesperson keeps one handy. You should too.

Sure, professionals can figure out rough dimensions of a room simply by pacing it off, one foot in front of the other. But if they need to be accurate, all they have to do is hook one end of the steel tape over a doorframe, for instance, and walk to the opposite wall, unreeling the tape as they go. After they get there, they bend the tape against the wall and get a precise number for the length or width of the room. Then they hit a button on the casing that releases the tape and automatically rewinds it. A steel tape is virtually indestructible and it's available in various lengths up to 30 feet.

Big deal, you say? Remember you can return uncut 2-x-4s to the lumberyard and be reimbursed for the expense. But if you order too much carpeting, you have to eat the cost — unless, of course, you can sell off the scrap pieces and even then, you'll probably get only a fraction of what you paid for it.

The most popular folded wood rulers measure up to 6 feet, so it takes two people to get accurate dimensions to ensure the ruler hasn't moved or slipped. Nevertheless there are times when this durable product comes in handy. It's good to keep a rigid 12-inch straight ruler and a yardstick handy as well. Splurge a little on these very inexpensive products and buy metal instead of plastic or wood and you'll never have to replace them.

Use a flat, metal *carpenter's square* to get precise right angles, determine whether joints and other surfaces are square, and to measure in inches and fractions. A *try square* with a handle riveted to the blade can do the job too. Another square sold is a *combination square*. It measures up to 12 inches and doubles as a ruler on one blade. It also has a moving head that you can use to mark 90- and 45-degree angles or draw a cutting edge parallel to a board.

You need a *level* to make sure your work isn't going up or down hill (see Figure 2-6). Quality means a lot when it comes to levels, so don't settle for a "bargain." Many of the cheaper products have bubbles that are "off" — the bubble doesn't center between the marked lines at each end of the bubble even if the level is on a perfectly flat surface. Or it may take more time for the bubble to center than it does with more expensive products.

**Figure 2-6:**
A three-bubble level keeps vertical and horizontal lines straight.

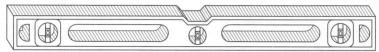

 Look for a level with a metal frame, not plastic, because it is more durable.

Always test a level before you buy it. Follow these steps:

1. **Place a horizontal edge of the level on a flat surface such as a shelf or countertop with the cutout up.**

2. **Note where the center bubble is positioned between the marked lines.**

3. **Turn the level around and test it again.**

4. **Is the bubble in the same place as it was in Step 2? If not, try another level.**

5. **Stand the level up vertically and place it up against a flat surface such as a display cabinet or sign.**

6. **Are the two end bubbles in the same place? If not, try another level.**

7. **Turn the level around and upside down.**

8. **Test it again along the cabinet edge to see if the bubbles stay the same as in Step 6.**

Don't purchase any level that doesn't pass this test.

## The ups and downs of ladders

If you own a home, you'll need two ladders — a 5- or 6-foot stepladder for indoor repair and decorating projects and an extension ladder for outside that can be extended 20 or 30 feet. Take a look at a *combination ladder* as well; it is a stepladder — shaped like an "M" when closed — that has three hinged joints. It can be turned into scaffolding for indoor use.

Made of aluminum, wood, or fiberglass, ladders come in three grades: Grade 3 for households, Grade 2 for commercial use, and Grade 1 for industrial use. Go with a Grade 2 ladder for your home because it's more durable than Grade 3.

The heaviest stepladders are made of fiberglass and they're almost twice the cost of aluminum (midrange) ladders.

Extension ladders, usually aluminum or fiberglass, can be extended 20 to 30 feet.

Aluminum is a good conductor of electricity so when you're moving one, be careful around power lines. Fiberglass doesn't conduct electricity and therefore ladders made of this substance are safer. They're extremely durable and stable, but also heavy and expensive. Nevertheless, if you can afford one that's the way to go.

In selecting a ladder, choose one that will carry the weight of the heaviest person in your house, plus materials, plus at least 10 extra pounds. Look for ladders with flat steps; it's easy to slip off rungs. For safety, always wear soft-soled shoes. And if the ladder has hinges, make sure they're locked securely when you open it up.

---

# Tools and equipment to rent

Sometimes it simply doesn't make sense to purchase tools and equipment that cost a lot. That's particularly true if you won't use them frequently, you're planning a one-time job, or you don't have space to store them. Your best bet then is to borrow the tool or rent it from a hardware, home improvement, or rental shop.

Some years after moving into a house, we realized that the family room floor was bouncy because of sagging floor joists. We borrowed a hydraulic jack to raise the joists, and reinforced them with 2-x-4s. The project took several weeks to complete and we've never needed a hydraulic jack again.

We also recommend renting instead of purchasing if you don't have a basement or garage.

When you don't have any place to put stuff, renting equipment just makes more sense.

You may be surprised at how little it costs to rent a staple gun or jackhammer. And stores have a variety of equipment — from power saws and drills to forklifts and backhoes. (Some rental shops carry heavy construction equipment and rent it to contractors and perhaps occasionally a venturesome homeowner.)

So think strategically. How often are you likely to use that tool? Does it really make sense to purchase it? Will storage be a problem if you don't have a basement or garage? And what accessories have to be stored as well?

# Part II
# Repairing Your Home's Interior

The 5th Wave                    By Rich Tennant

"I'll tell you where your tape measure
is if you promise to be more careful
where you put your wood glue."

## In this part . . .

In the following chapters, we help you get down to the bare bones of what's inside your home. What do you do when stairs and floors creak, windows and doors don't operate as they should, wall and ceiling cracks develop, or the cabinets, closets, and countertops drive you nuts because the doors or hinges sag, shelves threaten to collapse, or drawers stick and refuse to open? With the information in this chapter, you'll be armed to solve all kinds of glitches indoors.

# Chapter 3

# Taking the Creaks, Cracks, and Holes Out of Floors, Stairs, and Basements

## In This Chapter

▶ Restoring stairs and banisters

▶ Fixing problem floors

▶ Patching tile problems

▶ Eliminating vinyl problems

▶ Repairing carpets

▶ Keeping your basement dry

*I*n this chapter, we go over what happens to floors and stairs as buildings settle and age and explain what you can do to repair them. Whether loose, ripped, raised, or broken, floors and stairs can cause accidents and they should be fixed immediately. You can also get rid of the creaks, squeaks, and groans that sometimes make you wonder whether your home is inhabited by uninvited guests.

We also look at how to tackle those annoying holes and cracks that sometimes appear in finished flooring and carpeting. And finally, we give you plenty of tips for keeping your basement dry! So get out your hammer, screws, carpenter's glue, and any other equipment you need to do the job take a look at how to make those repairs.

## Fixing Creaky Stairs

If stairs creak and groan when someone steps on them, treads are loose or warped or risers need securing. You may be able to put up with the noise, but those squeaks are a signal for you to fasten the treads and risers before they get too bad. You don't want anyone to stumble on the stairs.

A *riser* (the vertical board behind the step) fits up to the underside of the *tread* (the horizontal board that you step on) above it. If the joint between the two isn't tight, stepping on the stair can create noise as the tread hits the riser.

## Working on risers under the stairs

It's easiest to fix open stairs, especially those in basements, because you can get at the unfinished underside to check for a gap between the riser and the tread above. Here's how:

1. **Ask an adult to step onto the stair while you watch for a slight deflection.** This tells you which is the problem step.

2. **Drive a thin, tapered wood wedge — a *shim* — into the space between the riser and tread.** Hammering it in will be difficult unless you put a wood block against the wedge and hammer the block instead of the wedge.

3. **When you can't hammer the shim in any further, cut off the protruding end.**

If the riser is loose, drill a pilot hole first, then insert a screw through the back of the riser and into the step that's just below it.

If you can't get a wedge in, reinforce the tread from underneath by nailing or screwing a piece of wood tightly up against the tread and riser. That will stabilize the boards. See Figure 3-1.

## Working on risers from the top of the stairs

If the stairway is finished underneath, you have to drive screws or nails into the top of the tread and through the riser. Here's how:

1. **Drill a hole at an angle into the tread and riser.** Place it just behind the overhanging edge. Be sure to use a bit that is smaller in diameter than the screw or nail that you will insert.

2. **Drill another hole, also at an angle.** Put this hole 6 or 7 inches away from the first if you're using screws. If you plan to nail the boards together, put the holes a couple inches apart.

3. **Insert the screws or nails, making sure that they're long enough to grab into the riser beneath the drilled hole.** See Figure 3-2.

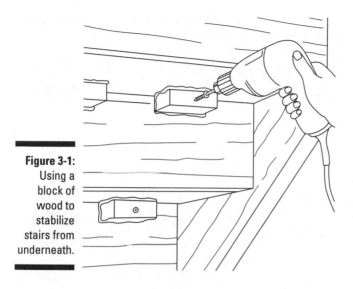

**Figure 3-1:**
Using a block of wood to stabilize stairs from underneath.

4. **Countersink the screw by inserting it below the surface of the tread.**

5. **Fill the resulting hole with a prestained wood plastic.** If you use wood putty, color it to match the treads before you use it. Dry putty stains unevenly and the patch will be noticeable unless you install carpeting on the stairs.

If your stairs are made of an exceptionally hard wood, you won't be able to drive nails or screws into them without first drilling a pilot hole. Make the hole with a bit slightly smaller than the nail or screw.

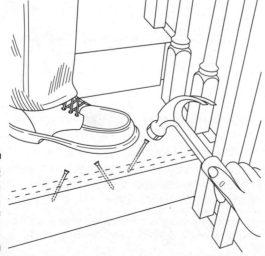

**Figure 3-2:**
Securing treads from the top of the stairs.

## Fixing split treads

Always repair cracked or split treads immediately before someone takes a serious spill, especially if the front edge is damaged. You may be able to glue the edges back together, and then insert screws to hold the split piece to the tread. Or you can take out the old tread and put a new one in. Here's how to glue the edge back to the tread:

1. **Squirt glue onto the edge of the tread and split piece.** If the nozzle of the tube is too thick, you can use a medical syringe or a spatula to get glue into the crack.

2. **Drill some small pilot holes into the wood.**

3. **With a hammer, drive small brads into the holes to hold the wood together while the glue dries.**

It may be easier to just replace the entire tread if the damage is extensive or covers a large portion of the tread.

These days, whenever you need new wood cut and planed, most hardware stores will do it for you, to your specifications. It's fast and easy and not expensive at all.

# Securing Loose Banisters

Wobbly *banisters* (handrails) don't feel safe because they aren't. They can contribute to accidents, especially if they break loose right when someone trips and grips them for security. In this section, we go over several different fixes for the problem.

If a banister comes loose in rental housing, the landlord is liable for any injuries. Private homeowners can be at risk too if someone stumbles and breaks a leg or hip. Take immediate steps to ensure safety in your home.

## Reattaching a rail to the wall

If the rail was fastened into the wall, it's probably coming loose because the screws aren't anchored to studs. To secure banisters screwed into walls, replace the screws with molly or toggle bolts. After you insert these anchors into walls that have only space behind them, the wings on the bolts expand and as you tighten the screw, it locks into place behind the drywall.

# Refastening the banister to posts

If the banister is breaking loose from the newel posts or the smaller *balusters* (small posts), here's what to do to refasten it:

1. **Squirt glue into the joint between the rail and the post or baluster.**

2. **On the underside of the banister, drill a pilot hole at an angle through the post or baluster and the banister.** See Figure 3-3.

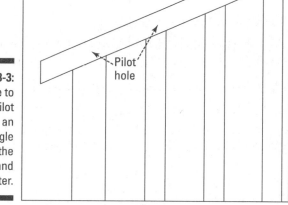

**Figure 3-3:** Where to drill pilot holes at an angle through the post and banister.

3. **Put a wood screw into the drilled hole and countersink it.**

4. **Drill another hole into the side of the newel post or baluster and into the banister.**

5. **Countersink another screw into the second hole.**

6. **Fill the holes with premixed wood filler matched to the color of the stairs.**

7. **After the filler dries, sand off rough edges and finish it if needed to make the fill invisible.**

# Reinforcing the railing

If the entire length of the railing is pulling free of its fastenings, you can add small pieces of wood to the underside of the banister, between each individual baluster and newel post. See Figure 3-4. Make sure the wood blocks you use are decorative!

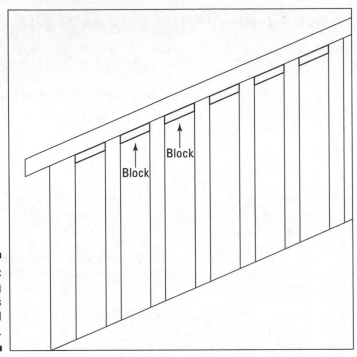

**Figure 3-4:**
Reinforcing
banisters
with wood
blocks.

When you reinforce the rail with pieces of wood, get lumber that will stain and match the existing handrail and posts. Don't expect pieces of oak to resemble cherry or teak railings. Here's what you have to do to reinforce the rail:

1. **Cut the wood into pieces that will fit tightly between each baluster or each baluster and newel post.**

2. **Angle the edges so that they fit into the angled corners of existing wood.**

3. **Glue the pieces, one at a time, onto the bottom of the handrail.** You may want to use scrap pieces of wood to prop the glued piece tightly against the rail. Leave them in place until the glue dries.

4. **When the glue is completely dry, drill pilot holes underneath the bridging, at an angle so that the bit goes through the new bridging, the baluster or post, and up into the handrail.**

   Remember to use a bit that's slightly smaller than the screws you will later insert.

5. **Insert the wood screws and countersink them so the head of the screw is concealed.**

6. **Fill in the hole with your premixed wood filler.**

# Quieting and Stabilizing Creaky Floors

Floors get squeaky — especially in dry weather — because the wood dries out Then you get one or more of four problems:

- ✔ Subfloor nails pop loose from the floor joists.
- ✔ Edges of unevenly spaced subfloors rub together.
- ✔ The floor joists are warped and twisted.
- ✔ Floorboards pull loose from the subfloor.

You can eliminate the noise by fixing the floor underneath, working in the basement or crawl space. You need a helper, chalk, shims, scrap wood, screws or nails, carpenter's glue, and possibly metal angles or cleats.

If there's a finished ceiling under the floor, your problem will be a little harder to fix. You may just have to be content with having a squeaky floor! Here's what to do when the subfloor squeaks:

1. **While you're in the basement, have your helper walk across the floor and stop when it squeaks.**

2. **Mark the spot with chalk where your helper is standing.** He may have to bounce up and down a couple times until you identify the exact location from below.

3. **If you notice the subfloor has separated from a floor joist, drive a shim between the joist and subfloor.** See Figure 3-5A. If one shim isn't thick enough to fill the space tightly, put a couple together and drive all of them in.

4. **If you have access below the floor, you can screw the subfloor to the underside of the finished floor to stabilize it.** See Figure 3-5B.

5. **Otherwise you can countersink screws or nails into the boards from the top.** See Figure 3-5C.

If you have a finished hardwood floor that you want to preserve, you can countersink the screws deep enough to add a matching plug on top of them. Sand and stain (or use a prestained wood filler) and varnish the board to match the floor.

Another option is to screw a metal angle or cleat to the subfloor. Here's what to do:

1. **Smear carpenter's glue on the top of the joist and underside of the subfloor just above it.**

2. **Have your helper stand directly above the squeak.** The weight pushes the floor down onto the joist.

3. **Attach a metal angle or cleat to the joist.** Your hardware store carries a variety of sizes for this purpose.

If you suspect subfloor edges are rubbing against each other and causing the squeaking, get a tube of carpenter's glue and, working in the basement or crawl space, squirt glue up into the subfloor seams. As you force the glue in, it will spread out in a T-shape between the floor and subfloor. After the glue dries, you may want to add a little more glue so that the subfloor joints are fully filled.

Another remedy for subfloor squeaking is to screw a screw into the crack where it's rubbing, forcing the boards apart.

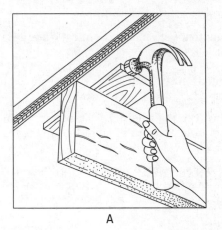

A

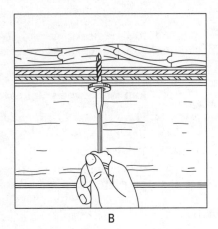

B

**Figure 3-5:**
Stopping subfloor squeaks by shimming (A), stabilizing from beneath (B), or stabilizing from above (C).

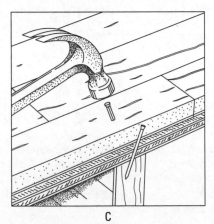

C

# Dealing with twisted floor joists

If you have a twisted or warped floor joist, the simplest way to correct it is to add a block — the same size as the joists or slightly smaller — between two joists. If the joist isn't vertical, put the block at an angle and then pound it up in to straighten the joist.

Another way to fix joists is to add diagonal bridging between the twisted joist and the ones on either side of it. See Figure 3-6. You need a hammer, long nails, a saw, and 16- or 18-inch-long scraps of 2-x-2s or 2-x-4s, depending on how far apart the joists are. You can also buy ready-made bridging at your lumberyard or home improvement store in either wood or metal. Here's how to do it:

1. **Saw the 2-x-2s to the appropriate size**

2. **Bevel the edge by sawing the corner off at an angle.** The bridging has to fit into the corner between the joist and subfloor.

3. **Nail one end of the 2-x-2 to the sound joist, then the other side of the bridge to the twisted joist.**

4. **Bridge the gap between the joists on the other side.**

5. **Repeat Steps 1 and 4, as needed, on other twisted joists.**

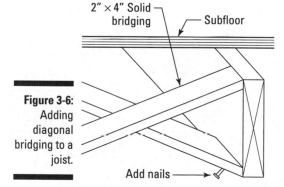

2" × 4" Solid bridging — Subfloor

**Figure 3-6:**
Adding
diagonal
bridging to a
joist.

Add nails →

# Fastening separated floorboards

To fasten separated floorboards to the subfloor, again work beneath the floor. You need wood screws, a tube of carpenter's adhesive, a drill, drill bits, and a screwdriver set. Here's what to do:

1. **From the basement, drill pilot holes through the subfloor so the screws will push in by hand.** Be sure to drill only far enough to have good starting holes for the screws.

2. **Then drill into the underside of the floorboards with a bit smaller than the screw.** Be careful not to drill too deeply or use a screw that will penetrate the finished floor.

3. **Put adhesive into the drilled hole.** It will adhere to the screw and make a tighter fastening.

4. **Insert the screw and tighten it securely.**

Most home improvement stores sell a specific glue for floor repair. It looks like a tube of caulk.

## Reinforcing bouncy floors

Floors bounce (and sometimes sag) because of construction problems. Years after moving into our home, we realized a bouncy family room floor had floor joists that were not stiff enough to handle the load. The contractor had used white pine (the weakest grade of wood) 2-x-10s for floor joists. If the wood had been a stronger grade, the floor wouldn't have deflected every time someone walked across it.

The easiest way to correct the problem is to reinforce each existing joist with a matching joist. See Figure 3-7. That works if there's no wiring or plumbing in the way. And because the new joist has to sit on supports, the problem is how to fit it onto each beam or wall plate, especially if the load has squashed an end of an existing floor joist.

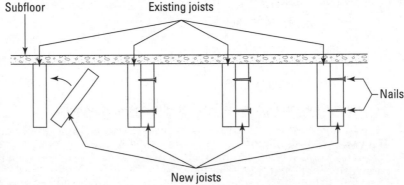

**Figure 3-7:**
Adding a
matching
joist to the
existing
joist.

Subfloor

Existing joists

Nails

New joists

If you're lucky, there will be a little more space at one of the ends so that the new joist can be pushed in. If so, then after one end is sitting on the beam, pull the joist out enough to get it onto the other beam.

If you're still game to tackle the job, you'll need a hydraulic jack, a hammer or mallet, and nails. You also need lumber. Get as many boards of the same size and length as the existing joists. Here's what you have to do.

1. **Using the hydraulic jack, raise the center of an existing joist until it is level.**

2. **Fit the new joist onto the support at each end of the span.**

3. **Nail the two joists together.**

If an end of the old joist is squashed so that you can't butt the new one against it, you can do one of two things. The best thing to do is angle the new joist in — forming a V; then pound it at the top until both joists are parallel. Or you can saw a notch on the bottom of each end of the new joist first and fit it onto the beams before nailing it to the existing joist. But the notched joist will not fit as tightly and, therefore, it may need to be shimmed with wedges after it's in place.

Beams and screw jack columns can help stabilize bouncy floors, but consult a structural engineer before putting them in. An engineer can help you decide where to reinforce the floor and whether you need footings under the columns so that you don't end up cracking the concrete basement floor.

# Correcting Scratched Floorboards

In an ideal world, solid wood floors look clean and shiny and never have problems. But in the real world, people drop things and pets have accidents. Take heart. You can make your floor as good as new.

Fix scratched floorboards by rubbing steel wool along the grain, then rubbing the area with mineral spirits. Deeper scratches have to be sanded first. Here's what to do:

1. **Sand along the grain with a lightweight sandpaper.**

2. **Fill the scratch with a premixed wood filler. Get one that matches the color of the floor.**

   Don't use wood putty unless you stain it yourself. Wood putty will not take color evenly after it has dried; therefore, the patch will be very obvious.

3. **Sand the filler after it has dried.**

4. **Refinish the board with varnish, polyurethane, or a similar product.**

5. **Wax the board so that it looks the same as the rest of the floor.**

For squeaky floorboards, follow the directions given for subfloors earlier in the chapter.

# Dealing with Ceramic and Clay Tiles

You can easily replace cracked and broken ceramic and clay tiles if you kept the remnants and extra grout mix. If the tiles were laid a long time ago, it may be hard to match the new one to the old. Look in the Yellow Pages under "Tile Contractors and Dealers" and then call to find out whether they serve the public — some are wholesale houses only. Then take a piece of the broken tile with you when you shop. Don't forget to look at what's offered in the home improvement stores.

If you can't exactly match the color, look for a similarly made tile in a different color. Then look at the floor and figure out if it's possible to create a random or regular pattern with a second color. It will be a little more work but in the end, a lot cheaper than putting in a new tile floor. Best of all, it's definitely a do-it-yourself project. Remember that the new tile needs to be the same size as the old.

When you go shopping take a piece of the old grout with you. Let the store employees figure out how you can match the color. Someone there will have the required expertise.

## Securing loose tiles

If a tile isn't broken or cracked, you're in good shape for fixing the floor. Here's what to do:

1. **Carefully lift the loose tile with a putty knife, working from center to edges on all four sides.** If the tile is 12-x-12, use a stiff spatula-type blade. The tile may feel loose when you walk on it, but that doesn't mean all the adhesive has broken loose. There still might be a patch holding some part of the tile.

   If you encounter difficulty, don't force the tile out; it will break. Heat the tile first with a warm iron to loosen the bond.

2. **When the tile is out, carefully set it aside and then work on removing all remnants of the old adhesive, using mineral spirits.** You want the floor absolutely clean before you apply new adhesive. If it's not, the

bond won't be as strong. It may also make the tile weaker if some of it isn't as flat as the rest.

While working on the tile and adhesive, make sure your scraper doesn't slip and damage surrounding tiles. If you encounter a stubborn spot, use the iron again to warm the adhesive, then scrape it out.

3. **Apply new adhesive to the cleaned-out patch.**

4. **Press the new tile in.**

5. **Clean off any adhesive that seeps through the seams.** Look at the manufacturer's suggestions for cleaning up excess adhesive.

Weight the tile with books for a day or two until you're certain the bond can't be broken.

## Replacing cracked or missing tiles

Replacing just one tile is pretty easy. Here's how:

1. **Cut around the cracked tile, between the tile and the grout.** Get a special tile cutter from a home improvement or hardware store.

2. **After the bond is broken, lift the tile out with a putty knife.**

3. **Remove the old adhesive with mineral spirits.**

4. **After the square is clean and dry, put new adhesive on the floor.**

5. **Set the new tile on top of it.** Position it correctly in the space.

6. **Regrout the new tile when it's positioned the way you want.**

If any grout has to be replaced, mix it to match the color of the rest of the grout.

# Giving Vinyl Sheets and Squares the Beauty Treatment

Don't throw away remnants or squares of vinyl flooring. You never know when they'll come in handy. A falling knife usually ends up blade down, leaving a small cut. Chairs can scratch, dent, and rip vinyl. And everyone knows what happens when a match or cigarette hits your vinyl floor. If you haven't kept the remnants or extra tiles, take a piece out of a closet or another spot where it won't be noticed. You need the scrap pieces, masking tape, a utility knife, a putty knife, floor adhesive, and a roller, such as a rolling pin. If you have a T-square or carpenter's square, you can cut a straighter edge. Use mineral spirits to clean up excess adhesive.

To remove stains and scuffs from vinyl, use mineral spirits. It takes everything off, including black heel marks, scuffs, tar, adhesive, and gum.

Patches won't show up in patterned vinyl because the pattern hides seams.

## Replacing part of a vinyl sheet

Sometimes, a piece of vinyl needs to be repaired. Here's how:

1. **Tape your scrap vinyl over the damaged area, matching the pattern.** You want to make sure the scrap won't slip.

2. **Using the square, draw lines on the patch where you will cut the vinyl.** Make the cut larger than the damaged area. If possible, use the pattern to minimize the visibility of cut edges.

3. **Cut through both layers of vinyl at once, the scrap and the flooring.**

4. **With the putty knife, remove the damaged vinyl.**

5. **Dissolve the old adhesive by rubbing it with mineral spirits.**

6. **Scrape out any remaining adhesive using the putty knife or a scraper.**

7. **Double-check the pattern and the fit.**

8. **Smear vinyl adhesive on the patch, then press the patch firmly in place.**

9. **Wipe up excess adhesive off the seams.**

10. **Use the rolling pin to press down harder so that the patch won't lift up.**

11. **Wipe the seams again with the mineral spirits.**

## Uncurling vinyl edges

You can try to put new adhesive under the curling edges, following Steps 5 through 7, and 10 and 11 in the "Replacing part of a vinyl sheet" section. But if adhesive doesn't hold down the edge, then cut a patch of scrap vinyl to fill in the curled edge.

## Replacing vinyl tiles

Buckling, scratching, and staining can ruin vinyl tiles. But they're easy to replace if you've saved the extra pieces. If not, scavenge a replacement tile in a closet or from somewhere a missing tile won't be noticed. You need a replacement tile, a putty knife, a heat gun or warm iron, mineral spirits, tile adhesive, a notched trowel, and a rolling pin. Here's what to do:

1. **Warm the tile with the heat gun or iron.** You want to make the adhesive soft, but *don't* melt the vinyl.

2. **Use the putty knife to get under the old tile and lift it out.**

3. **Dissolve the adhesive on the floor with mineral spirits.**

4. **Scrape the adhesive with the putty knife or a scraper.**

5. **Coat the underside of the new tile with adhesive.**

6. **Put the new tile in place.**

7. **Roll it with the rolling pin.**

8. **Clean up excess adhesive with the mineral spirits.**

# Restoring Damaged Carpets

Many things can damage carpets. Treat spills, stains, and accidents as quickly as possible before they have to chance to really lay claim to you carpeting. If you don't, it will take more work to get the stain out.

If you get a new carpet, keep the remnants. You never know when they may come in handy.

## Carpet stains

Treat spills and stains immediately. If you treat a bloodstain immediately, cold water usually takes it out with repeated dabbings with a wet cloth. After blood dries, use an enzyme stain remover. Enzymes also are great for treating stains caused by pets and effectively remove strong cat odors. You can get them at a pet shop. You can use white vinegar on wine or food stains without worrying about color changes or more damage. If a stain persists and you have carpet remnants, you can cut out the stain and replace the stained carpet without leaving a trace. Here's how:

1. **Use a utility knife or buy a special carpeting tool called a cookie cutter to cut through the remnant and the stained carpet at the same time.** (You twist a the cookie cutter back and forth in a circular motion to make the cut.) See Figure 3-8A.

   Cut a piece that's larger than stained area and if the carpet has a pattern, be sure to match the remnant pattern so that it isn't obvious after it's glued in place.

2. **Put double-sided carpet tape on the floor.** See Figure 3-8B.

3. **Press the new patch into the cutout area.**

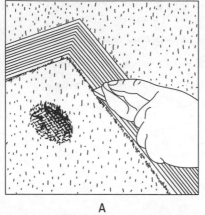
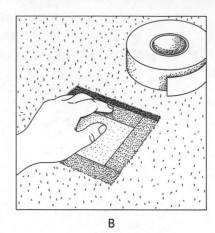

**Figure 3-8:** Cutting out (A) and replacing (B) a patch of damaged carpet.

A                                      B

Low- to high-pile carpets have a nap. You have to put the patch in so that the nap runs in the same direction; otherwise, it will look different from the rest of the carpet. To determine what's right, follow these steps:

1. **Push the nap in one direction and compare it to the rug.**

2. **Push the nap in the opposite direction and compare that.** You'll notice that in one direction the color and pattern blend in; the other way, the patch stands out from the rest of the carpet.

3. **Squeeze seam adhesive on the edges will prevent the loops and strands from unraveling.**

For carpet burns, cutting the carpet should be a last resort. It's much easier to repair the damage by cutting a few fibers off the carpeting in an adjoining closet, or somewhere else where the cut won't be noticed. Then glue them in so that they conceal the burn. You can keep adding more fibers, if needed, or try again if the initial repair isn't quite right.

## Fixing ripped carpet

When something sharp falls, it may cut the carpet. But most often, tears are likely to occur along a seamed edge or at the edges of badly worn carpeting. If a seam comes loose, fix it right away before something catches on the lifted edge and tears the carpet. You need heat-activated carpet tape and a seam iron, available at most rental stores. Here's what to do when a seam comes loose:

1. **Remove the carpet tape that's under both edges of the seam.**

2. **Cut a length of heat-activated tape.** You want a strip long enough to fill the entire lifted edge.

3. **Put the tape down, shoving it under both edges of the seam.** You want to fasten both seam edges firmly to the tape.

4. **With a seam iron, heat the tape so that it becomes sticky.** Then push down one edge of the seam and then the other.

5. **Continue heating the tape and fastening both edges until you come to the end of the seam.**

# Patching Basement Floors (and Walls)

Water collects on basement floors and walls during damp, humid weather. It happens because when moist air hits cold basement walls and floors, it condenses. Sometimes water collects during hard, fast rain storms, coming in between window frames and casings, through cracks in the foundation, or up through the sewer lines. The problem compounds if your yard slopes toward the house instead of away from it.

Basements also get wet if they're deep and the water table in the area is high. For that reason homes in the South — and New Orleans cemeteries, for instance — are constructed above ground.

If water pools against the house, it can cause tiny cracks to form in poured concrete, concrete block, brick, and stone foundations. And eventually, these holes will get larger. Just think about how water carves rocks, changes the flow of rivers, and creates huge underground caverns. In the following sections, we show you how to stop water leaks and get rid of moisture and bad odors that are caused by mold and mildew building up.

## Stopping water leaks and seepage

You can take steps to minimize, if not permanently eliminate, water leaks:

- Start outdoors by looking at the downspouts and gutters. Make sure they aren't clogged because that will contribute to your problem.

- Buy downspout extensions at a hardware or home improvement center and attach them to the downspouts. You want water coming out to drain farther away from the house. Place the ends of the spouts as far away as possible without encroaching on your neighbor's property.

- The next time it rains, go outdoors and look at the yard. If water pools up against the house and stays there long after it's stopped raining, the yard may be sloped towards the house.

## Did a dam break?

What do you do if disaster strikes and your basement or crawl space becomes flooded by excessive rain, plumbing problems, or some other emergency? Other than calling your home insurer in a blind panic, the obvious thing to do is to get all the water out. Water can damage the inner workings and foundations of your home. A flooded basement requires a high-volume pump to get the water out, so you need to call a plumber who has the equipment, or rent it yourself from a hardware store. For smaller flooded areas, like crawl spaces, you can buy your own portable pump. These small, light pumps, sometimes called "trash pumps," cost less than $75 and are well worth keeping around the house, because they're useful for pumping water in a variety of situations. Hook a garden hose up to one for drainage, place it in your crawl space, plug it into a secure outlet, and it will work away for as long as you need to move all of the water out of your crawl space and into an outside ditch or drainage area. After the water is gone, you can then determine what other repairs need to be made to your home. If the flooding occurred because of a clogged sump pump, Chapter 9 tells you how to fix it. And if you don't have a sump pump, we tell you about sump pump installation in this chapter.

We had a problem with water ponding on the patio. So after removing the old concrete, we changed the grade by bringing in sand, and after changing the slope so that the yard was lower, we built a new patio. Now water drains from the house down toward the yard. If changing the grade of the yard doesn't solve the problem, there are several other more costly solutions:

- **Consider replacing basement windows with glass block.** We had one window that always leaked during heavy rainfalls. The water never damaged anything, but we decided to install glass block windows. That completely stopped the seepage and, as a bonus, warmed up the basement in the winter months.

- **Install a sump pump in the basement.** Built into a drain at the lowest point of the basement floor, it pumps water collected to a drainage ditch or to a drain area in your yard.

- **Install drain tiles in the yard.** They collect water and carry it to a low spot in the yard farther away from the house.

- **Dig a trench around the foundation to get at the exterior walls and waterproof them.** For more information, see Chapter 14.

### Eliminating excess moisture in the basement

You can reduce moisture in the basement with a few simple steps. Your first step is to buy a dehumidifier. You should also wrap insulating tape around cold water lines because they sweat in hot weather. Buy tape that has an adhesive backing. Wrap the fittings, as well as the pipes, because they sweat, too. If you have a long pipe to wrap, you may want to use a sleeve that fits around the pipe. You can get them at home improvement and hardware stores. Wrap the pipe in the sleeve and then tape the sleeve together.

### Waterproofing the walls

Seal the foundation with a premixed, waterproofing paint. You need a wide, stiff brush, a roller or a sprayer, and a hose. The paint has some concrete in it and is thick and hard to work with. Plan on spending almost a full week to complete an average-size basement. Waterproofing will keep the walls from feeling clammy, but it will not seal small cracks that water comes through.

Always clean the foundation wall first. You want to get rid of dirt, loose mortar, and any grease or powder. Also be sure the wall is dry.

### Fixing settlement cracks

Sometimes, settlement cracks in the foundation contribute to moist basements. It's not usually a problem, but if you see a layer of mold on the edges of the crack, water is seeping in. So fill the hole with a quick-hardening sealant such as hydraulic cement or epoxy putty. These products expand to fill the hole. Here's what to do:

1. **Use a cold chisel to enlarge the hole or crack and bevel the edges.** This will help the patching compound to hold better.

2. **On cracks caused by settlement, work the sealant into the hole or crack with a trowel or putty knife.** Skip to Step 5. (A structural engineer can look at your cracks to determine whether they were made by settlement.)

3. **To seal dry patches in the concrete, mix one part cement to two parts sand and enough water — added slowly — to make a dough of the cement and sand.** Be sure to follow the manufacturer's recommendations.

4. **Work the sealant into the hole or crack with a trowel or putty knife.**

5. **As the sealant hardens, push it farther into the hole.**

6. **After it dries a few minutes, put more of the cement mix on the patch.** Smooth it off with a putty knife or trowel.

### Installing a sump pump

If your basement is damaged because you need a sump pump to get rid of water that comes up through the basement floor itself, call a contractor to do the work. (See Chapter 18 for tips on hiring an expert.) It's difficult to put in a sump pump by yourself because you have to make a hole in the floor at a low point in the basement.

## Getting rid of musty basement odors

If a basement smells musty, the moisture in the basement may have caused mold and mildew. Sometimes standing water can also smell before mildew and mold occurs. You can do three things to immediately reduce the problem:

✔ Get a dehumidifier and run it constantly as soon as hot, muggy weather sets in. In the northern tier of states, that's usually until fall when the furnace kicks in.

✔ Use a fan to dry out the damp area. Then use a bleach and water solution to clean it.

✔ Get a sump pump to handle excessive moisture. It will kick in at any time of the year when water collects in the drain.

If you shop for sump pumps or talk to contractors, be sure you get a pump that is large enough to handle all of the water you get. And consider a battery-operated backup for power. Sump pumps don't operate when the power goes off and that's precisely when the most water damage occurs. You want another source of power to take over during storms.

If you use a dehumidifier, be sure to empty the reservoir every day. Otherwise, the dehumidifier will shut off when it's full and the captured moisture will slowly evaporate, putting moisture back into the air.

In northern climates, basement dehumidifiers "freeze up" when temperatures drop. To defrost a frozen one, turn it off and don't turn it back on until after the area warms up and the ice or frost has melted. Be sure to maintain the dehumidifier as directed by the manufacturer.

# Chapter 4

# Conquering Door and Window Headaches

oors stick and sag. Windows are often painted shut or have to be re-roped as they get older. Glass breaks, screens tear, and those annoying plastic parts snap off. Meanwhile, don't overhead garage doors seem much heavier today than they were yesterday? If your exits are blocked and you feel blocked because you don't know where to call for help, liberate yourself. In this chapter, we show you how easy it is to fix most exit-entrance problems and what tools you need to have on hand.

## Doctoring Doors

Ever notice the first thing people do when they lose their temper and leave the room? Bam! You can almost hear echoes as the door reverberates, the glass rattles, the space between the trim and the wall opens up, and the hinges continue their downward trend. And if you've got teens clumping through the house, they don't even have to be annoyed to give your doors a "bang" every time they go through one. In fact, they'll argue, "I didn't slam it." Or, "It wasn't me!"

Fortunately, you don't need a carpenter to fix a problem door. If you don't have a handy friend or family member, why not do it yourself? The following sections show you how to make the most common repairs to various types of door and lock problems.

## Unsticking sagging doors

When a door sticks or sags, you can usually blame the hinges or the weather. There are a few quick fixes that won't involve much effort:

- ✔ Before you try anything else, check the hinge plates to see whether the pin is all the way down or any screws are loose. If the problem is with the pins, tap them in place with a hammer.

- ✔ Hot, humid weather causes wooden doors to expand, but don't try to "fix" sticky doors during the summer. Wait until the temperature drops and the moisture abates. Then if the door still sticks, sand it.

- ✔ If a wooden door sticks only slightly, you can sand it at that spot only. (You need to sand more of the edge than is necessary to give clearance for the paint you'll be adding to that edge.)

- ✔ If the door binds at the doorknob and lock edge, then look at the hinges; 99 percent time it's the hinges that are at fault.

  If a door is sagging because of worn hinges, replace them before doing anything else.

If the screws are loose, follow the directions in the next section.

### Tightening screws and filling stripped holes

If the screws in the hinges are loose, tighten them as explained in the following steps. You need a wedge, a screwdriver, a hammer, toothpicks, Elmer's glue and a lubricant such as WD-40. Now here's what to do:

1. **Look at the door to find out where it gaps and where it sticks.**

   - If the door binds at the top (leaning against the knob-side frame and touching the floor below it), you need to work on tightening the top screws. (If the door rubs on carpeting, however, it needs to be cut off on the bottom.)

   - If you have trouble finding where the door binds, chalk the edges, then slowly open and close the door. You can then see where the door binds because the chalk will rub off in those spots.

2. **Open the door and stick a wedge under it on the side that opens.** You have to prop up the door so you can work on the screws in the hinge plates.

3. **Unscrew the screws and lift up the top or bottom hinge plate.** If the screws simply need to be tightened, go to Step 8.

4. **If the holes are stripped, fill them with white glue (Elmer's will do).**

5. **Fill those holes with toothpicks; tap them in one at a time, until no more will go in.**

6. **Let the glue dry, then cut the toothpicks off flush.**

7. **Punch a hole in the wall where the center of the screw hole in the hinge falls, so you can put in new screws.**

8. **Tighten the screws in the holes.**

### Taking a door off its hinges

If that doesn't work, you can take off the door to work on the screws. Here's how to remove the door:

1. **Remove the pins on the bottom hinge.** Place the tip of the screwdriver under the head of the pin and tap the screwdriver gently with the hammer until you raise the pin. If it doesn't budge, use a large nail in the hole directly under the pin to raise the pin enough to get a screwdriver under the head. Take it out.

2. **Repeat Step 1 on the top hinge.** Hold the door so it doesn't fall back on you.

3. **Lift off the door and lay it down.**

4. **Take out each screw in the hinge plates, lift the plates, and check the wood behind them.** If a screw won't tighten, repair the wood it fastens into.

5. **Repeat Steps 3 through 7 in the "Tightening screws and filling stripped holes" instructions.**

6. **Using new screws, refasten the plates, but don't tighten them yet.**

7. **Hang the door by hooking it onto the hinge plate.**

8. **Clean and lubricate the pins with petroleum jelly so they'll be ready to put back in place.** See the section "Silencing squeaky hinges" for more information.

9. **Reinsert the pins and tap them all the way down.**

10. **Now tighten all the screws.**

## Silencing squeaky hinges

Just like the rest of the house, hinges get dirty and they may rust. But unlike the dust and dirt on floors and tables, hinges talk back. If you hear them squeaking every time someone opens and closes the door, remove the pin, wipe it off, lubricate it with petroleum jelly, and stick it back in. If the hinge doesn't have a removable pin, just squirt the hinge with WD-40. That's all it takes.

## Adjusting a striker plate

The striker plate is the metal plate that the door lock or latch slides into when you close the door. When a striker plate is out of alignment and the latch or lock won't secure properly, first look at the top hinge to make sure it's tight or not too worn. Tighten the screws or replace the hinge if necessary. If the bolt still won't go into the hole on the striker plate — usually caused by settlement, worn hinges, or too many coats of paint — you have to adjust the plate up or down, or in or out. Most often, striker plates have to be moved up or down, but the process is the same for moving it in or out. Here's what to do:

1. **Remove the screws and take off the plate.**

2. **Fill existing screw holes with toothpicks and glue.**

3. **Use a utility knife to change the recess so that the plate can be moved up or down.**

4. **Put the plate back on.**

5. **Punch a hole where the screws will go, using a nail or icepick.**

   Don't drill a pilot hole, because jambs are usually made of soft wood such as pine. A drill will remove too much wood and you'll have to fill the new hole with toothpicks and glue and start all over again.

6. **Reinsert the screws.**

## Working on balky locks

Locks can cause problems all by themselves. When that happens, start out by using a lubricant, such as WD-40. Put it on the keyhole only — not the lock cylinder or on the key because that will attract dirt and eventually gum up the cylinder.

If lubricating the keyhole doesn't work, take apart the doorknob assembly. (See Figure 4-1.) All types of locks, including deadbolts, can be cleaned and lubricated as described in the following steps. You need screwdrivers, a lubricant, and powdered graphite (to lubricate the lock cylinder). Here's what to do:

1. **Unscrew all connecting screws on the latch plate and faceplate.**

2. **Pull the doorknob out of the door, then pull the bolt from the faceplate hole.** (See Figure 4-1.)

3. **Put the screws, knob, and other pieces down on paper or the floor. Keep track of the screws.**

4. **Spray lubricant (all-purpose or silicone) on all moving parts, except the lock cylinder, and clean them.**

5. **Clean all accumulated dirt and excess lubricant off the pieces.**

6. **Coat the lock cylinder with graphite.**

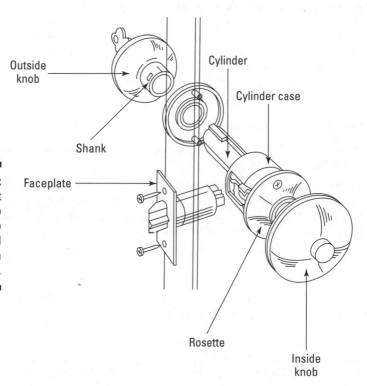

**Figure 4-1:**
Taking apart doorknob locks to clean and realign them.

Outside knob

Cylinder

Cylinder case

Shank

Faceplate

Rosette

Inside knob

Now you will reassemble the knob assembly:

1. **Push the latch assembly back through the hole.**

2. **Install the outside doorknob first, making sure the spindle and holes for the screws are aligned properly.**

3. **Loosely insert screws into the latch assembly.** They'll be tightened after you put in the doorknob.

4. **Put the doorknob on the shaft, matching screw holes with the screws.**

5. **Tighten the screws almost all the way.** If they don't line up, take the doorknob off and try again.

6. **Test the door by turning the knob and locking the lock.**

7. **Tighten the screws all the way.**

## Trimming wooden door bottoms

Carpets have high, low, or no nap. When you install a new carpet, it may be necessary to trim a wooden door so that it clears the carpet. If you don't take this step, the door can damage the carpet by wearing it down unevenly. If a throw rug is causing the problem, it might be better to remove it. Here's what to do when you have to trim the door:

1. **Figure out how much has to be trimmed off the door.**

2. **Place painter's tape all the way around the door so that your cut is in the center of the tape.**

3. **Carefully mark the door along the trim line.** If the surface is veneer, run a utility knife along the cutting line. Keep a straight edge on the door until you've scored all of it. The straight edge will keep the knife from slipping off on a tangent. Scoring the veneer helps reduce the risk of splintering it.

4. **Cut through the door with your handsaw or power saw.**

Place a board on top of the door and use it to guide the saw along the scored line. And don't let the piece you cut off drop prematurely. Prop it up until you know you've sawed through the whole width of the door.

## Straightening warped wooden doors

If a wooden door warps, you can try to unbend the bowing by first removing the door and then weighting down the bad area. Use a pile of books or one of the weights in your weight set and keep them on the door for at least three days.

You can also try adding another hinge. If it's in the middle of the door, weight will be distributed more evenly and the extra hinge may straighten out the door.

## Sliding stubborn patio doors

Opening a sliding patio door gets difficult when it needs a new roller or when the tracks get dirty or bent. You don't need to run out to the store to buy a new door. Just get the track working again.

It's easy to see excessive dirt or buckled tracks. If you have either or both conditions, start out by vacuuming the track to get all the loose dirt and fur out of it. Then clean off the caked-up dirt with a small, stiff brush. Use water and detergent if necessary. Finally, lubricate the track and the rollers to get the door working smoothly. Use WD-40 or a similar lubricant on the rollers and graphite or paraffin on the track.

To straighten a bent track, run a block of wood, the width of the track, through the track. Whenever you come to a bowed area or blockage, lightly tap the metal track with the wood block behind it to straighten it out.

If a track is in terrible shape, take out the door (by lifting it up and over the existing track) and install a new track. When you head to the home improvement store, take a portion of the track with you so you can buy an exact replacement.

You also can reposition the track by taking out the screws in the track and readjusting the track.

If you notice the door sags towards the opening edge so that you have to lift the door to move it, you need to readjust the height of the rollers or replace them. Here's what to do:

1. **Remove the door from the track.** It's heavy. Get someone to help you hold it up and set it down out of the way.

2. **Take the old rollers off the bottom of the door.**

3. **Screw in the new ones.**

4. **If package directions tell you to lubricate the new rollers, do it lightly.**

5. **Adjust the rollers — usually with a large Phillips screwdriver in the hole in the ends of the door.** Turning the screws clockwise raises that roller and that end of the door. Then do the other side.

## Replacing door thresholds

Thresholds on outside doors get a lot of abuse — people walk on them as they go in and out, sometimes with wet or muddy shoes. Nails pop up, wet wood rots, doors drag, and heavy furniture, shoved over a threshold when you're moving, can cause cracking and splintering, especially when the threshold is made of soft wood. Thresholds are also stressed when a house settles, sometimes causing misalignment. When your thresholds are in trouble, you can usually replace them yourself with ease. In this section, we show you how.

Wood and metal *thresholds* on outside doors create a seal to keep cold air and water from creeping into a house underneath the door. Metal thresholds usually don't get damaged unless they get dented by something heavy dropping on them. But wood thresholds can crack, split, or break, or you may have to replace one because you're replacing an adjoining floor. When you want to put in a new threshold, we recommend that you get a metal replacement with a rubber insert because they're easy to install and adjust. Now we explain how to put in a new metal threshold:

1. **Take out the old threshold by removing the nails and prying up the wood.** If necessary, you can cut it into three pieces (see Figure 4-2A). Remove the centerboard first.

   When you're taking out the old threshold, be careful not to damage the flashing beneath it.

2. **Measure the threshold and buy one that's metal. Be sure to get one that has a rubber insert in the center. See Figure 4-2B.**

3. **Using a hacksaw, cut the metal to fit under the doorjambs.** Use the old threshold as a pattern to cut the notches.

4. **Tap the threshold in place to check for fit and space under the door.** Adjust the threshold height if necessary by loosening or tightening the screws. If it's a non adjustable type threshold, use shims under it. Screw it securely to the floor. See Figure 4-2C.

5. **Cut the rubber insert to fit into the space between the door frames.**

6. **Snap the rubber into the channel on the top of the threshold.** The rubber should just touch the bottom of the door.

7. **Check for clearance and fit again, making adjustments as needed.**

8. **Use a clear caulk on the edges to seal them.**

If the space under the jamb is tight, use a chisel to trim the bottom of the wood. Be sure to do a little at a time so you don't take out too much or damage the jamb. See Figure 4-2B.

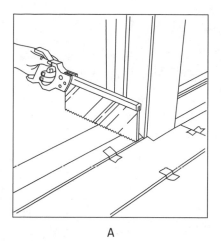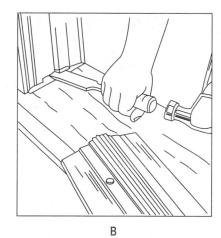

A         B

**Figure 4-2:**
Removing
the old door
threshold
and replac-
ing it with a
new one.

C

# Working On Windows

New windows ain't anything like old ones. Over the years, the old ones may have been liberally swathed in paint, making them balky or totally inoperable. And if they're really old windows, they most likely operate with a rope-and-pulley system — another reason why they may need attention. And windows are costly to replace, especially if they're not standard sizes. So until you are able to make the investment for new windows, you have to contend with what you have and give your windows the attention they need. See Figure 4-3 for the anatomy of a double-hung window.

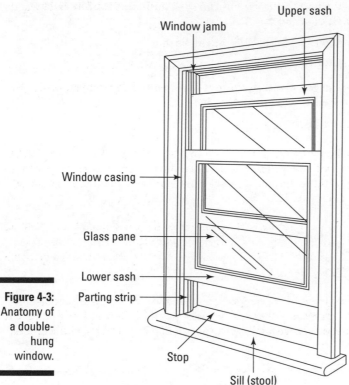

Window jamb

Upper sash

Window casing

Glass pane

Lower sash

Parting strip

Stop

Sill (stool)

**Figure 4-3:**
Anatomy of
a double-
hung
window.

## Unsticking windows

Generally, windows stick because paint oozes into the crack between the sash and keeps the window from moving smoothly. Sometimes, the channels need to be cleaned and lubricated. In extreme cases, windows may have been painted shut when the room was redecorated.

To get windows moving, wrap a cloth around a block of wood, place it against the window frame at the bottom, and tap it gently with a hammer. Be careful not to break the glass. Then go to the other side and do the same. Go back and forth between both sides of the sash until you've reached the top of the window frame. Another way to break a bond is to insert a stiff-bladed putty knife into the cracks and tap the handle gently with a hammer. You can also work from outside, using a pry bar and a block of wood. Here's how:

1. **Put the pry bar under one end of the sash and rock the bar backwards, over the block of wood.**

2. **Repeat Step 1 on the other side of the sash.**

3. **Go back and put the bar under the sash on the first side.**

4. **Repeat these steps, working the pry bar toward the center, until you've lifted the entire bottom sash.**

5. **Try lifting the window.**

If that doesn't work, run your utility knife or a single-edge razor blade in the crack to break the paint seal. Then rattle the sash — again working gently — to free it from the window frame. It's a slow, tedious process so be patient and work slowly and carefully. Then try raising the window.

If it's still stuck, you have to take off the window stops with a pry bar. Follow the steps in the section on "Re-roping old windows." Take out the window sash, then sand the edges of the sash and stop. Rub them with soap or hard candle wax to lubricate them.

Sometimes, it takes even more work to get a window to operate smoothly. Look for excessive paint in the crack on both sides of the window and on the bottom, between the sash and sill. Scrape it all off with a putty knife, chisel, or a Paint Zipper.

## Re-roping old windows

New and replacement windows are cordless, but the double-hung windows in old houses still have *cords* — the mechanism that allows them to open easily, stay open (without a stick propping them up), and shut. Over time, the cords fray and break, disconnecting the weights. Some windows have chains instead of ropes and over time, they, too, can break. But the process of fixing them is the same as re-roping.

You don't have to be frustrated by your inability to throw open the sash to catch gentle summer breezes. You can replace the cords (or chains), which were constructed with weights tied to the end that give balance to the window. See Figure 4-4. Here's how to remove the window:

1. **Remove the window stop from the frame.** If the window and frame have been painted, cut through the paint with a razor blade or utility knife.

   You want to make it as easy as possible to get under the stop so that it won't break as you lift it out.

2. **With a stiff putty knife (or a small pry bar), raise the stop wherever there's a nail.** Start at the bottom and work your way up, removing nails after they're loosened from the sash. See Figure 4-4A.

3. **Remove the parting strip.** (The *parting strip* is a piece of wood that separates the tracks of the upper and lower sash.)

4. **Push the lower sash up high enough that you can clear the windowsill and lift it out of the window frame.** Pull the bottom toward you.

5. **On each side of the lower sash, near the top, detach the cord from its slot.** Now you're ready to work on the jamb.

6. **Unscrew the access plate (or cover) from each side of the lower jamb to uncover the pulley and weight.** See Figure 4-4B. Put the plates aside.

   If the jambs don't have plates, you have to remove the window casing to get at the cords, weights, and pulleys. Lift the wood gently with a putty knife or pry bar to loosen the nails, then remove the nails and finally, the wood. Work carefully so you won't have to replace the casing.

7. **Take out the weights from each side of the jamb.** See Figure 4-4C.

8. **Remove the upper sash.** You'll see the weight pulleys on each side of the upper jamb.

9. **Clean out any debris from inside the access panel.**

To repair your rope or chain, follow these steps:

1. **Use WD-40 or another lubricant on the pulleys.** Clean them first if they look like they need it.

2. **Tape the ends of the new cord or chain to the old cords.**

3. **Pull the old cords out, feeding the new cords or chains up and over the pulleys.**

4. **Feed the cords or chains through the hole in the weights, and knot them together.** If using chains, use wires to secure the ends to the weights. See Figure 4-4D.

5. **Put the weights back in the jamb.**

6. **Test the new cords or chains by pulling the weights up to the pulleys to see whether the cords and weights operate smoothly.**

7. **Put the upper sash in.**

8. **Place the lower sash on the windowsill.**

9. **Hold each cord, in turn, firmly against the window.**

10. **Three inches below the hole in the side window sash, cut the cord.** Repeat this on the other side.

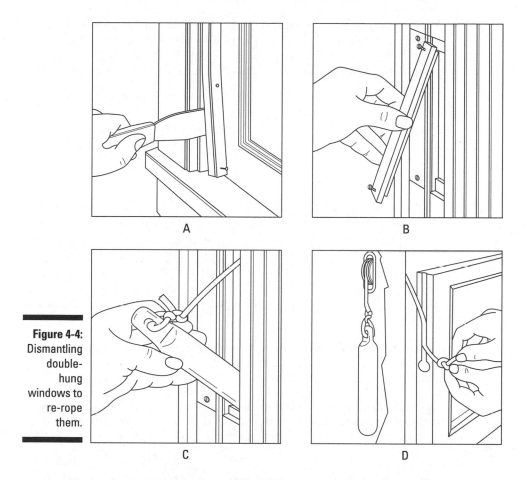

A

B

**Figure 4-4:**
Dismantling
double-
hung
windows to
re-rope
them.

C

D

11. **Tie a knot in the ends of the cords and reinsert them in the slots and holes on the sides of the lower sashes.**

12. **Put the lower sash back into the window frame.**

## *Replacing and reputtying glass*

When the old putty around a window cracks and falls out, the best-quality window in the world can't keep heat and cold from getting into your house and racking up your utility bills. You can put new putty in by following these steps:

1. **Using a putty knife, take out the old putty.** Be sure to remove all of it.

2. **Put the new glazing putty around the window.** You can use a rope of putty or the canned type.

3. **Press down on the putty with the putty knife, forming a triangular shape.** Be sure to press firmly, so it adheres to the frame and the window. If the putty is too stiff or if it rolls up, take it off and knead it with a little mineral oil until the mineral oil is worked in. Then put it back on the window.

4. **Let it dry for a few days.**

5. **Paint the putty to protect it from getting too dry.** Be sure to use an oil-based primer first because putty is an oil-based product. The paint can be water based.

## Putting in new glass

Baseballs, wild birds, elbows — you name it. We watched in amazement one morning years ago when a hyperactive dog leaped through the lower pane of a storm door. It was January and freezing outside, but the sun was bright and the shards and tiny pieces of glass glittered and sparkled as they sprayed out behind him. A beautiful, unforgettable sight. (The dog was fine — not a mark on him!)

It's easy to put in a new pane, although if it's a storm door that shattered, you'll probably have to settle for a clear acrylic panel or some other shatterproof glass. Purchase double-strength glass as a replacement. It is stronger — the dog wouldn't have been able to sail through it. And it is more energy efficient. Have it cut by the hardware or home improvement store. It should be ⅛ inch smaller than the opening in the window frame. Be sure to measure accurately or else take the frame with you when you go for glass. To replace your window glass:

1. **Take out the window putty and glazing points (the little metal things that your putty knife catches on when scraping the putty out).** They hold the glass in.

2. **Carefully remove the old glass.** Grab it with an old rag or wear gloves to protect your fingers and hands.

3. **Put the new glass in.**

4. **Push glazing points into the wood.** They hold the glass tightly against the sash. Put two per side on small panes and four to six per side for larger windows.

5. **If you have a wooden frame, put some oil on the sash.** Use linseed oil or a similar product. That prevents the oils in the glazing compound from soaking into the frame.

6. **Put a ribbon of canned or rope glazing compound around the new pane, where the glass meets the frame.**

7. **Use a putty knife to angle the compound against both surfaces and press down hard on the angle.** You want to make a tight bond.

8. **After the compound dries for a couple days — although it will still feel somewhat pliant — you can prime the compound with oil-based primer, then paint it.** That will prevent it from cracking.

## Rejuvenating rotted sills

Windowsills rot because moisture has penetrated the finish. Even though the sills slope out to resist moisture, you may have a problem in cold weather if the windows are old and single paned. Before we got replacement windows, ice used to form on the sills in extremely cold weather because of the discrepancy between the outside and indoor temperatures. Eventually it caused the painted sills to flake and chip.

Preventive maintenance is recommended, so inspect sills at least once a year, usually in fall. Keep the sills caulked and painted to reduce rot.

To find out whether any of your sills are rotted, probe into the wood in spots that have lost their finish. You can use a pick for getting the meat out of nuts or an ice pick. Stick it into the bare spot. If it goes in easily, then your sill has "dry rot." If the sill is still in good condition, the pick won't go into the wood. If the wood isn't rotted, you should take steps to refinish it quickly before it goes bad. See Chapter 14.

If the whole sill is bad, you should call a carpenter to put in a new sill because it's a complicated job that takes special skills. If just small patches are rotted, you can, and should, repair it before it gets worse. We explain what you have to do below. You need a chisel or utility knife, some wood filler or epoxy, a putty knife, sandpaper, and paint or another finishing product. Here's what to do:

1. **Chip out the rotted area with your utility knife or a small chisel.** Be sure to get all the bad wood out.

2. **Kill the fungus causing the rot by using Git Rot or dump bleach in it if the surface is flat.**

3. **Fill in the patch with wood fill or epoxy.** If the hole is deep, fill it several times, waiting between applications. Be sure that the filler gets into every crevice.

4. **With a small knife or putty knife, shape the patch.**

5. **Apply a preservative, such as Thompson's Water Seal.**

6. **Wait 24 hours, then coat the patch with linseed oil.** That will keep it from drying out and shrinking.

7. **After that dries, prime and paint the sill or stain and finish it to match the window frame.**

## Working on casement hardware

The hardware on casement windows sometimes needs adjusting so that the window can operate smoothly. Some windows open with a rod sliding through pivots mounted on the sill and window. Other windows have a metal bar (called a *sliding shoe*) mounted on the sill; a rod slides through a channel in the middle of the shoe. Still others open when you turn a crank that's attached to a gear. (See Figure 4-5.)

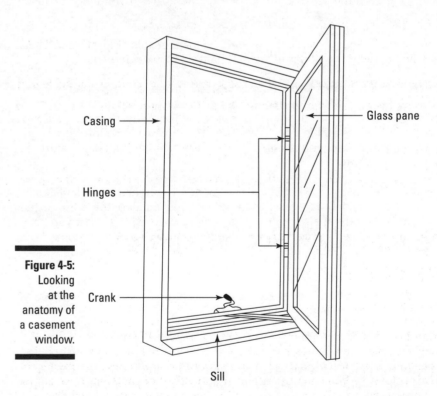

Casing

Glass pane

Hinges

**Figure 4-5:**
Looking
at the
anatomy of
a casement
window.

Crank

Sill

All three mechanisms need fine-tuning periodically — basically cleaning and lubricating. Here's what to do with sliding rods:

1. **Clean off all dirt and built-up paint on the rod, using steel wool.**

2. **Lubricate the rod by rubbing it against a bar of soap or paraffin.**

3. **Tighten screws and lubricate them with WD-40.**

Here's what to do with rods and sliding shoes:

1. **Take out the screws on the channel.**

2. **Clean the channel and the sliding shoe.**

3. **Use paraffin wax or soap to lubricate the channel.** Wax is the best choice.

4. **Screw the channel back into the sill.**

5. **Tighten all other screws.**

6. **Use WD-40 or a similar lubricant on pivot points.**

Here's what to do with cranks and gears:

1. **Clean the track after you open the window.** Use a stiff brush to clean it.

2. **Spray inside the track with silicone or petroleum jelly.**

3. **Lubricate moving parts on the crank handle with WD-40.**

4. **Wipe off all excess lubricant.**

That's all you have to do. This should take care of your problems for a while.

# Caulking and Weather Stripping Windows and Doors

Caulking keeps windowframes and doorframes weather tight. Moisture can't get into the cracks between the structure of the house and the window or door and wind is prevented from whistling through, eliminating drafts and making the inside temperature much more cozy in cool or cold weather. But you can't caulk all potential trouble spots. Doors and windows are meant to open and close, so you can't seal them shut. Instead of caulking those edges, you can weather strip them. In this section, we show you how to caulk and weather strip your doors and windows.

## Caulkin' without squawkin'

When your windows and doors were installed, the seams were caulked as a matter of routine. But caulking dries out over time, and then it can crack and fall out. So if your house feels drafty when it's windy or cool, go around the house finding out where the draft is coming from. Obviously, you can also just inspect the windows and door caulking, but in some spots you may not notice where the caulking has come loose. If you've checked your windows and the house still seems drafty, carry a lighted candle around the house on a windy day. You may notice it flickering where the draft is coming in.

Besides caulk and a caulking gun — the metal holder and handle that squeezes caulk from the tube — you need a putty knife and an old toothbrush or something with a similar handle.

Caulking also comes in an easy squeeze tube, but only in small quantities, so it's primarily useful for small projects. You can cap the tube, which gives it a longer shelf life, and you don't have as much waste as you get with a caulking gun. When you use a gun, it's hard to stop the flow of caulk. But for large projects, the tube and gun may be the only way you can keep costs down. Here's what you have to do:

1. **Inspect each window and door, in turn.** Check the caulk around and under the outside edges of the frames.

2. **If you see any slightly cracked, broken, or missing caulk or if it looks like the caulk has dried up and pulled away from the house or frame, use the putty knife to remove all the old pieces.**

   It's best to take out *all* the old caulk, but if you're in a hurry or don't have time to redo all of the caulking, just chip out all of the broken or shriveled chunks.

3. **After you've removed all the old putty, cut the tip off the putty-tube nozzle and put the tube in the caulk gun.** You also have to puncture the foil seal; use a thin screwdriver, coat hanger, or the wire attached to the better caulking guns to make a few holes.

4. **Squeeze a bead of new putty into the gap.** Apply it liberally, and then work it into the crevice with the putty knife.

   Try to use a smooth, continuous motion, squeezing lightly and moving the tube as you go along the crack. You don't want to jerk the gun or press too hard on the trigger; if you do, the caulk will clump in some spots and be too thin in others. Try not to get frustrated. It takes a little practice to get caulking right. If you're not happy with how it looks, take out the caulk and put down another bead.

5. **Push the caulk further into the space firmly.**

6. **Smooth the caulk using a wetted implement.** A Popsicle stick, toothbrush, your finger, or a plastic spoon are all good choices for the job.

7. **Repeat these steps on the next window or door.**

For leaky windows that you want to open in the summer, use a removable caulk on the inside and peel it off in the spring.

## The wonders of weather stripping

With the cost of energy mounting, renters and homeowners alike want to keep the lid on increases in gas, oil, and electric bills. You can help do that by weather stripping doors and windows so the furnace doesn't have work overtime to heat up the cold air coming through the cracks inside window-frames and doorframes. Weather stripping also prevents loss when you're using your air conditioner. It reduces the dust coming into your home, as well as the number of insects and spiders. And you won't hear aggravating outside noise — heavy traffic, yipping dogs, and the deafening music of the teens next door. Fortunately, weather stripping is an easy job you can do yourself. And weatherstripping is generally easy to install or take off if you want to use it only seasonally.

Your first step is deciding what kind of weatherstripping to use — how durable you want it to be and how much you want to spend. (Keep in mind there are always new products on the market and different brands.)

Weatherstripping is available in tape-backed foam that goes around windows and doors, and also sweeps or shoes that go under doors. The cost is nominal, compared to the cost of heat or air conditioning.

Don't forget to put a weatherstrip on the bottom of exterior doors and windows. There's always a gap between the door and threshold and even locked windows have air coming in or going out if there's no weatherstripping.

When you're sealing doors and windows, the weatherstripping is placed on the outside of the frame. Follow package directions carefully.

## Replacing and Mending Screens

It doesn't cost much to have the local hardware store replace a torn screen — and put in those troublesome plastic corners. But it's another job you can do yourself quite easily. And you can do it in a couple of hours instead of waiting days to make it to the top of the store's waiting list.

You can buy aluminum and/or fiberglass netting at a hardware or home improvement store. But fiberglass is easier to work with and so we'll concentrate on replacing it. It comes in prepackaged widths and lengths or off a bolt. The bolts also have various widths and, of course, you can match exactly the length you need. (You'll probably find prepackaged widths at a home improvement store.) The store should also carry an assortment of plastic replacement pieces.

The plastic pieces should be replaced before the new screen is installed.

Measure the length and width of the frame, and then add on an extra two or three inches to each side. It is easier to install a screen if it overlaps the frame slightly. You can trim off the excess after the screen is done, before you set it back into the window or door.

## Putting in new mesh

Before you replace the mesh, you need the screen, new spline (*spline* is the finishing piece or vinyl rope that keeps the edges of the screen in place), and a spline tool, which is inexpensive and useful. See Figure 4-6. Even if the old spline looks good, it shrinks and is probably brittle, so you won't have enough for the new screen. Here's how to replace the mesh:

1. **Put the screen on the boards or table where you'll be working.**

2. **With a screwdriver or small pliers, lift the spline out of the groove running along the inside edge of the screen frame.** See Figure 4-6A.

3. **Lift out the mesh.**

4. **Clean the groove.**

5. **Put the new mesh down, hanging the excess over the window frame.** You want a few inches of mesh hanging on each side. Keep the horizontal and vertical lines straight, not running diagonally. See Figure 4-6B.

6. **Put the spline on top of the draped mesh.**

7. **With the spline tool, push the spline — along with the mesh — into the groove on one side.** See Figure 4-6C.

   Don't put the mesh in the groove first because then when you push the spline, it will push more mesh in, leaving no space for the spline.

8. **On the opposite side, push in the mesh and spline in next.**

9. **Keep tension on the mesh while you're working so that it won't look rippled or bowed in or out after you've finished.**

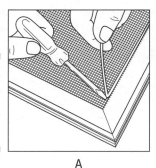
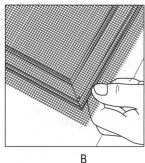
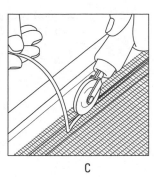

**Figure 4-6:**
Replacing
torn screen
with new
mesh.

A                    B                    C

10. **Then do the last two sides the same way.**

    Do the left and right sides first, then the top and bottom. Don't worry about the excess. You'll trim it off when you're done. See Figure 4-6.

11. **If any side is bowed in, pull out that spline, loosen the mesh, and redo it.**

12. **When all sides look straight, try it in the window or door to see if it fits right.**

13. **If it does, use a single-blade razor or utility knife to cut along the outside edge of the spline.** Then pull off the excess mesh.

14. **Put the screen back in the window.** You're done.

## Mending a tear

If a metal screen has a small rip, you can fix it very easily without replacing everything. All you need is a piece of screening, slightly larger than the tear itself. You can't use fiberglass to patch a metal screen; you have to get a piece of aluminum screen. Here's what to do:

1. **Lay the screen on a couple boards, the floor, or a table.** (If you use furniture, protect the surface with newspaper.)

2. **Flatten the ripped edges of the screen by pressing down on the tear.**

3. **Cut a rectangular patch from a piece of mesh.** It should be longer and wider than the tear.

4. **Bend the edges of the patch.** You want the patch to look like the cover of a box.

5. **Put the patch — bent edges down — on top of the tear.** Be sure the patch overlaps the entire tear.

6. **Push the bent wires through the mesh and bend them in, toward the tear.**

7. **Press down so the edges are totally flat.**

# Troubleshooting Garage Doors: What You Should and Shouldn't Do

Garage doors are tricky because there are certain things that absolutely must be left to a professional. However, there are minor fixes you can do yourself that will help keep your door functioning properly for a good long time and reduce your need for a repair specialist. In this section, we go over the things you can do yourself.

Keeping your door in good working order helps the electronic garage door opener work more efficiently. Because the information in this section deals only with the doors, if you need to know more about the garage door opener refer to Chapter 7.

*Never* try to adjust a garage door on your own. It is extremely dangerous because of the weight of the door and the possibility of wires and pulleys snapping loose. Always call a garage door service if you're having problems with the opener chain, the gears, binding tracks, tension on the springs, or the sprockets, bearings, and pulley.

Most garages aren't much different from the outside temperature in the winter or summer — and when you cool or heat your house, the air seeps into your garage. Attached garages may share one or two walls with the house. Compounding the energy loss is that an overhead door, tightly sealed in the summer, may not be as tight during the winter months: Ground frost causes concrete driveways to heave. You may notice a gap under the door or that the locking mechanism won't lock.

Short of heating the garage, you can minimize heat loss by weather stripping overhead doors. It will help reduce, at least a little, what you have to pay for utilities. And you can easily do the work yourself. To cut down on the loss of energy, install a moderately priced seal:

1. **Take off the old weatherstripping.**

2. **Measure the width of the door and purchase an overhead door seal.**

3. **Cut it ⅛ inch narrower than the door itself.**

4. **Be sure the sweep will block the gap between the door and floor after it's installed.**

5. **If your door is metal, screw the sweep onto the door; if wood, use roofing nails, which won't rust.**

Other garage door fix-its homeowners can do include:

- ✔ **Refastening loose screws and bolts.** They can put the door out of alignment. Most rolling garage doors, particularly wooden ones, consist of panels held together with screws and bolts that can wear away or become loose through a lot of use. You can prevent some door problems by checking panel-type garage doors once a year to make sure the bolts are still tight.

- ✔ **Realigning the track.** If anything blocks the track, the doors won't completely open or close. If the tracks are bent or out of alignment, call a qualified door service company.

- ✔ **Cleaning and lubricating the hinges and rollers.** Use a degreaser from your hardware store to clean them. To lubricate sticky and sluggish doors:

  1. **Put a couple drops of lightweight oil on the hinge pins, rollers, pulleys, and cables.** It smoothes the way when garage doors get balky.

  2. **Wipe the cable with a rag dipped in oil, especially if the cable is starting to look a little rusty.**

  3. **If the door still sticks, look at the trim around the door to see whether you notice any spots where the door may be rubbing against it.** If this is the case, you can pry off the trim and then remount it, just a little farther from the edge of the door.

     Don't lubricate the tracks because it attracts dirt, and if you brush against them, you'll get lubricant on your clothes.

  4. **If the door still sticks after lubricating it, check the vertical and horizontal level of tracks on each side of the door.** If one side of a track is bent or further away from the other at any point along the track, the door won't operate smoothly. The mounting brackets of tracks usually have slots in the mounting holes that can be adjusted with a wrench. A professional should fix this.

Old wooden doors that sag due to worn fastenings or warped wood usually have to be completely replaced.

Call in an expert if a spring needs adjusting or refastening and it is mounted above the door on the wall. If a spring breaks loose while you're working on it, it will virtually explode. You won't have time to move out of the way and the door will cause you serious injury.

# Chapter 5

# Closing In on Walls and Ceilings

● ● ● ● ● ● ● ● ● ● ● ● ● ● ● ● ● ● ● ● ● ● ● ● ● ● ● ● ● ● ● ● ● ● ● ● ● ● ● ● ● ● ● ● ● ●

*In This Chapter*

▶ Fixing problems with drywall

▶ Replastering cracked walls

▶ Substituting tiles

▶ Repairing wallpaper

▶ Restoring paneling

● ● ● ● ● ● ● ● ● ● ● ● ● ● ● ● ● ● ● ● ● ● ● ● ● ● ● ● ● ● ● ● ● ● ● ● ● ● ● ● ● ● ● ● ● ●

*I*n this chapter, we discuss ways to fix the most typical wall and ceiling problems, including loose seam tape, sagging drywall, and those annoying pop-outs caused when nails back out of wallboard. And you won't have to hunt down a plasterer — almost an ancient skill — because we tell you how to replaster small cracks and holes yourself. Because we're talking about walls, we decided to throw in some tips on how to patch holes in wallpaper and repair scratched or damaged paneling for good measure.

## Correcting Drywall Problems

Since World War II, drywall has taken the place of plastered walls and ceilings, mainly because it's cheaper and quicker to install. Nailed or screwed to studs, drywall is ready to prime and paint after the seams are taped and covered with a joint compound. (Drywall is also called sheetrock, gypsum board, wallboard, or plasterboard. It comes in various sizes from 4 x 8 feet to 52 inches x 16 feet.)

Popped nails, damaged corner joints, loose tape, and holes, dents, and gouges are the most common drywall problems, but panels can sag as well.

Drywall can be repaired with a variety of different patching compounds — hard drying, fast drying, or chemically set. These aren't interchangeable with a ceiling-patching compound, which must be stiff enough not to fall out before it dries. In contrast, a wall-patching compound is mixed with water and can be made thicker to fill holes or thinner to fill cracks.

When applying coats of patch over a scratch or hole, it's best to put on several thin coats, about ¼ inch thick, rather than one big glob. Thin coats will dry faster and you'll have better control over the repair. You also won't have the work of sanding all that excess mud down.

Drywall compound for textured ceilings is different from other types, but it can be used in the same way. It dries harder and is whiter than mud for regular drywall, but that doesn't matter if you plan to paint it to match the rest of the ceiling.

## Reattaching popped nails

The most frequently needed drywall repair is refastening popped nails. A *popped nail* means that either the compound placed over the nail head falls out or the head of the nail starts poking out of the wallboard. This happens when a house settles or the nail wasn't fastened to a stud. Sometimes, pops occur when people walk through the house and the floor bounces or moves. You can hide popped nails by using a screwdriver, drywall screws, a patching compound, fine sandpaper, primer, and paint. Here's what to do:

1. **Fasten a drywall screw slightly above and below the popped nail.**
   *Dimple* the screws — that's inserting them below the wall's surface. Work carefully so you don't break through the paper that covers the wallboard. You have to mount the screw onto wood; if you don't, move it over ¼ inch and try again. It doesn't matter if you have a few extra holes in the drywall; you can patch them with the patching compound in Step 3.

   The easiest way to find studs is with a stud finder, an electronic device that senses the difference between drywall and drywall with wood behind it. You can find them for less than $5 at hardware and home improvement stores.

2. **Dimple the popped nail.**

3. **Put the patching compound over the dimples.** Read and follow manufacturer's instructions.

4. **Coat the dimples again as needed.**

5. **Sand the patches, then clean them.**

6. **Prime the area, then paint the surfaces.**

## Securing sagging drywall

When drywall sags from the ceiling, it may not have been adequately fastened or it may have been softened by water leaks. If you have a leak from the outdoors or an upstairs bathroom that's damaging drywall, turn to Chapter 14 for help on stopping the leak. If the drywall hasn't been severely damaged by water, you can refasten it after the leaks are fixed and the drywall thoroughly dries. Here's how:

1. **Find one of the ceiling joists with an electronic stud finder — available in hardware and home improvement stores — or by thumping on the ceiling.** The joist under drywall has a solid sound; between joists it sounds hollow. After you locate one stud, the next will be either 16 or 24 inches away.

2. **Place pairs of drywall screws into the joist 2 inches apart along the length of the ceiling joists where the ceiling sags.** Space the pairs 6 to 12 inches apart.

3. **You may have to tighten all of the screws a little at a time so the sag will lift evenly.**

4. **Recess the screws a little.**

5. **Fill the recesses.**

6. **Sand and paint over the screws.**

## Resealing loose tape

*Drywall tape* is plain paper that adheres to drywall patching compound — also called *mud* — and hides the joint where two sections of drywall come together. The tape comes loose if the drywall installer didn't use enough compound under the tape, the mix was too thin, or too much seeped out when the seam was smoothed out with the trowel.

To reseal loose tape, you need scissors or a utility knife, a stiff putty knife, drywall tape, joint compound, sandpaper, primer, and paint. Here's how:

1. **Mix thin drywall mud.**

2. **Put some on a putty knife, slide it under the existing tape, and spread it wherever the tape is loose.** The thin mix will reactivate the old mud so the bond will be strong when it dries.

3. **Press the tape down and smooth it with the putty knife or trowel.**

If only ¼ inch of the 1½-inch-wide tape lifts, you can tape on top of the lift. Just put mud along the edge and onto the wall, and place another piece of tape on the new mud. Spread another thin layer of patch on top of the new tape and adjacent wall. When it dries, sand, prime, and paint it.

For tape that gets badly damaged after it lifts, here's what to do. You need scissors or a utility knife, a stiff putty knife or trowel, drywall tape, joint compound, sandpaper, primer, and paint. Here's how:

1. **Cut off any tape pieces damaged beyond repair.**

2. **Prepare a thin mix of compound, about the consistency of toothpaste.**

3. **Cut new pieces of tape to the same length as those you removed.**

4. **Spread the compound with a putty knife.** (See Figure 5-1A.)

5. **Place the tape in the compound and smooth it on the remaining damaged tape with the putty knife.** (See Figure 5-1B.)

6. **Add more compound and smooth it with a trowel.**

7. **When the compound dries, sand and clean the area.**

8. **Prime and paint the repairs.**

> **TIP**
>
> When you're putting mud on drywall, it's better to layer it ¼ inch at a time than to do one thick application which could take a long time to dry.

**Figure 5-1:**
Resealing
drywall
tape by
spreading
compound
over the
seam (A)
and retaping
it (B).

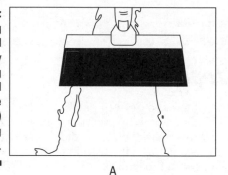 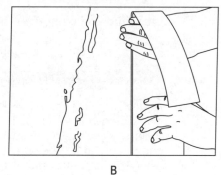

A       B

## Repairing holes in drywall

There are basically three sizes of holes in drywall. Small and medium-sized holes can be repaired using only drywall mud. Larger holes should be patched with a piece of drywall. You get small holes — up to about 1 inch in diameter — if you miss a nail and the hammer punches a hole in the wall. Medium-sized holes are about as big as a fist.

Both can be patched by building them up with the patching compound. Put some mud at the bottom of the hole, let it dry, then add another layer until the hole is filled. You can also add coats of mud, ¼ inch at a time, until the surface of the patch is even with the wall.

Small pieces of net can be stuffed into small holes or placed on top of them to provide backing for the repair. Get them at hardware or home improvement stores.

To repair a large hole, you need a utility knife, a board that's 6 inches longer than the length or width of the hole, a piece of drywall the size of the hole, patching compound, drywall tape, screws, and a screwdriver. (This only works if no studs or joists are exposed.) Here's what to do:

1. **Trim the rough edges of the hole so that all loose drywall paper and pieces of gypsum are removed.** You'll probably enlarge the hole to get smooth edges, but that's okay. And it doesn't matter what shape the hole is; however, it's easier to tape if the hole is square.

2. **Using your precut board, hold onto it in the center and put it into the hole so that each end overlaps the sides of the hole equally.**

3. **Screw through the drywall to one end of the board.** Make sure the board pulls up tight to the back of the wall.

4. **Fasten the other end to the drywall.** Now you can let go of the center.

   It's not necessary to fill the hole with boards; one across the center is enough.

5. **Insert a screw into the center of the patch; this is your handle.**

6. **Fit the piece of drywall into the hole, screw it to the board, and then remove the screw used for a handle.**

7. **Use mud on the seams.**

8. **Press drywall tape over the seams that are covered with mud and smooth it with a putty knife.**

9. **Put more compound on top of the tape.**

10. **Smooth it with a putty knife or trowel, feathering out the edges on the adjoining drywall.**

11. **After the compound dries, sand, prime, and paint the repair.**

## Getting rid of waterlogged drywall

Not too long ago, we smelled mildew every time we walked into the front hallway, but for months couldn't figure out why. Finally the water seeping from a toilet that needed reseating soaked all the way through the ceiling, leaving an ugly wet patch. To get rid of the stain — and nasty odor — we cut out the ruined drywall and filled it with a piece of drywall stored in the basement.

A toilet needs to be reseated when the wax ring that fastens it to the floor breaks loose because the toilet is loose and rocks. Usually when this happens, you see water on the floor around the toilet, but in our case, it leaked onto the ceiling below. To learn more about putting in a new seal, see Chapter 9.

You, too, can get rid of water stains caused by leaking roofs or bathroom overflows and ruined drywall. Just cut out the water-damaged drywall, making the hole slightly larger than the damaged area. Then follow the steps for patching small or large holes. If you expose one or two studs or floor joists in the process, great. Make sure you cut the damaged piece out only to the center of the joists. This leaves a solid backing for the seam of the old and new drywall.

If you see any mold on any wood studs, ceiling joists, or framing wood after you cut out the damaged drywall, you need to spray it liberally with straight bleach to kill the mold and keep it from spreading.

## Repairing drywall dents and gouges

Dents and gouges can be fixed by patching the area, then painting it with a primer and matching paint. You need a utility knife, a patching compound, a stiff putty or drywall knife, primer, and paint. Here's how to repair gouges and dents:

1. **Cut off the loose paper and damaged pieces of gypsum with a utility knife.**

2. **Brush the pieces out of the dent or gouge.**

3. **Spread the patching compound into the hole or dent and overlap the edges a little.**

4. **After it dries, sand the surface smooth.**

5. **Prime and paint it.**

## Refastening damaged corners

Where drywall panels meet at the corner, they're usually held in place by metal edges that are covered with patching plaster. Sometimes, corners get damaged, particularly when furniture is being moved. You need drywall screws, a hammer, patching mud, sandpaper, primer, and paint to refinish the corner. Here's what to do:

1. **Reform the metal with a hammer and insert additional screws to hold it flat.** If the edge is rough, file it with a metal file.

2. **Dig out any loose or cracked mud.**

3. **Apply mud to the edges to fill and smooth them out.**

4. **After it dries, sand the corner smooth, then clean off excess dust.**

5. **Prime and paint the edges.**

# Fixing Small Plaster Cracks

Drywall is easy to install and maintain; therefore few new homes are plastered unless the owners specify its use. But plaster has to be maintained in millions of older homes. Settling and drying out cause tiny and large cracks and holes, particularly if anything bangs into a wall. Plaster, a mixture of lime, water, and sand, can also absorb excess water, causing it to fall apart or develop bulges.

Plaster repair is much more difficult than fixing drywall. Unless the repair is small, plasterwork should not be attempted by anyone without prior training or experience. It's easier to replace a wall or ceiling panel with drywall.

Although plastering a room is difficult, patching cracks and small holes is pretty easy. You can purchase a patching compound or patching plaster in hardware and home improvement stores. You also need sandpaper to smooth the patched surface, a putty knife, a masonry chisel, and a screwdriver. For finishing, use a vacuum cleaner, primer, and paint. Here's what to do:

1. **Using the chisel, make the crack wider.**

2. **Remove loose plaster with the tip of a putty knife.**

3. **Following manufacturer's directions, fill the crack with the patching material that you chose.**

4. **Sand the patch, starting with a medium-grade sandpaper.** You want a totally flat, smooth surface.

5. **Prime the patch and paint it to match the rest of the ceiling or walls.** Of course, you may have to repaint the whole room.

# Replacing Broken Tiles

If a wall tile cracks, you can fix it the same way you replace floor tiles, as we explain in Chapter 3. First, check to see whether you have any spares left over from when the tile was installed. If not, go to a few stores that specialize in tile or a home improvement center that may have the same tile or a close match.

If that doesn't work, consider taking out several good tiles as well and getting a small box of decorative tiles to put in their place. You can find a variety of solid colors or patterned tile that will look good. Be creative.

You need a hammer and chisel to break out the old tile, possibly some gypsum board if the wall behind the tile has deteriorated or gotten wet, tile adhesive, and grout that matches the rest of the wall. Here's what to do to replace tiles:

1. **Crack the tile into pieces that you can chip out easily. Be sure to wear safety glasses during this step.**

2. **Chip away all bits of adhesive or mastic adhesive that held the tile to the wall.**

3. **If necessary, replace or repair the wall by filling it with some new wallboard.**

4. **Put adhesive on the back of the replacement tile.** See Figure 5-2.

5. **Press it to the wallboard.**

6. **Put Popsicle sticks into the seams that will be filled with grout to keep the tile from slipping while the adhesive dries.**

7. **Grout the seams.**

In order to match existing grout you may have to experiment several times by mixing a small amount of dry grout, colorant, and water. Be sure to let the mix dry before you decide whether or not you've got the proportions right. Dry grout will not be the same color as wet grout.

**Figure 5-2:** Chipping out the old tile and putting adhesive on the replacement.

# Patching Torn Wallpaper

Despite the expertise of the hanger, your wallpaper can end up with tears, bubbles, and loose seams and edges. But put down that stripper. If you still love the wallpaper you chose, just fix the imperfections (assuming you kept some remnants from the roll).

You need wallpaper patches for some repairs, scissors, an adhesive for wallpaper, a utility knife, a syringe (or something similar for squirting glue under the loose paper), a sponge, and a roller for the seams.

## Putting in a wallpaper patch

Get your scrap wallpaper and carefully select an area that matches exactly with the paper that's torn. You need the patch, scissors, a utility knife, a damp sponge, adhesive, and the roller. (A rolling pin will do if you don't have a wallpaper roller.)

1. **Look at the scraps and choose one that is exactly the same as the portion that you want to repair.** Be sure to color match edges and everything above and below any forms. Don't look at the center only. Depending on the pattern and repeat, you may have a form that repeats frequently, but on several different colors. Paisley patterns are a good example.

2. **Cut the scrap larger than the area to be patched.** Double-check that it exactly matches the pattern you want to cover.

3. **Rip the edges of the patch carefully by holding it in one hand and tearing the waste off away from you.** A square or rectangle with straight lines will be more noticeable than a random edge.

4. **Remove any loose wallpaper in the area of the tear.**

5. **Scrape or clean with a damp sponge any straggling bits of wallpaper.** Bumps under the glue will be very noticeable.

6. **When the wallpaper is dry, put wallpaper adhesive on the back of the patch.**

7. **Press it down on the wall, carefully aligning all patterns and colors.**

8. **Smooth it down, using the damp sponge.**

9. **After the adhesive dries for a quarter-hour, roll the edges with the roller to squeeze out excess glue and form a strong bond.**

## Refastening lifted edges and seams

Sometimes too much of the adhesive seeps out when wallpaper edges and seams are rolled. When this happens, the bond weakens, and eventually the edges and seams lift or curl. To fix this, you need a knife or Popsicle stick, a damp sponge, a tube of seam adhesive with a pointed nozzle, and a roller. Here's what to do to glue down wallpaper edges:

1. **Sponge the wall lightly so that it's moist.**

2. **Raise the lifted edge with a knife.**

3. **Squirt the adhesive underneath the edge, seam, or tear.** See Figure 5-3.

4. **After 15 minutes, roll the seam or edge with the roller.** Don't press down too hard, because you'll take out too much of the glue and the edge will lift again.

## Squashing bubbles

There are two kinds of bubbles in wallpaper: one is caused by a glob of wallpaper paste that wasn't smoothed out when the paper was hung, the other appears later if the bond between the wallpaper and wall is weak and the wallpaper lifts. Fixing an air bubble takes about 5 minutes. You need a utility knife, a syringe, and glue. Here's what to do:

1. **Use the utility knife to slit the bubble.** See Figure 5-4. Be sure to keep the slit as small as possible so it won't be visible when the repair is done.

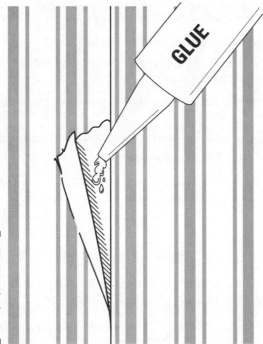

**Figure 5-3:**
Gluing down a lifted wallpaper edge or tear.

2. **Push down on the bubble to get all the air out from under it.**

3. **You can squirt some glue into the opening, but try pressing it down without glue first.** If that doesn't hold, then use some glue in a syringe.

To get rid of blobs of paste, carefully slit the bubble with a utility knife or single blade razor. With a damp sponge, clean off the paste. Don't rush because you don't want to damage the paper.

**Figure 5-4:**
Slitting
bubbled
wallpaper.

# Cleaning unwashable wallpaper

Some wallpaper is too fragile to wash. Check on the back of your remnants. Usually manufacturers stamp papers as being washable or unwashable. If there's nothing that says it's washable, don't take a risk; use one the following methods. (Or you can test wash a remnant to see whether it will withstand harsher cleaning methods.)

To clean fragile wallpaper, rub the marked area gently with one of those soft gum erasers — yes, the kind that crumbles easily. You can find one in an office or art supply store.

Sanding the area with a slice of rye toast also works; just don't use butter and jelly!

To get rid of greasy marks, get some cornstarch and cleaning fluid. Here's what to do:

1. **Make a paste from cleaning fluid and cornstarch.**

2. **Apply it to the stain.** Rub it in gently (remember you have to use this cleaning method because the wallpaper is fragile).

3. **After it dries, use a brush to take it off.**

4. **Repeat as many times as necessary.**

If you have fingerprints all the way up your stairs or in hallways, we can almost guarantee there are kids in the house. To clean those spots, you need a damp cloth and cornstarch. Here's what to do:

1. **Use a damp cloth on the prints to remove them.** Don't get that rag too wet.

2. **Put a light coat of cornstarch on top of the area you just cleaned.** It will take away excess moisture so it doesn't damage the paper.

# Repairing Wood Paneling

Good wood paneling is elegant. It gives a den, office, or family room a rich patina — until it gets dirty or scratched, or it buckles, becomes loose, or the nails pop out. But it doesn't have to stay that way for very long because you can clean and fix most faults.

## Cleaning paneling

You can find wood cleaners at the grocery, hardware, and home improvement stores, as well as department stores that sell everything imaginable at low-end prices. Ask friends and acquaintances where they get their cleaners and whether they like them.

Our favorite for paneling is Murphy's Oil Soap Household Cleaner. We also use Duster Plus for dusting and cleaning, then wipe the wood with Pledge to give it a shine. Cascade liquid for dishes and warm water also works great at cleaning (don't try the generic brands; in this instance they aren't equal). We follow it up with a coat of Pledge.

Cascade liquid is good for lightening and brightening painted drywall and taking soap scum off tile. You don't even have to rinse.

## Touching up small scratches

Get one of those furniture touch-up sticks in a color that matches the wood. Apply it to all the small scratches. That should make them blend in quite well. If the surface looks dull after the touch-up dries, apply a little paste wax and buff it until it blends in with the rest of the area.

Some like liquid products for small scratches, but we prefer Wax Stix, which shines when you rub it. Or we use Weldwood Blend Stick, Minwax Blend Fil Pencil, or Minwax Wood Finish Stain Marker. Old English Scratch Cover is a good liquid product for scratches, too.

## Flattening buckled areas

If a portion of a panel has lifted or buckled, hammer a few nails into the groove where it's buckled. If the extra nails hold it flat, countersink them and fill the surface with a premixed wood putty.

If the panel still pulls up — usually because of moisture — take the panel off the wall and reglue it. You need a putty knife, pliers, wood adhesive, a hammer, paneling or finish nails, and a touch-up stick. Here's what to do:

1. **Use a stiff putty knife to lift the panel.**

2. **Press the panel back down and pull out the nails.** They should be easy to get at if you lift the panel first.

3. **Apply the adhesive to exposed studs, furring strips, or the drywall.** *Furring strips* are narrow strips of wood used either to raise the surface, level the surface, or otherwise smooth out a rough surface to prepare it for paneling.

4. **Let the adhesive sit until it thickens and feels sticky.**

5. **Push the panel firmly against the adhesive.**

6. **Nail the panel in place by starting in the center and working outward.** Sink the nails into the grooves as much as possible; they won't be as noticeable there.

7. **Use the touch-up stick to hide scratches or the nail heads, if necessary.**

8. **If any adhesive comes out of the seams, and it cleans up in water, wipe it off immediately with soapy water.** However, if you're using an oil-based adhesive, leave it in place until it until it dries, then cut it off with a utility knife.

# Chapter 6

# Tending to Cabinet, Closet, and Countertop Glitches

....................................................................................

## In This Chapter

▶ Renewing cabinet and closet doors

▶ Straightening out your shelving problems

▶ Working on countertops

▶ Fixing drawers

▶ Working with hardware

▶ Refastening towel bars and toilet paper holders

....................................................................................

*W*hen you think about it, cabinets, countertops, closets, and drawers take a lot of abuse and don't get a lot of attention until something goes wrong. The kitchen is the hub of a home and that makes the kitchen cabinets especially vulnerable to wear and tear. And in bathrooms, excessive moisture can cause warped cabinets and drawers. Closet and cabinet doors sag, as do shelves. In this chapter, we show you how to resolve common problems and fix malfunctioning hardware. We also talk about different kinds of hinges, closers, and brackets.

## Restoring Cabinet and Closet Doors

We open and close kitchen cabinets constantly to get food, snacks, plates, glasses, cups, pots and pans, detergent, and cleaning utensils. Kids, and perhaps even adults, tend to hang onto the door as they peer into cabinets. Then they bang doors shut; using force much greater than they'd ever acknowledge. No wonder the hinges come loose or shear off.

Closet doors are opened less frequently than those in the kitchen, but that doesn't mean the hardware lasts forever. That's especially true of oversize doors and bypass doors that operate on tracks or hang off hardware mounted on the doorframe. But even those doors that have side-mounted hinges need attention when screws and hinges pull loose. In the following sections, we explain how to reverse these common door problems.

## Straightening sagging cabinet doors

Doors sag when a screw or hinge comes loose, when the hardware is damaged, and when the wood underneath the hinge is stripped or gouged by a loose screw. You need a screwdriver. (A helper makes it easier to hold the door in position while you work.) Here's what to do:

1. **Open the door.**

2. **If the top hinge is loose, push the door up and back to straighten the door.** The bottom hinge rarely goes bad because there's no pressure on it, but if the screws are loose, tighten them.

3. **Tighten the screws while your helper holds the door in that position.** If you don't have a helper, prop it up with your foot and lean into the door while you tighten the screws.

4. **Let the door hang by itself.**

5. **Open and close the door several times to make sure the screws don't work loose right away.** If they do, then the screw holes need repair.

### Filling enlarged and stripped holes with toothpicks

If you can't get the hinge secured, back the screws all the way out, take off the hinge, and look at the wood beneath it. If the hole is too large or has been stripped, you need to fill it in and then drill a new hole. You need a drill, a screwdriver, toothpicks, and a liquid white glue such as Elmer's. Here's what to do:

1. **Squirt some liquid glue into the hole.**

2. **Stuff the hole with toothpicks until it won't take any more, and then cut or break them off flush.**

3. **Drill a pilot hole through the toothpicks, using a bit that's much smaller than the circumference of the screw.**

4. **With a screwdriver put the screw back in.** If the screw is stripped, put in a replacement that's the same size.

5. **Let the glue dry.**

You can repair surface mars or dents with wood filler, but filler won't hold screws. They need to be inserted in wood, and if the hole is too large, it should be filled with toothpicks first.

After your hinges are secure, keep them that way. Periodically tighten the screws, but don't overdo it. And lubricate the hinge. A drop or two of WD-40 on each is sufficient. You don't want the lubricant dripping down the doorframe.

# Closing cabinet doors that won't close

When doors won't close, determine whether the door itself is getting stuck or the hinge is keeping it from moving freely. We talk about hinges in the "Straightening sagging cabinet doors" section. But the door itself may be at fault. Wooden doors can absorb moisture and warp in hot, humid weather. One way to find out if that is the cause is to wait for dry weather. The wooden door will shrink when the humidity drops. Placing a fan in front of the door also will help evaporate the moisture. That should solve the problem. Occasionally, it doesn't; then you should lightly sand the edge where the door sticks. Very likely you will also have to refinish the sanded portion, using paint or stain.

Sometimes, doors need to be sanded extensively on the bottom, side, or top edge. If that's the case, you need to take the door off the hinges after you determine where it's sticking. You need a hammer, a screwdriver, pencil or chalk, coarse sandpaper, a clear primer, and paint or finish. Here's what to do:

1. **Determine whether the hinges are loose or have worn pins and repair them before continuing.**

2. **Open and close the door as much as you can several times to determine where it's rubbing — on the bottom edge, the side, or top.**

3. **Using a pencil or chalk, mark the edge to show exactly where you have to work.**

4. **Put the screwdriver under the hinge pins and tap the bottom with the hammer to raise the pins.**

5. **Take out the pins.**

6. **Lift the door off the hinges.**

7. **Lay it down with the side that needs work up, or close to the top.**

8. **Use coarse sandpaper.**

9. **Periodically put the door back in to see if it swings free.** Don't take off more wood than you need to.

10. **Smooth the cut edge with fine sandpaper.**

11. **Prime and finish the edge to match the door.** That will keep it from absorbing excess moisture on another humid day.

12. **When the door is finished, hang it on the hinges, lubricate the pins, and put them in.** Again use the hammer to tap them in place.

# Tackling Cabinet and Closet Shelves

We never have enough storage space for everything we accumulate. To get it out of sight, we shove it onto shelves. It's easy to underestimate how much stress this places on them, as well as the hardware that's supposed to be holding the shelves up. No wonder shelves sag or crack and brackets come loose. One way to reduce the strain on shelves is to get rid of stored items that you don't use. That might work for neatniks, but for the rest of us, forget it. We'd rather spend a little time strengthening the shelf than throwing out something the might come in handy another day.

## Loose shelving supports

To do their intended job, brackets need the right kind and size of fasteners and the fasteners should be anchored in studs, not drywall. If a stud isn't available at one end of a closet shelf, then use a molly bolt for a fastener, not just a screw or nail. *Molly bolts* have wings that pop open after they're screwed in, holding the bolt securely against the drywall. But even when the support is fastened to a stud, a screw can strip the wood, enlarging the hole. You can repair the wood, and then refasten it. But before you do, look at the bracket and make sure it isn't damaged. If it is, replace it. Take the shelf off the supports and unscrew the bracket. Then follow Steps 1 through 5 in the "Filling enlarged holes with toothpicks" section.

## Raising sagging shelves

Closet and cupboard shelves sometimes sag because of the inferior quality of wood or particleboard used for the shelf or because supports are insufficient to hold shelves up. All shelves are held up on brackets at either end, but the hardware may not be sturdy enough to hold the weight. And the greater the span of the board, the more support it needs. You may need to add more brackets or hangers along the length to bear the weight after the shelf is filled. You might be able to reduce the sagging by redistributing the weight or finding a new place to store some of it. Here are a few more tips:

- Another quick trick is to turn the board over. Let the other side bear the weight for a while. This trick may even straighten the board.

- You can replace wood and particleboard shelves with a better-quality product or get rid of the board altogether. Put in one of those lightweight wire shelf systems sold in hardware and home improvement stores, but again, don't go for the one that's the least expensive. You want a quality product that won't fall apart almost instantly.

✔ Upgrade the hardware. If you replace something, get hangers and brackets that are stronger. And buy a few extras to screw into the studs behind the walls to provide added support for the items stored on the shelf.

✔ If the shelves are mounted on wooden cleats on either end, you can add more support by adding a cleat the full width of the back.

# Restoring Countertops

Any time you open a kitchen drawer or cabinet there's a risk that the countertop will be damaged. Heavy cans fall off the shelves, knives you're using drop and slip, and glasses and plates drop and break, marring the surface. You're probably not a stranger to splashes and spills that stain. And you can burn some types of counters if you put a hot pan directly on them.

## Repairing laminates

You can repair vinyl laminate countertops, cut out a bad section and replace it with a cutting board or glass insert, glue down lifted edges and corners, and take care of small stains and scratches.

### Regluing bubbled countertops

A laminated counter is similar to furniture veneer. Thin sheets of vinyl laminate are glued onto a wood surface with an adhesive. And like veneer, sometimes the bond breaks and the laminate forms bubbles or the edges pop loose. You can reactivate the adhesive easily. See the section on repairing veneer in Chapter 13.

### Refastening lifted edges

When a laminated edge lifts, it's still the glue you should concentrate on. If reactivating the glue doesn't work, then get a liquid adhesive, a small sheet of wax paper, and a syringe or a knife with a slender blade. Here's what to do:

1. **Put some glue in the syringe.**

2. **Gently lift the loose edge.**

3. **With the syringe, push glue under the laminate.** Another option is to put glue on the knife and insert the knife under the laminate. Spread the glue onto underside of the laminate, and then put more glue on the knife and work it onto as much of the wood as possible.

4. **Immediately put pressure on the edge.**

5. **Wipe off excess glue, and then wash the side and top of counter and anywhere else the glue might have oozed.**

6. **Put the wax paper on the counter, then weight it with books.**

7. **When you're finished, excess glue can be removed with lacquer thinner on a rag.**

Laminate glue also comes in an aerosol can, which works well for getting under loose countertops but is hard to clean up if the area is oversprayed and not protected with paper and tape. Use it only as a last resort.

### Hiding small cuts and scratches

A sharp knife is great for preparing food but if it slips, you end up with small cuts or chips in the countertop. You can fill small holes with a product called SeamFit, available in about 20 colors. Get it at a home improvement center. If you or someone you know is good at blending colors, you can come up with the shade you need by mixing your own. The product has a satin finish when it dries, but there's a gloss additive for surfaces with more shine. Follow the instructions on the package.

### Getting rid of stains

Common household products attack most stains effectively. Automatic dishwasher soap is one that's handy and cleans up most stains. Two other good products to use are Soft Scrub or straight bleach on tougher stains. And keep a bottle of mineral spirits around. It gets that stubborn adhesive off countertops.

## Refurbishing butcher blocks

Butcher blocks are gorgeous, but after a while, they may be marred with cuts from knives, scorch marks left by hot pans, and water marks. To get rid of these marks, you need fine-grit sandpaper, a steel scraper, and mineral spirits. Here's what to do:

1. **Rub the area along the grain of the wood with a steel scraper, placing it on a 60-degree angle.** See Figure 6-1. While using a scraper, keep the beveled side up. If there's a deep scorch mark on the butcher block, you can scrape away wood fibers with a utility knife. Gently, please.

2. **Sand the area with fine sandpaper.** If you dip the sandpaper in mineral spirits, it will lubricate, as well as smooth, the surface.

3. **If the scorched area is still apparent, put bleach on a cotton ball and dab it until it fades.**

4. **If the mark needs to be filled, use wood filler to match.**

5. **Buff the wood with three coats of a nontoxic finish such as mineral oil warmed for easier penetration.** Don't use olive or vegetable oil because they will turn rancid.

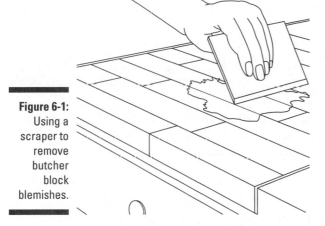

**Figure 6-1:**
Using a
scraper to
remove
butcher
block
blemishes.

# Restoring ceramic tile countertops

Ceramic tile countertops are resilient. You can't burn tile even when you take a hot pan from the oven and put it directly on the surface. But tile can be chipped or cracked and it may break if a heavy object, such as a soup can, falls on it. And while tile doesn't stain, the grout does, especially if it's light-colored. Even though you seal grout, it still gets dirty and there's a risk that mold will form if you don't clean it regularly with an antibacterial cleaner.

### Replacing tile

You can replace a broken or cracked tile, but it's more work than cleaning the grout. You have to cut into the grout along the edges of the tile, remove the grout and the tile, and after putting in a new tile, regrout the edges. You need a tile cutter; look for it at a home improvement, hardware, or paint store. You also need replacement tiles, adhesive for tile, a trowel, a utility knife, a rubber mallet, dry grout mix, colorant if needed, a Popsicle stick or spacer, and warm soapy water. You can get Popsicle sticks at craft stores or wash and save old ones. Here's what to do:

1. **Use a utility knife to cut between grout and damaged tile, and between grout and adjacent, undamaged tiles.**

2. **Pull out the grout, prying under it with a putty knife or wide-tipped screwdriver, if necessary.**

3. **Use a putty knife or chisel to get under the damaged tile.** If it doesn't work out easily, drill a few holes in the center and tap the tile with a rubber mallet to break out the pieces. Put a block of wood over adjacent tiles to protect them as you pry out the tile.

4. **When the tile is out, use the putty knife to scrape out all the old adhesive.**

5. **Put adhesive on the new tile and fit it into place.**

   Place Popsicle sticks into the cracks to straighten the lines, but be sure to overlap the corners of adjacent tiles. Tile spacers can be used instead of Popsicle sticks; they're available wherever tile is sold.

6. **Push the tiles down so the adhesive makes a good bond between the tile and plywood.**

7. **Let the adhesive dry, keeping the Popsicle sticks in place.**

8. **After 24 to 36 hours, remove the Popsicle sticks.**

9. **Mix a batch of grout according to package instructions.**

10. **Put it in all the cracks.**

11. **Push down on the grout — use the edge of one of the Popsicle sticks.**

12. **Compress it to get out air bubbles.**

13. **Put more grout along the seams, especially if you see any indentations.**

14. **Push it with the Popsicle stick again until all of it looks level.**

15. **Immediately scrape off excess grout with as many clean Popsicle sticks as you need.**

16. **Wash grout residue off the tiles.**

17. **Grout sealer may be used to keep the grout from absorbing dirt and stains.**

18. **Let the grout set up for a couple days before you start using the tiles.**

### Patching cracked and missing grout

Occasionally grout cracks, falls out, and it has to be replaced with fresh grout. To repair grout, follow Steps 8 through 15 in the "Replacing tile" section.

# Reversing major counter damage

You don't always need to replace a whole countertop when just one part of it looks awful. Odds are that the damage is adjacent to a sink or range — high-risk areas. So all you have to do is cut out the damaged section and in its place, put in a cutting board, a sheet of glass, or some decorative tiles, and guests will think you got the idea from a magazine focusing on upscale homes. In the following sections, we explain a how to refurbish the counter-top without spending a lot of money.

Before you make a decision about what to do, look underneath the damaged area to find out whether any supports or braces would be damaged if you cut a hole in the counter. If there are, you'll have to rout the surface instead of cutting all the way through it. Also, keep in mind that these steps are for the more adventurous do-it-yourselfers. If they don't work, you still have to replace the countertop.

## Adding a cutting board

The logical place for a cutting board is right next to a sink where you can wash vegetables, chop them, and scrape the scraps directly into the garbage disposal. You may also want one next to the stove so as you cut, you can dump the pieces into a pot. You need a good-quality cutting board or piece of butcher block with beveled or finished edges. The piece needs to be slightly larger than the damaged portion of the countertop. You also need a square and ruler, a pencil, a saber saw with a long tapered blade or a router, a level, clear silicone caulk, adhesive, and a metal frame that the wood piece can fit into. Look for them in the kitchen area of home improvement stores. Here's what to do:

1. **Measure the damaged area.**

2. **Purchase a cutting board or butcher block that's larger than the damaged area.** You want the board to be surrounded completely by undamaged laminate so that it doesn't look like you patched the counter.

3. **Now measure and mark the laminate.** Use a square and ruler to mark each side precisely.

4. **Make sure the new piece will be level from side to side and along the front before you start cutting.** Make sure that it's level with the edge of the counter, not the back wall. Most walls aren't completely straight, but the counter edge should be.

5. **Carefully cut the countertop along those marked lines with a saber saw if you intend to go all the way through the counter.** Go slowly enough that the saber saw doesn't head off on a tangent.

   Or you can use a router to make a shallow cut into the plywood in the counter, to make a base to support the cutting board or butcher block.

6. **Starting in the center or well inside a cut seam, pry up the vinyl laminate and plywood under it.** If you start inside the cut edges, there's less risk of nicking the surrounding countertop.

7. **If you used a router, level the surface and sand it if necessary so that the board will fit into the hole tightly without rocking.**

8. **Apply adhesive to the surface of the cutout.**

9. **Set the board in place, pressing down on it to make sure it bonds tightly.**

10. **Cover the board with cloth and weight it until the adhesive forms a tight bond.**

11. **Squeeze a thin line of clear silicone caulk all around to seal the joint between the countertop and board.** That will keep food out of the cracks and prevent mold from forming.

### Adding tempered glass

If you decide you want a glass inset to take the place of damaged laminate, purchase tempered or heat-resistant glass. Then you can put a hot pan or baking dish directly onto it without worrying about breaks or cracks, as you would if you put cold glass that isn't heat resistant into a hot oven. Tempered glass, available at home improvement stores, has to have a metal frame and you have to cut all the way through the countertop to install it. You need a square, a ruler, the glass, the frame, caulk, and a saber saw. The bolts or screws come with the frame. Here's what to do:

1. **Measure the damaged area.**

2. **Purchase a piece of tempered glass that's larger than the damaged area.** You want the piece to be surrounded completely by undamaged laminate so that it doesn't look like you patched the counter.

3. **Now measure and mark the laminate.** Use a square and ruler to mark each side precisely.

4. **Level the area from side to side and along the front edge before you start cutting.** Make sure that it's level with the edge of the counter.

   Most walls aren't completely straight. But even if yours isn't, it won't be as noticeable as having the front and side edges of the board climbing a hill or walking down a plank.

5. **Carefully cut the countertop along those marked lines with a saber saw.** Go slowly enough that the saber saw doesn't head off on a tangent.

6. **Hang the metal rim off the cut edges.** See Figure 6-2.

7. **Put the glass into the center.**

8. **Put lug bolts through the frame, working underneath.** See Figure 6-3.

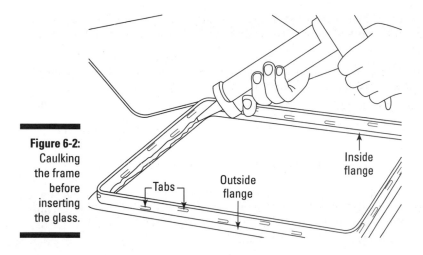

**Figure 6-2:**
Caulking
the frame
before
inserting
the glass.

Inside flange

Outside flange

Tabs

9. **Fasten them to the anchor pad.**

10. **Apply adhesive to the surface of the cutout.**

11. **Set the board in place, pressing down on it to make sure it bonds tightly.**

12. **Cover the board with cloth and weight it until the adhesive forms a tight bond.**

13. **Take excessive caulk off the glass and frame.** You may have to use a putty knife or some other stiff blade.

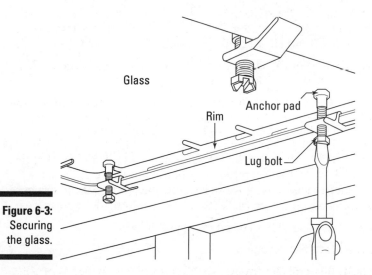

Glass

Anchor pad

Rim

Lug bolt

**Figure 6-3:**
Securing
the glass.

# Repairing Wooden Drawers

It's bad enough that drawers jam because they're overstuffed. But even partially filled drawers jam at times and we wonder what's going on. Blame it on the runners (also called rails or guides) that slide on the cleats. If you know the drawer is falling apart, the possibilities are that the corners aren't square or the bottom hangs down too much, especially if the drawer is overstuffed or the bottom is warped. You can get those old drawers running smoothly again by refastening the hardware, lubricating the rails, replacing broken rails, or rebuilding and regluing the drawer. See Figure 6-4.

If the only time the drawer sticks is when it's hot and humid out, sit back and relax. You're having problems because the wood has absorbed moisture and expanded. You can wait for better weather or turn on the air conditioner or dehumidifier. Then the drawer will work just fine.

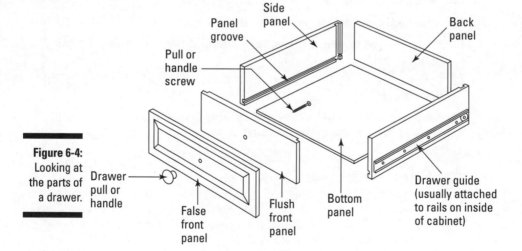

**Figure 6-4:**
Looking at the parts of a drawer.

Side panel

Panel groove

Back panel

Pull or handle screw

Drawer pull or handle

False front panel

Flush front panel

Bottom panel

Drawer guide (usually attached to rails on inside of cabinet)

When a drawer sticks because it's too full, pull out the drawer underneath it. Push up on the bottom panel with one hand while pulling on the drawer pull with the other. It should work loose — that is unless something in it is sticking up out of the drawer. If you can't fit your hand into the drawer, use a screwdriver or metal ruler to try to knock it down enough that the drawer will pull free.

# Unsticking drawers

If you know there's nothing in the drawer keeping it from pulling out and the weather hasn't caused the wood to expand, pull the drawer all the way out of the cabinet or chest so you can determine what the problem is.

### Lubricating the rails

Undamaged rails and cleats slide better if you periodically lubricate them. Rub them with a bar of soap, some candle wax, or bee's wax if they're wood, and use WD-40 on the rollers if they're metal. Push the drawer in and out several times until the drawer slides smoothly. Another quick fix to try is to put thumbtacks on the runner to build it up. See Figure 6-5.

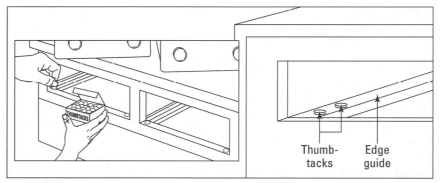

**Figure 6-5:**
Using thumbtacks to build up the rail surface.

Thumb-tacks    Edge guide

### Sanding the rails

If more drastic action is needed, use medium-grade sandpaper on wood rails to remove any burrs or minor obstacles. Do it lightly and test the drawer by pushing it in and out after you sand just a little. After the drawer slides easily, put the sandpaper away and seal the edge with a wood sealer, varnish, or paint to keep it from absorbing moisture. (While the drawer's out, lubricate the rails and guides on the side of the drawer.) You need sandpaper and soap, candle wax, or bee's wax. Here's what to do:

1. **Sand the surface to make it smooth.**

2. **Rub soap or wax on it for lubrication.**

3. **Test the drawer.**

You don't have to be a detective to spot a cracked, split, missing, or worn wooden rail. But also check the hardware to see whether it's damaged, whether a screw is missing or loose, or whether the screw has stripped the wood or enlarged the hole. If the rails are metal or plastic, look for obstructions, dents in metal or cracks in plastic, and loose hardware.

### Realigning side rails

If a wood rail is out of alignment, you need a small square, wood glue, wood filler, a screwdriver, and recessed screws. Here's what to do:

1. **Using the square, check that the rails are perpendicular to the front of the drawer.**

2. **Straighten the side rail.**

3. **Fasten it with the recessed screws.** See Figure 6-6.

4. **Squirt glue behind the rail to secure it to the sides of the chest or cabinet.**

5. **Lubricate the rails with wax or soap.**

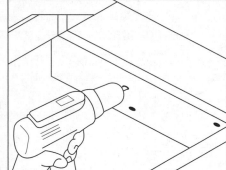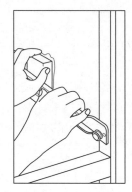

Figure 6-6:
Realigning
the side rail.

### Fixing stripped holes in rails

If you can turn the screw around with your fingers, the hole is stripped. Here's what to do:

1. **Fill an enlarged hole with toothpicks and glue.** See the steps in "Filling enlarged holes with toothpicks."

2. **Drill a pilot hole for the screw.** The bit should be smaller in diameter than the screw.

3. **Insert the screw and tighten, using a screwdriver.** That's all!

Another option is to take out and throw away the old screws and replace them with screws that are longer and larger in diameter. Then you know the screw will be tightly fastened. Before you put them in, however, make sure they won't obstruct movement of the drawer or damage the cabinet itself.

### *Regluing cracked and split pieces*

If the wood is cracked or split, you need carpenter's glue, a screwdriver, and a vise, a C-clamp, or weights to hold it. Here's what to do:

1. **Take out the drawer.**

2. **Unscrew the rail and take it out.**

3. **Glue the break and put the pieces back together.**

4. **Using a vise, weights, or small C-clamp, hold the pieces together until the glue dries.**

5. **Refasten loose screws if there's no damage to the wood or the metal.** If the hole is stripped, refer to the steps in "Fixing stripped holes in rails."

### *Replacing rails*

You don't have to put up with damaged rails. You can easily put in new wood or metal. You need a screwdriver and new rails. Here's what to do:

1. **Take out the problem drawer and any others that will be in the way while you're working.** You have to get inside the cabinet to fasten the new rails.

2. **Unfasten the rails.**

3. **Inspect them and the drawer to see how they're supposed to work.** Some drawers hang off rails and have hardware on the drawer itself. If that's how your drawer was made, then you'll have to hang it from the new rails too.

4. **Purchase similar rails.**

5. **Fasten the rails to the cabinet.** Make sure they're level and perpendicular to the front of the drawer.

## *Fixing loose corner joints*

When corner joints get loose, a drawer becomes difficult to open and close because the sides may bow out or collapse. The bottom of the drawer may work loose, catching on the frame of the cabinet when you try to open the drawer. You can fix this problem with a putty knife, carpenter's glue, a screwdriver, and a mallet or hammer wrapped in cloth so it won't mar the wood. Here's what to do:

1. **Pull out the drawer.**

2. **Remove any screws or small nails fastening the sides to the front, back, and bottom panels.**

3. **Gently tap the drawer to crack any glue bonding the pieces together.**
   If you don't have a rubber mallet, wrap the hammerhead in cloth so you
   don't mar the wood. You can also place a piece of wood against the
   drawer and hit it to soften the impact.

4. **Gently wiggle the sides back and forth until they separate from the
   front and back.**

5. **Remove the bottom of the drawer.** See Figure 6-7.

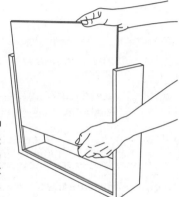

**Figure 6-7:**
Sliding the
bottom out
of a drawer.

6. **Remove any dried glue from the pieces.** If you glue over them, the
   bond of the new glue will be weak.

7. **Reglue the pieces.**

8. **Reassemble the drawer.** See Figure 6-8.

9. **Wrap a ratchet clamp around the drawer.** (See Chapter 2.)

While you're putting on the clamp and tightening it, keep measuring the
drawer front to back diagonally. The distance between the right front
and left rear corner should be exactly the same as the left front to right
rear corner. That means that the corners are square. If one diagonal is
different from the other, readjust the drawer and pressure while the glue
is still wet.

**Figure 6-8:**
Reassem-
bling
drawers
with square
corners.

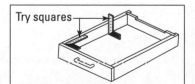
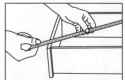

Try squares

10. **Let the glue set, following manufacturer's instructions.** If you want to be safe, don't touch it again for 24 hours.

11. **Slide the bottom panel back into the frame.** Don't glue or nail it in.

## Building up sides

Worn edges can make a drawer difficult to open and close. You can glue a piece of wood to the bottom edges. You need carpenter's glue, a ratchet clamp, and strips of wood. Here's what to do:

1. **Remove the drawer from the cabinet.**

2. **Glue strips of wood to the bottom edge.** The strips should be just as long as the bottom edge of the drawer.

3. **Use the ratchet strap to clamp the edges.** Wrap it all the way around the drawer and pull it tight, making sure that it stays square and you don't distort the drawer by tightening it too much.

4. **After the glue is dry — follow the manufacturer's instructions as to how long — sand the new edges with sandpaper until they're level.**

5. **Put wax or soap on the bottom edges to lubricate them.**

6. **Put the drawer back in.**

You can get plastic caps to fit over the bottom edges of the sides of drawers in a home improvement or paint store to make the drawer pull smoothly. Ask for self-adhesive vinyl wall-corner molding. It just sticks on the wood. Buy a long strip, and then measure and cut it to fit. This works on drawers where rollers ride on the wood of the drawer. You can also "iron" the bottom to try to flatten it or cut a new bottom panel with similar wood, using the old bottom as a pattern. See Figure 6-9.

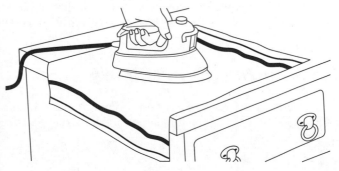

**Figure 6-9:**
Using an iron to flatten a warped drawer bottom.

## Fastening loose and broken pulls

You can refasten loose pulls with a screwdriver. But if the wood underneath is stripped, see the "Filling enlarged holes with toothpicks" section for information about patching it or filling enlarged holes with toothpicks. If a metal pull is damaged, think about replacing all of them. It will give new life to the pulls and a decorative touch to all the drawers. To refasten a pull, you need a screwdriver and slightly larger screws if you're using the same pulls; if you want to replace them, count how many you need and head to the home improvement or hardware store to see what's available. Take the old pull along so you can try to match the holes that are already in the drawers. We talk about hardware at the end of this chapter. Here's what to do:

1. **Tighten the screw with the screwdriver.**

2. **If it spins loose easily, take out the screw.**

3. **Try one that's larger.** Or fill the hole with toothpicks, following the steps in the "Filling enlarged holes with toothpicks" section.

4. **Screw the pull in.**

5. **Reinsert the drawer.**

# Handling Door and Cabinet Hardware Problems

If the hardware that fastens, hangs, or operates your doors, drawers, and shelves isn't durable, you may notice problems opening and closing doors and drawers. Less expensive hardware often includes metal that is easily bent. And then you have a problem with the doors, drawers, and shelves. They rub against frames, bind on top, or hang at one corner. The metal may eventually shear off and you'll need to replace it, as well as repair or replace any stripped or damaged wood. Buy the best quality hardware you can afford.

## Latching on to cabinet doors

In general, five types of latches are used on cabinet doors. Which one you use often depends upon how the cabinet and door are constructed. Here are some examples (also see Figure 6-10):

- **Spring-loaded roller** and **friction latches** are especially strong and durable. You find them on good cabinets.

- **Bullet latches** usually are mounted on cabinets with narrow edges.

- **Touch latches** are especially popular today. To use them, all you have to do is push down to open the door.

- **Magnetic latches** are also popular because there have no working parts that can break. They may occasionally need to be repositioned if they slip out of place.

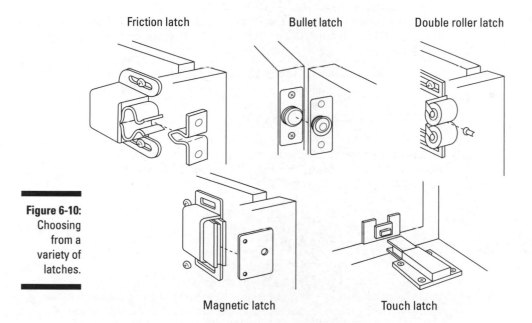

Friction latch        Bullet latch        Double roller latch

**Figure 6-10:**
Choosing from a variety of latches.

Magnetic latch        Touch latch

## Getting a grip on handles and knobs

Handles and knobs can be functional and decorative. Made of metal, vinyl, ceramic, and other materials, they rarely break. But they work loose and the screws securing them to the door or drawer need to be refastened and some-times replaced. If you leave the handle or knob loose for too long, the screw may strip the wood or fiberboard underneath it. Most of the time, all you need is a screwdriver to refasten the handle. When the base it's secured to gets stripped, a screw can often be replaced by one that's slightly larger. Or you can fill the hole with toothpicks and glue and drill a new pilot hole into the wood. That will keep the screw tight for a long time. We explain how to do that in the section "Filling enlarged holes with toothpicks."

## Scrutinizing screws and hinges

People choose hinges for two reasons: based on the type of door they're securing and to add decorative features to the cabinet itself. We explain what to look for when you want to replace worn out hinges with a new-style hinge. Here are a few examples (also see Figure 6-11):

- **Butt or leaf hinges:** These are commonly found on flush doors, meaning the surface of the door is mounted into the frame so that it doesn't go any higher or lower than the cabinet itself. That means the hinge has to fit into a *mortise* — usually a rectangular hole cut into the edge of the frame. The surface of the hinge, recessed into the hole, is flush with the surface of the cabinet. These hinges are rarely elaborate or decorative.

- **Overlaid hinges:** This type of hinge is fastened onto the surface of the cabinet. They overlap all four edges of the frame. If they get out of alignment, they're easy to adjust. And they can be easily replaced. You can't see any seams when the doors are closed and the space behind the door isn't obvious when the door's closed.

- **Inset hinges:** One end of this hinge is fastened around the edge of the cabinet and door and the other end, usually larger and quite decorative, is mounted on top of the frame. Inset hinges add ambiance to kitchens and baths, and are often used in country-style rooms. These hinges are easy to install.

**Figure 6-11:** Choosing from a variety of hinges.

Invisible hinge

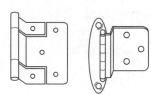
Partially concealed hinge

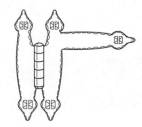
Decorative hinge

## Choosing brackets for shelving

Shelf brackets can be fixed in place or adjustable, depending on whether they're mounted to studs in the wall or to standards. *Standards* are metal bars with evenly spaced holes into which the brackets are placed. See Figure 6-12. If you're concerned about how your shelving looks, perhaps in the living areas of the house, wooden brackets are better and they're very sturdy. Metal standards can be used in bedrooms, closets, and basements. Fitted brackets and standards have to be level if you want the shelf to be straight. They work best when mounted to the middle of studs so that they're strong enough to hold what you store on the shelf. If there isn't a stud behind a fixed bracket, you should use a molly bolt to hold it against the drywall — and avoid putting anything heavy on the shelf.

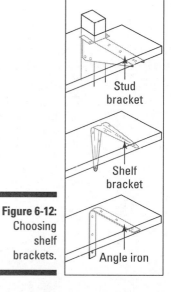

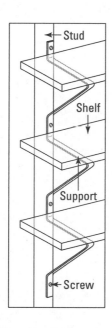

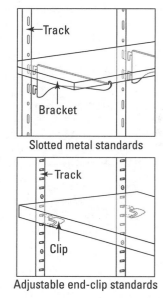

**Figure 6-12:** Choosing shelf brackets.

# Fixing Towel Bars and Toilet Paper Holders

You wish towel bars and toilet paper holders would stay fastened, but they don't. If they come loose because the screw stripped the hole:

- Use molly bolts to refasten holders if the holes in the wall aren't too large.
- If the holes are large, use toggle bolts.
- If you're lucky enough to have a stud behind the holder, simply get a longer screw.

Any of these options should keep the towel bar tight for a long time.

# Part III
# Conquering Simple Electrical, Air, and Plumbing Repairs

The 5th Wave    By Rich Tennant

Okay, this is a little more complicated than I thought. Bring me my canoe paddle, a large balloon and a can of spray cheese.

# In this part . . .

Who starts life as a plumber or electrician? They're learned skills, just as keeping furnaces and air conditioners purring are. Even if you never wanted to learn "the trades," we have advice on how to keep these essential home components working as they should. That allows you to cut down on unessential service calls and keep your budget intact. Don't worry. A trade-school diploma isn't necessary for you to follow our advice and easy instructions.

# Chapter 7

# Don't Blow Your Fuse: Minor Electrical Repairs

. . . . . . . . . . . . . . . . . . . . . . . . . . . . . . . . . . . . . . . . . . . .

## In This Chapter

▶ Going over some safety tips

▶ Understanding the basics

▶ Working on switches, dimmers, and thermostats

▶ Fixing wall outlets and fixtures

▶ Recharging doorbells

▶ Opening garage doors

. . . . . . . . . . . . . . . . . . . . . . . . . . . . . . . . . . . . . . . . . . . .

**Y**our whole home is humming with electricity: wires, cords, wall outlets, lights, electronic equipment, electrical devices, appliances, doorbells, thermostats, heating and cooling equipment, water heaters, stoves. But you don't have to call an electrician or repair specialist every time something goes out. In this chapter, we tell you how to take care of minor electrical problems on often-used household items.

Before you start fixing things, we give you the skinny on safety when working with electricity. We also go over some electricity basics. These background topics help you understand what you're working with when you start to fix switches, dimmers, doorbells, and the like.

## Going Over Electrical Safety Tips

If there's ever a time to be cautious, it's while doing electrical work. You never know who was working on the wiring before you or how knowledgeable that person was. So if you aren't careful, you can shock yourself, and we don't mean the little zap you get from static electricity or the mild buzz that travels up your arm from some malfunctioning appliances.

Electrical shocks can kill, so don't do repairs when you're tired, distracted, or rushed. You should always be cautious. Make sure to follow a routine and double-check yourself each step of the way. Here are some extremely important safety tips when dealing with electricity:

- **With electricity, never assume anything!** Just remember that even though hot wires are supposed to be colored and the neutral wire, white, people change things around, especially if they don't know what they're doing.

- **Unplug any appliance you plan to work on and turn light switches off.** Double-check that it's still unplugged before you start the work. Flip the light switches on and off a couple times to ensure they're dead.

- **Turn off the circuit breaker or unplug the fuse that feeds electricity to the outlet or switch you want to work on.** If in doubt, turn off all power to the house.

- **Review the instructions several times until the sequence is fixed in your mind.**

- **Examine cords and wires carefully so that you know which part is hot (carrying the power) and which is neutral.** Black or colored wires are supposed to be hot. The white wire is neutral. We explain more about power lines and wires in the sections below.

- **Look at the plugs so you know which prong is hot and which is neutral.** The narrow prong always carries electricity; the wide prong is neutral. And these plugs can fit only in outlets that have a wide and narrow slot.

- **Never overload a circuit or fuse by plugging in too many appliances and lights.** Have an electrician put in new outlets if you need them or at the very least, use a power strip outlet that has an overload safety-trip feature.

- **Never work in or near water with power equipment.**

- **Don't open the service panel to change a fuse or turn on a circuit breaker while standing in water.**

- **When working with wiring, clearly label wires and bend them, in different directions.** Make sure the labels are out of the way of each other so you don't have one hot wire accidentally touch the other or put two hot wires together by mistake.

- **Check that the power is still off before you twist or splice wires together.** Match color to color; don't cross them.

- **Always review each step along the way to make sure you did it right, especially before turning the power back on or plugging in an appliance.**

For more information on electrical safety, visit the Electrical Safety Foundation International Web site, at www.esfi.org.

And keep in mind that if your "easy fix" doesn't work and you're reluctant to go further, or if you're really leery about handling a "hot" wire, call a licensed professional (see Chapter 18). We all have limits and there's nothing wrong with reaching one — especially when working with electricity.

# Understanding the Electrical System

Most homes get electricity from power lines strung by the electric company outdoors from one utility pole to another or via a buried underground cable. Buildings along the route of the power lines tap into that source of energy via individual lines that run from the main power line to each home.

Three wires come into each building through an electric meter, two of them hot wires and the other neutral. The black and colored hot wires connect to the main power shutoff in your *service* (supply) panel. The *hot* (live) energy flows through these wires. The third wire, white, is the *neutral;* it connects to the neutral bus (also called the common bar) in the service panel and is the return path for the electricity that flows or circles through the house.

Electricity makes a complete circuit (circle) through your home. The *service panel,* commonly known as the circuit breaker box or fuse box, distributes the electricity that flows into it from the lines outside. That power goes into the fuses or breakers in the service panel and they distribute electricity via hot wires to every outlet, switch, or appliance in your home. Then it flows back to the service panel, via the neutral wire and the neutral bus bar, completing the loop.

*Circuit breakers* and *fuses* are designed to be the weak links in the power supply chain that exists within your home. These safety devices *trip* or *blow* when a line in the house is overloaded or has a short, shutting off electricity to the outlets, switches, and appliances along the overloaded line. Simply put, breakers and fuses protect people from shocks and homes from fires.

If you don't know whether your house has fuses or breakers, go look at the service panel, a metal box that's typically in the basement or near a utility area. If your house has fuses, the box contains a number of fuses with round, glass tops that are screwed in. (They typically are found in homes built before the 1960s.) When a fuse blows, it's *dead* and you have to replace the fuse to turn the electricity back on.

If your house has a circuit breaker box instead of glass fuses, you'll see a number of switches or buttons (usually rectangular). The switches are similar to light switches. Buttons, which were used when builders transitioned from fuses to circuit breaker boxes, have to be depressed if you want the power on. When a circuit breaker blows, the breaker switches to off or the button pops up and there is no electricity in that part of your home until you turn the power back on. Circuit breaker and fuse boxes also have a master control — if that pops, everything electrical in your home is shut off. See Figure 7-1.

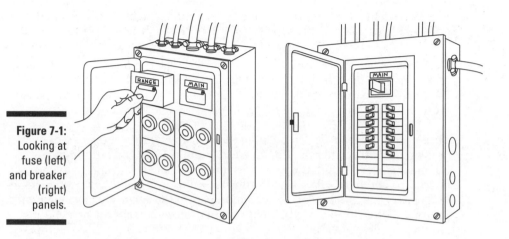

**Figure 7-1:** Looking at fuse (left) and breaker (right) panels.

## Labeling your service panel

You should label every breaker , button, or fuse in your home so you know what circuit it controls. In addition to being an important safety measure, labels save you a lot of time in identifying the right breaker or fuse when you want to turn off power to one particular room or appliance. However, keep in mind that each breaker controls multiple lights or outlets (in combination). So, when labeling breakers, be sure to find out exactly which switches and outlets the breaker controls and where they're located. Don't assume that if there's no electricity in one part of the kitchen, for example, that everything in the kitchen is off. Usually large appliances are on an individual circuit. And one room may have power coming into it by two or more circuits. So if you turn off the breaker for the light over the kitchen table, never assume that all the rest of the lights are off.

People have been electrocuted because of unlabeled breakers. So for safety and ease of troubleshooting, label them all with a comprehensive list.

## Understanding shorts and opens

Many folks think that any malfunction in the electrical system is automatically a short — but some malfunctions are actually opens.

A *short* is an inadvertent or unintentional connection of a hot wire to ground or neutral. And when a hot wire connects with a ground it will blow a fuse or trip a breaker or a ground fault outlet. This can happen in the house wiring, outlets, electric boxes, and appliances or cords. (An overloaded circuit will also blow a breaker, as will a weak breaker, but those aren't shorts.)

An *open* is a break in the wire, a loose connection, a light bulb going bad, a bad switch, or a bad outlet. Opens don't blow fuses or breakers but they do cause lights to blink or go off and on all by themselves and appliances to work intermittently; you may have to wiggle something to make it work. A loose wire or connection is dangerous, however, because it may lead to arcing and heat — and that can cause a fire.

# What to Do When the Power Shuts off

If all of the power to the house is off, go outdoors and see whether your neighbors' lights are on. If it's dark out and there are houselights, your neighbors are obviously getting power. During the day, phone or ring your neighbor's doorbell and ask. If no one in the vicinity has power, call the utility company and report it. It's probably a transformer or main line that's down. Here are other checks to make:

- ✔ If your neighbors have power, check your breaker panel for tripped breakers before calling the service company. The power line from the street to your home may have trouble, or your service box, mounted outside your home, may have malfunctioned.

- ✔ If just one light goes out, plug that light into another outlet. If it works there, test the original outlet with a different lamp or appliance to see if the outlet itself is faulty.

- ✔ If the test appliance works, you know there's power coming into the outlet and the outlet is fine. Your TV or light might have a problem. To find out what could be wrong with it, see Chapter 11 for information on checking small appliances or "Testing and rewiring table lamps" in this chapter.

- ✔ If the appliance or light doesn't come on, you have to look at the service panel to find out if a breaker tripped or a fuse blew. If they're all still on, then the outlet needs to be replaced. (We talk about "Replacing outlets" later in this chapter.) If the breaker tripped, it needs to be turned on. If the fuse is blown, replace it.

Even if you forgot to buy more fuses, *never* replace the one that burned out with a larger size (higher number) fuse. It's dangerous. There's a huge risk of fire, along with other problems.

If a circuit breaker or fuse keeps popping, no matter what's plugged into the outlet, the breaker may be getting weak or going bad and you may need to replace it. Refer to the section "Checking circuit breakers" later in the chapter.

## Flipping a switch when a breaker trips

When a breaker trips, look at each one in the panel box. If there are switches, one will be leaning toward off. First push it to off, and then push it in the other direction to on. If you try to turn it on from a tripped position, it won't stay: It must be shut off first. Some boxes have buttons that pop out instead of switches. To turn the power back on, push the button down or in.

If you want to protect appliances and electronic equipment, shut them off or unplug them before turning on the power. Then you won't have to worry about damage from a surge in power.

After the power is on, restart the appliances and equipment. If the breaker trips again, it might be faulty. Refer to Figure 7-1.

## Replacing screw-in fuses

When a fuse pops, the metal strip under the glass is either broken or black. Always replace a fuse with another that's the same size, never bigger.

## Checking cartridge fuses

Some homes have cartridge fuses that turn off power. They have to be removed with a fuse puller sold at hardware and home improvement centers. You can test an old cartridge fuse by touching both ends of it with the probes of a continuity light but do it only after it is removed from the fuse box. If the light turns on, then the fuse is still good. If the light doesn't come on, replace the fuse. Here's how:

1. **Unscrew the two metal ends**. If they don't unscrew, then the fuse is not repairable. Buy a new cartridge.

2. **Remove the pieces of broken link.**

3. **Buy the same amp replacement link.**

4. **Install the link in the fuse cartridge.**

5. **Bend the link over the ends.**

6. **Install the end caps.**

## Checking circuit breakers

Before you call an electrician, test the circuit breaker to see whether it's faulty. Remove the front cover to the panel. Using a 110-volt tester, touch one prong to the terminal screw on the breaker and the other to the ground. If the light doesn't turn on, there's no power and the breaker is faulty. It will have to be replaced. Here's what to do:

1. **Shut off the main circuit breaker or switch to the service panel.**

2. **Remove the cover to the circuit breaker service panel.**

3. **If you have push-button circuit breakers, loosen the screws that hold the damaged breaker and pull it from the panel.**

4. **If it's a breaker, insert a screwdriver between the bad one and the one behind it and pry the old breaker out.** It rocks out towards the wire side.

5. **Before you disconnect the wires, identify them so you will be able to reattach them correctly to the new breaker.** Review and follow the safety tips at the beginning of the chapter.

6. **Remove the wires connected to circuit breaker.**

7. **Make sure the new breaker has exactly the same amps as the damaged breaker.**

8. **Attach wires to the new breaker while it's out of the box and in your hand.** Don't rush. Double-check your work. Read the labels on the wires to make you've got the wires connected correctly.

9. **Mount and fasten it to the service panel.** (Some will snap in, others have to be fastened with screw fasteners.)

10. **Turn on power.**

 For your own safety, always wear rubber shoes when you work on a control panel because rubber doesn't conduct electricity. Also, make sure the floor underneath the panel is dry. Water is an excellent conductor of electricity and you don't want your body to become part of the circuit.

 Any time a fuse or circuit breaker pops, you have to look at a sequence of receptacles and switches, usually on a straight line from the area closest to the service panel. If your service panel is located at the front of your home, the electric circuit will flow to the back of the house. To identify what's connected to that circuit, work with a helper who can turn on appliances and lights, and then let you know which ones go off when you turn a circuit breaker off. Remember a major appliance should be the only thing on a 240-volt circuit, but test outlets and lights in the vicinity just to make sure.

## Fixing flickering lights

Don't worry about ghosts if lights start to flicker on and off; your house isn't haunted. You may have a bad outlet or switch that's causing the problem. Or it may be just a bad bulb. Replace it before continuing. To find the faulty outlet or switch, you have to test every one of them on the line, starting with those located nearest to the place where the problem is occurring and then continuing to the next. The easiest way to do this is by turning on lights, and plugging in a radio or another appliance to find out if they work.

A bad outlet outside the building might also be on a line that controls outlets in the family room, kitchen, and porch. So when you're trying to find the one that's causing the problem, always start at the electrical device that's nearest to where the problem is occurring.

# Testing and Replacing Switches

Overhead lights turn on or off when you flick a wall switch to its on and off positions. *Off* breaks the flow of electricity going into the light; *on* switches it back on. Table lamps and most appliances have their own switches, but they function the same way. Most switches last between 5 to 20 years, depending upon how well they were constructed, what materials were used, and how much use — and abuse — they get. When a switch stops working, you should check to see whether wires have come loose or whether there's no power coming into the switch. If you see sparks in a switch or the electricity is arcing, act immediately. These are two potential fire hazards that need immediate attention. Shut off the power.

If you plan to buy a new switch, get one that is graded for commercial use. These switches are better built and will last longer, taking more abuse, than typical household switches.

You can get new switches from hardware and home improvement stores. If you want something special, then go to a store selling electrical supplies or a store specializing in lighting, accessories, and parts. To test and replace a switch, you need screwdrivers, a continuity light, wire stripper, pliers, electrical tape, and masking tape. Follow these steps:

1. **Turn off the circuit breaker or take out the fuse in the service panel.**
   If you don't know which one feeds that switch, turn off or take out the master switch or fuse.

2. **Double check that the power is off, and then remove the switch plate.**

3. **Disconnect the switch by unscrewing the top and bottom screws that secure the switch to the electrical box behind it.**

4. **Pull the switch out enough to expose the wires on the side and back of the switch.** See Figure 7-2.

5. **If any of the wires in Step 3 are loose or broken, you know that that's what is causing the problem.** Go to Step 7 if the wires are connected securely.

6. **If necessary, tighten or secure those wires.**

7. **Label the wires with masking tape so you know how to reconnect them.** Make sure you record, for instance, which color wire goes on what color, in which position, or on which screw. Then loosen the terminal screws on the switch.

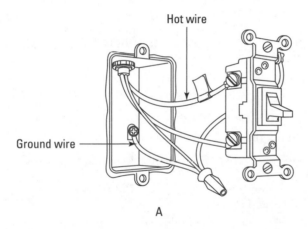

Hot wire

Ground wire

A

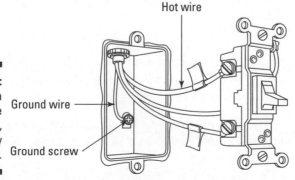

Hot wire

**Figure 7-2:**
Wiring in a
single-pole
(A) and (B),
a three-way
switch.

Ground wire

Ground screw

B

8. **Take the wires off the terminal screws.** Some switches may have wires that are inserted into holes at the back of the switch. If this switch does, push a small screwdriver in the hole below the wire. That should release it.

9. **Put one probe of your continuity light to one terminal and the other probe to the other terminal.**

10. **Flip the switch to the on and off positions.** If the continuity light doesn't turn on when the switch is on, get a replacement switch and continue with Steps 11 through 17.

11. **Strip about ½ inch of the insulating cover off the wires, using a wire stripper.**

12. **Again using the stripper or pliers, bend the end of the wire into a half circle.**

13. **Wrap that bent end around the terminal screw in a clockwise direction.** See Figure 7-2. If the switch doesn't have screws, put the straight wires into the holes at the back of the switch. Make sure they are in the right hole; you don't want to cross the wires.

14. **Tighten the screws.**

15. **Put the new switch into the terminal box, making certain it's straight up and down and from side to side and that "on" is up.**

16. **Screw the cover back on.**

17. **Turn the power on and test the switch to see that it works.**

Most lights are operated by one switch only. But there also are three-way switches, typically found in hallways, on stairs, or at exit doors. Three-way switches operate the same light or lights from two different locations. They're convenient and useful for illuminating areas in which safety might be a factor.

Three-way switches have three, not two terminals. The third terminal functions as a common terminal. A three-way needs the third wire going to the third screw (on lower right of switch), and the ground wire needs to be connected to the ground screw. See Figure 7-2B. If you have to replace a three-way switch, make sure you label the wires leading into it. If the wires are connected wrong, the new switch won't function properly.

# Troubleshooting Dimmers

Ah, dimmers. Nothing beats low light for relaxing, leisurely meals, especially when you want to add a touch of romance to the setting. Dimmers malfunction, too, which is anything but relaxing. Here's how to replace and repair them:

1. **Shut off the power to the room you're working in.**

2. **Remove the dimmer dial, pulling it firmly towards you.**

3. **Take the cover plate under the dial off.** It looks just like the cover plate on a standard switch.

4. **Unscrew the screws on the cover plate and carefully pull the dimmer out of the electrical box.** See Figure 7-3.

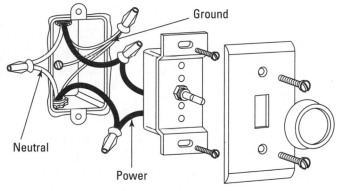

**Figure 7-3:** Labeling the wires in a dimmer switch: black is hot or power, white is neutral, and bare is the ground.

Ground

Neutral

Power

5. **Remove the wire nuts from the leads.** (There are no terminals on a dimmer switch.)

6. **With your continuity light, test the dimmer for power by touching one probe to one wire and the other to the other wire.**

7. **Use electrical nuts to connect the dimmer wires on the new switch to the power wires.**

8. **Reassemble the switch going from Steps 5 to 1.**

# Repairing Indoor and Outdoor Wall Outlets

Wall outlets look indestructible, but they crack, short out, and get loose enough that plugs easily slip out with the least bit of tension on a cord. In addition, they become unsightly with spattered paint or don't "go" with the newly decorated room. Now you have five good reasons to replace them. But before putting in a new outlet, figure out what's causing the old one to malfunction. Then you won't have to worry about damaging expensive appliances when you plug them in.

Purchase or borrow a receptacle analyzer — they're very inexpensive. You also need screwdrivers, pliers, electrical tape, a wire stripper, and wire nuts. With an analyzer, you can test outlets safely without turning off the power or going into electrical boxes. They have three lights and, depending on the manufacturer's design, indicate the source of electrical problems. We recommend getting one with a ground fault circuit interrupter (GFCI) button because it also tells you whether the outlet is grounded.

## Testing outlets

Testing outlets is easy. All you need is a circuit analyzer, which tells you which circuit breaker or fuse in the service panel controls power in the outlet and whether the circuits are properly wired and grounded. With an analyzer, you can identify all the outlets in the house and easily label the service panel. For more info, see the section "Labeling your service panel" earlier in the chapter. Here's what to do:

1. **Plug the circuit analyzer into one receptacle on the outlet.**

2. **If the outlet isn't working, see whether it's controlled by a wall switch that has to be turned on and turn it on.**

3. **The circuit analyzer will show whether there's power and — just as important — whether the wires are hooked up correctly.**

4. **Be sure to check both receptacles of an outlet.**

5. **If there is no power coming out of an outlet, then it needs to be replaced.**

## Replacing outlets

To replace a wall outlet follow these directions:

1. **Shut off power and confirm it's off with the circuit analyzer.**

2. **Take the cover off the wall.**

3. **Unscrew the mounting screws.** Be careful not to touch any wires or the terminals.

4. **Pull out the receptacle but don't remove any wires.**

5. **Place the new receptacle next to the old one and use masking tape to identify the wire connections.** See Figure 7-4. You want to know exactly how to wire the new outlet after the old one is disconnected. If you don't use labels, make a diagram. If you have enough wire, you can move the wires one at a time. Sound confusing? Don't worry. We all started out this way.

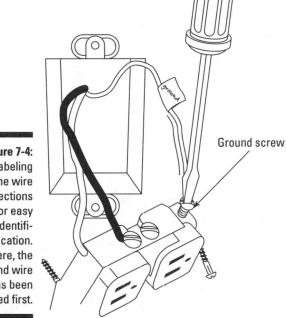

Ground screw

**Figure 7-4:**
Labeling
the wire
connections
for easy
identifi-
cation.
Here, the
ground wire
has been
labeled first.

Some receptacles have terminal screws on the side of the terminal. Others come with holes on the back, through which the bare wires are inserted. You will also find receptacles with a combination of both. See Figure 7-5.

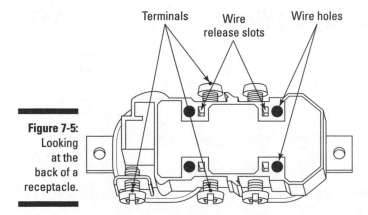

Terminals    Wire
release slots    Wire holes

**Figure 7-5:**
Looking
at the
back of a
receptacle.

6. **Unscrew the terminals.**

7. **Carefully pull off the wires.**

8. **Inspect the wires from the circuit.** Clean them, if needed, so that they don't have dirt or bits of insulation on them.

9. **If there isn't about ½ inch of exposed wire at the ends, use a wire stripper to take off the excess.**

10. **Attach each wire to the new receptacle, putting it in exactly as you found it.** The white wire (neutral) goes to silver terminal. The black or colored wire attaches to the brass colored terminals.

11. **Wrap electrical tape over all the terminals and bare wires to insulate them.**

12. **Push the new receptacle into the electrical box/wall.**

13. **Replace the cover and turn on the electricity.**

14. **Double-check your work with the receptacle analyzer to make sure the outlets are functioning correctly.**

# Rewiring Fixtures

Most homes have two types of light fixtures: fluorescent and incandescent. Fluorescent lights usually are tube-shaped; incandescent lights are the ones with rounded bulbs that generally screw into a socket. Both types of fixtures can have problems other than the bulb or tube burning out.

## Fixing fluorescent lights

Fluorescent lights have three main parts — starters (which are found mostly on lights that are more than 10 years old), *ballasts* (wire transformers), and switches. Each can malfunction. When a fluorescent light won't turn on, make sure the power's on and check the cord. If it's bad, follow the directions for replacing the cord in Chapter 11. When the power's on and the cord is okay, then look for defects in the starter or ballast. Most other problems are caused by the tube or the starter. Typically check them when:

- The light goes on, but isn't as bright as before.
- The ends light up, but not the center.
- The light flickers.
- The light flashes on and off.

Sometimes the pins in the socket holding the tube get bent and don't hold the tube securely. If that happens, you have to replace the socket.

Fluorescent tubes last a long time and aren't expensive, but they're very fragile and release inert gas and phosphor if they break. Handle them carefully.

### Replacing the starter

Lighting technology has changed, and new fluorescents don't have starters. But if you want to keep the old light, we show you how to replace the starter. Here's what to do:

1. **Turn off the power.**

2. **Lift up the diffuser or cover — if there is one — on the fixture.**

3. **Take out the tube so you can get at the starter — a round plug-in component that's either under the tube or on the side of the fixture.**

4. **To remove it, twist the starter counterclockwise ⅛ turn and pull it out.**

5. **Get a new one that has exactly the same part number and rating from a hardware or home improvement store.** Take the old one with you to be sure.

6. **Twist the new starter into position.**

7. **Put the tube back in.**

8. **Replace the cover.**

9. **Turn the power on.**

### Replacing the ballast

The ballast is the most expensive part of a fluorescent light. It's defective if there is tar leaking from it, if it gets extremely hot (warm is okay), or if the fixture is burned around the ballast. If it needs to be replaced, consider getting a new light instead; it might be less expensive. But if you decide to fix the fixture anyway, here's what you have to do:

1. **Turn off the power.**

2. **Remove the diffuser, the tube, and cover plate if there is one.**

3. **Disconnect the wires leading to the ballast.** It's large and near the center of the fixture.

4. **Take it out.** Be careful because it's heavy.

5. **Put the new ballast in place.**

6. **Reconnect the wires in the same way you took them apart.**

7. **Replace the cover plate, tube, and diffuser.**

8. **Turn the electricity on.**

### Replacing the socket

Follow these steps to replace a socket on your fluorescent light:

1. **Turn off the power.**

2. **Take the diffuser, tube, and cover off the fixture.**

3. **Disconnect the socket wires.**

4. **Disconnect the socket and take it out.**

5. **Get an exact replacement socket.** Take it with you to the store.

6. **Reconnect the wires.**

7. **Put diffuser, tube, and cover plate back in.**

8. **Turn on the power.**

## Repairing incandescent light fixtures

Everyone knows how to replace burned-out light bulbs with thin tungsten wire filaments inside the glass. They're fragile and if the light goes out, you should always check the bulb first. But other things can turn off lights too: especially loose wires, worn sockets, and overloaded circuits. So if a new bulb doesn't work, find out whether other things on the circuit are working. If they are, then look at the fixture to see what's wrong. You need screwdrivers, wire cutters, and a continuity light to test the circuit. Here's what to do if you need to replace a ceiling fixture:

1. **Turn off the circuit breaker.**

2. **Take off the shade or cover on the light.**

3. **Unscrew the bulb.**

4. **Disassemble the hardware securing the fixture.** Most are held up with a cap on a threaded nipple or sometimes two screws. And some fixtures have trim on top of the fasteners. That will have to be removed first.

5. **Pull the fixture out or down.** There's an electric box behind it.

6. **Disconnect the ceiling fixture wires from those in the electric box.** They may be connected with electrical nuts or tape. See Figure 7-6.

7. **Go to a hardware, home improvement, or electrical parts store with the fixture.** It's important to match the wattage, as well as the mounting holes.

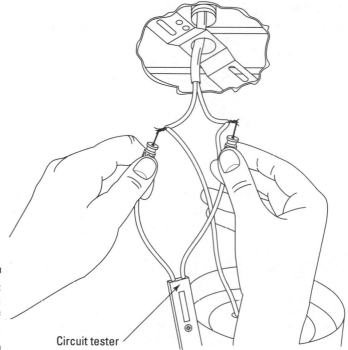

**Figure 7-6:**
Pulling the
fixture off
the ceiling.

Circuit tester

8. **When you get back home, strip at least ½ inch of insulation off the ends of the new wires.**

9. **Connect the black wire to the black wire in the electric box, and the white to white.** Use electric nuts or tape to make the connections. If the new light has a bare ground wire attached and the box doesn't have the corresponding bare wire, wrap the wire around a screw in the box or add a screw. See Figure 7-7.

10. **Attach the new fixture to the electric box using mounting screws.**

11. **Tighten the screws.**

12. **After the fixture is attached, put in a new bulb.**

13. **Turn the power on and test the light.**

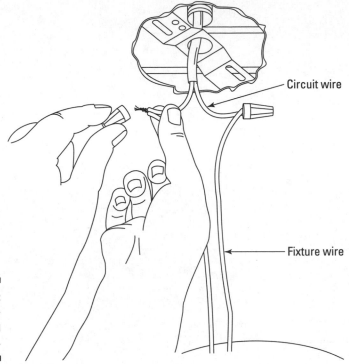

Circuit wire

Fixture wire

**Figure 7-7:**
Recon-
necting
the wiring.

## Testing and rewiring table lamps

Although table lamps are accessories, not a part of the house itself, they also aren't appliances. So we included them in this chapter. They're simple to test and rewire. Just follow these steps:

1. **Unplug the power cord, and remove the bulb and the shade yoke.**

2. **Squeeze the socket to get it out of the lamp.** There's an inner and outer shell with a cardboard insulator between them. If the outer sleeve is damaged, get a new unit.

3. **Look for loose wire connections on the terminals in the threaded shell.** Figure 7-8 shows the end of a wire beneath a terminal screw that probably doesn't have a secure enough connection.

4. **Tighten the connections.**

5. **Put the lamp back together and test it to see whether it works.** If it does, you're done.

6. **If the wires aren't loose, disconnect them.**

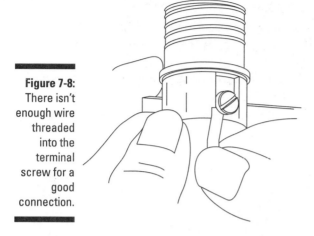

**Figure 7-8:**
There isn't enough wire threaded into the terminal screw for a good connection.

7. **Using a continuity wire to check the plug, put the probe on one exposed wire in the lamp and the other on a prong of the plug.** See Figure 7-9. If the light goes on, that prong is okay. Now check the other prong and wire. If neither test turns on the continuity light, get a new plug and cord.

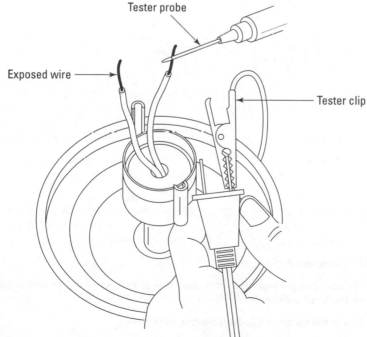

Tester probe

Exposed wire

Tester clip

**Figure 7-9:**
Testing the plug and cord.

8. **If the plug and cord are okay, replace the lamp socket.**

9. **When installing the new socket, connect the ridged insulation wire to the terminal with a silver screw.** The other wire, which is smooth, hooks up to the brass screw.

10. **Put the inner socket in place, the cardboard sleeve over it, and then the outer part of the socket.**

11. **Adjust the socket so everything lines up, so that the switch fits into the notch in the sleeve.**

12. **Press the socket down until you hear it lock into the lamp fixture.**

13. **Put the rest of the lamp pieces together, including the bulb, and turn the light on.**

# Getting Doorbells to Work

Not long ago, all doorbells in homes were hardwired into the door frame or very near it. They didn't present problems for years. But, inevitably, they no longer worked and you had to take them apart to repair them. Now you have options. You can fix the original doorbell, buy a new one that chimes or sounds much nicer than the old, or purchase a remote-controlled doorbell and leave the original alone.

## Calling all intercoms . . .

The most common problem that people encounter with intercom systems wired into homes is excessive buzzing or humming coming from the wall units. If a unit starts buzzing for no apparent reason, check and make sure that all the wires and connections are tight. If you hear buzzing on just a couple of units, then it may be a problem with those stations. It all units are buzzing, then the problem probably lies with the master unit. Make sure the ground terminal on the master unit is connected. If all connections are fine, then the buzzing or humming may be coming in over the wiring, which may have to do with the location or the wiring of your home. In that case there's no easy solution.

Most wired-in intercom systems are installed by companies that have technical support or customer service available for repairs. If your wired-in intercom stops working, you might want to weigh the cost of calling in a technician versus buying a new wireless system. Wireless intercoms are becoming more advanced than the old wired-in kind. They're very practical and user friendly, especially since they're portable and no wires are involved!

Remote doorbells have a variety of sounds and when they malfunction, all you have to do is get new batteries for the receiver. We opted for a wireless remote a couple years ago when the original bell — now corroded and permanently silent — stopped ringing. The only drawback is that someone in the neighborhood has a remote the same frequency. The neighbor's remote makes our bell ring only occasionally; but after answering the door, we announce, "It's just our ghost."

You don't have to put up with ghosts or phantoms if you don't want to. Fixing old doorbells or buying replacements is an option. We explain what to do in the following sections.

## Working on hard-wired doorbells

Wired doorbells have a bell, a junction box with a transformer on it, and the button at the door. See Figure 7-10. Ringing the bell connects the ground wire together, which activates the circuit. But several things can go wrong: loose wires, button defects, short circuits or a power failure, corroded connections, an accumulation of dirt on parts, and malfunctioning bells or transformers. You need pliers, screwdrivers, wire strippers, electrical contact cleaner, fine sandpaper, isopropyl (rubbing) alcohol, and a cotton swab or old toothbrush.

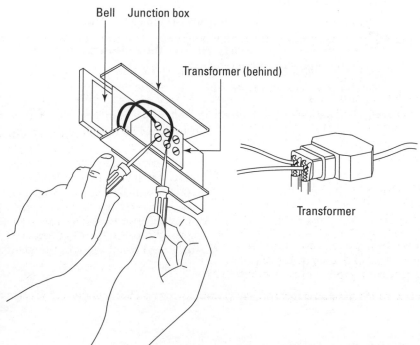

Bell   Junction box

Transformer (behind)

Transformer

**Figure 7-10:**
Looking inside a doorbell and transformer.

When the bell doesn't ring, look at the circuit breaker or fuse box. If it hasn't tripped, turn off power to the doorbell. Now follow these steps:

1. **Check the wires behind the button, in the junction box, and on the transformer.** They may be damaged or loose. If they're loose, tighten them; if damaged, go to Step 2.

2. **Cut out the damaged area.**

3. **Strip 1 inch of insulation off the ends of both wires so you can twist them together and then tape them.**

Although doorbells don't emit much voltage, the transformer is connected to a 120-volt wire in the house. Turn off the power before you start working on the doorbell.

If the wires are sound, look for corroded terminals. Here's what to do:

1. **Remove the plate from the button and look at the terminals.** They may be corroded.

2. **Clean the terminals with electrical contact cleaner.** You can also take the screws off the wires and sand off the corrosion using fine sandpaper.

3. **Test the button after turning the power back on.**

4. **Put the plate back on.**

To test the bell or chimes and transformer, follow these steps:

1. **If it chimes continuously, remove the button plate.** Make sure the wires aren't pinched or touching.

2. **Tighten the screws.** Be sure to keep the wires separate.

If the bell sounds as though it's buried under blankets, it probably needs cleaning. Use a cotton swab or soft toothbrush dipped in isopropyl (rubbing) alcohol to clean it.

Never oil any part of the bell or chime. It will only make the sound worse and may even cause the device to collect more dirt.

The grommets holding the chimes can deteriorate when they get old, causing a muffled sound. Get some new ones and replace the old ones. Also look at the hammer to see whether it's bent. If so, straighten it out by using pliers. Be careful not to damage it.

# Testing and fixing push-button doorbells

Here's how to test and fix push-button doorbells:

1. **Loosen the screws that hold the button in place.** If there are clips instead of screws, raise them with a screwdriver blade slipped under the clips. Go slowly so you don't damage the clips.

2. **Test the button by placing a screwdriver bit across the terminals to see if the bell rings.** If that causes the bell or chimes to ring, the button (switch) has to be replaced. Follow Step 3. If there is no sound when you use the screwdriver, you have to test other parts of the doorbell.

3. **Take the wires off the terminals on the switch.**

4. **Put in the replacement switch.**

5. **Loop the wires around the terminal screws.**

6. **Tighten the screws.**

7. **Press the doorbell button to make sure it rings.**

8. **Turn the power back on.**

# Testing and replacing sounding devices

Exposed to the elements, doorbells rust and get dirty after time. Clean yours up before replacing the bell or chimes unless your heart is set on getting a nicer one. Use a cotton swab dipped in isopropyl (rubbing) alcohol for the job.

# Replacing chimes and bells

To replace a sounding device, follow these steps:

1. **Turn off the power to the doorbell at the service panel.**

2. **Tape and label the wires so they can be reinstalled the same.**

3. **Loosen the terminal screws and take the wires off.**

4. **Using a screwdriver, unfasten the bell or chimes from the wall.**

5. **Put the wires into the back of the replacement unit.**

6. **Attach it to the wall.** When you attach each wire, loop the end clockwise around the terminal screw. Make sure you attach the previously marked wires to the correct terminals. Then tighten the screws.

7. **Put the cover on the new unit.**

8. **Turn on the power and test the doorbell.** It should work now. If it doesn't, replace the transformer.

To replace the transformer, here's what to do:

1. **Purchase a new transformer from a hardware or home improvement store.** Make sure it's the same voltage as the old one.

2. **Shut off the power to the circuit at the breaker panel.**

3. **Disconnect the doorbell wires and house cable wires from the old transformer.**

4. **Put the leads from the new transformer through the hole in the panel and attach wires.**

It doesn't matter which wire connects to the black or white wires in the house electric box and you can put the low-voltage wires on either way also.

# Fixing Garage Door Openers

Garage door openers work off the electrical current in the house; the controller transmits a radio signal or an infrared light. The signal activates an electric motor attached to the track and pulleys that open and close the doors. They generally don't have problems other than having to replace batteries. Typical garage door opener glitches include:

✔ **Motors not responding to signals.** If the door doesn't respond to the signal, make sure the cord from the motor is plugged into the outlet. Then wait 15 minutes to let the opener cool off before trying to open the door again. A hot motor can restrict the door from opening. Replace the batteries in the controller. If you have a second controller, find out whether it works. Also check the antenna on the motor to see if it's intact.

✔ **Doors that open, but don't close.** When the door goes up but will not close, the electric eyes or the open/close limit switches (see Figure 7-11) may be out of alignment. Read the manufacturer's instruction manual to find out how to realign them.

✔ **Doors that raise without a command.** Sometimes the opener has a mind of its own. When the door opens of its own accord, look at the button on the remote to see if it's stuck, or the controller could be bad. There also might be a circuit board that's faulty. If it is, you will have to get a new one.

✔ **The remote button doesn't work.** If the remote button doesn't work, the wires may be loose or damaged, or the switch could be corroded or bad. Disconnect the wires from the button and check the button with a continuity light.

✔ **Doors that reverse when they're closing.** And if the door suddenly reverses while closing, make sure nothing is blocking the electric eye. To adjust the eye, just make sure each side is pointed at the other. The down limit switch may be out of adjustment so you need to reset it. If the door reverses when it's opening you have to readjust the open-limit knob. Refer to your instruction manual.

✔ **Your neighbor's garage door also opens when you use your remote.** If your remote also operates a neighbor's door, you're both on the same frequency. Look at your owner's instructions to see if you can reset the frequency and if so, how to do it.

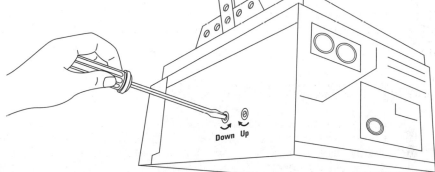

**Figure 7-11:** Readjusting the open/close limits of a garage door opener.

 When working on your garage door opener, you should also do any minor repairs or maintenance needed on the other garage door workings. When they're in good shape and working well, your garage door opener will work much more smoothly. See Chapter 4 for information on basic garage door hardware fixes.

As you may have guessed, any time you're not sure where a part is, refer to your owner's manual for specific illustrations and instructions on what to do.

 Always call for service if you're having major problems with the garage door itself, as trying to do the repair yourself can be extremely dangerous. See Chapter 18 about hiring a professional. For more information on the types of garage door fixes that you *can* do yourself, see Chapter 4.

# Chapter 8

# Handling Your Heating, Cooling, and Air Quality Systems

### In This Chapter

▶ Tinkering with furnaces

▶ Fixing furnace humidifiers

▶ Making air conditioners more efficient

▶ Dealing with ducts and air returns

▶ Getting fans to work

▶ Improving your air quality

**Y**ou can do a lot to improve comfort and air quality throughout your house. In this chapter, we tell you what you should look for when there's a problem with heating and cooling systems and the gadgets we use to improve the air we breathe. And, yes, you who own older furnaces will also get some easy fix-its you can do on Friday nights and all through the weekend.

What do you do when your furnace goes out on a weekend? Call for service at emergency weekend rates, abandon the house until Monday, or try to figure out what you can do. Most of you, no doubt, will start tinkering. If the furnace is relatively new, however, it probably has electronic parts that make it difficult for homeowners to tackle. With an older furnace, you have more options and might get it running yourself. In this chapter, we give you some pointers on determining what you can do yourself and what you should leave for the pros.

# Maintaining and Repairing Furnaces

Most homes are heated by forced air furnaces — fueled by gas, oil, or propane. Forced air furnaces are efficient, relatively cheap to install, and relatively easy to maintain. That doesn't mean they don't have problems: motors and some of the moving parts get old and need to be replaced, a pulley loosens or breaks, or the pilot light goes out. Sometimes, furnaces don't work efficiently because people block air returns with large pieces of furniture or they fail to change the filter regularly or clean the heat ducts. And sometimes, a furnace is simply too small to warm a particular house. Most repairs should be left in the hands of a professional (see Chapter 17), but there are a few things you can do to at least check to make sure a major repair is necessary.

Gas furnaces are the most common furnaces, but with increasing gas prices, all-electronic furnaces are becoming more popular. You can't work on an electronic furnace, though, because all the "brains" or controls are sealed up. So, if you have a problem getting your all-electronic furnace to operate properly, call for service.

## Gas furnaces

These are still the most common furnaces found in homes. They usually hum along without any trouble, as long as you change your filter regularly and have a professional service technician come out once a year to inspect the furnace and clean the pilot. (See Chapter 18 about hiring a professional.) When something goes wrong with a gas furnace, you have to be careful because of the dangers presented by the gas.

Older gas furnaces have a pilot light, much the same as gas stoves do. See Figure 8-1 for the inner workings of a gas furnace and the pilot. Newer furnaces use a spark igniter, glow plugs, or a hot-surface igniter.

When you move into a new home, or if you don't know where it is on your existing home, find out where the gas-shutoff valve is located. It's usually next to the gas meter outdoors. That way you'll be able to locate it quickly and shut off the gas to your home if there's an emergency.

There are some things you can do safely, and should do, to keep your gas furnace in good working order. We explore those things in the next sections.

If the gas burner doesn't turn off, shut off the electricity and turn off the gas inlet valve, both located on the outside of the furnace, and call the gas company right away. There might be a short circuit or something wrong with the automatic gas valve or furnace limit switch. Don't try fixing them yourself.

### Relighting pilot lights

If the gas pilot light on the furnace goes out, it only needs relighting, just as on old stoves when the pilot blew out. The furnace pilot light is accessible after you lift the front cover off the furnace. Refer to Figure 8-1.

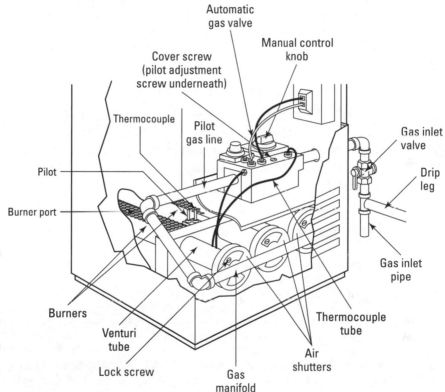

**Figure 8-1:** Looking inside a typical gas furnace.

Automatic gas valve

Manual control knob

Cover screw (pilot adjustment screw underneath)

Thermocouple

Pilot gas line

Pilot

Burner port

Gas inlet valve

Drip leg

Gas inlet pipe

Burners

Thermocouple tube

Venturi tube

Lock screw

Gas manifold

Air shutters

If the pilot is out and there *is* a gas smell, it could indicate a buildup of gas. If that happens, get everyone out of the house, turn off the gas supply valve on the outside of the house, and call the gas company. Use your neighbor's phone or a cellphone.

Here's what to do when the pilot light goes out.

1. **Check whether the furnace is turned on, and if there's a safety reset button on it, make sure that it didn't pop up and shut off the unit.** Also check whether anyone closed the gas inlet valve.

2. **Remove the cover at the front of the furnace and read instructions on the furnace itself or in the manual that came with the furnace when it was new.**

3. **Turn off the gas flow. The control knob is located on the automatic gas valve inside the furnace.** See Figure 8-1.

4. **Wait 5 to 10 minutes.** By then any gas that's in the pipes will have dispersed.

   If you have a furnace operating on bottled gas (propane) wait at least 30 minutes; bottled gas lingers longer than natural gas.

5. **Turn the thermostat way down.** You can turn it up to its regular setting after the furnace is running again.

6. **Inspect the pilot orifice to see whether any dirt or debris is plugging it up.** See Figure 8-2. Clean it off with a wire brush.

7. **Turn the furnace control knob to pilot.**

8. **Push the knob down and hold it, light the pilot, and continue to hold knob down for 45 to 60 seconds.**

9. **Turn the knob to on.**

10. **Turn up the thermostat.**

11. **Look at the pilot flame.** It should look bright blue with a softer blue in the center. It shouldn't have a yellow tip.

### Changing filters

Furnaces can't operate efficiently unless the filters are changed monthly throughout the heating season (do this year-round if you have central air). Most furnaces have a narrow compartment between the furnace and the duct system. The filter pulls out easily and if it's dirty, replace it. See Figure 8-3A. You can buy a similar filter or one of the new accordion-pleated types just as long as it has the same dimensions as the old one. While you're at the hardware or home supply store, get a box of filters so that they're on hand when you need a new one.

Dirty filters can cause the blower motor to fail prematurely. That will cost more money and aggravation than keeping a year's supply of filters on hand.

For more suggestions on how to maintain heating systems and control the climate in your home, get *Home Maintenance For Dummies* by James and Morris Carey and *Home Improvement For Dummies* by Gene and Katie Hamilton (both published by Wiley). Both books are full of advice for keeping furnaces, air conditioners, and other equipment at peak performance.

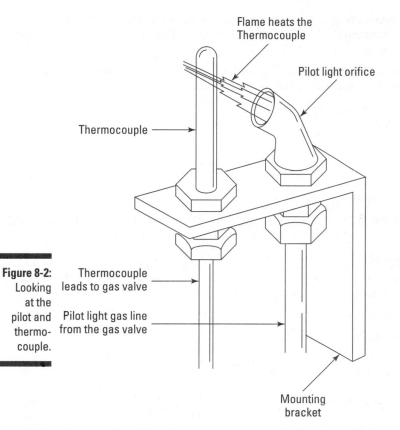

Flame heats the
Thermocouple

Pilot light orifice

Thermocouple

**Figure 8-2:**
Looking
at the
pilot and
thermo-
couple.

Thermocouple
leads to gas valve

Pilot light gas line
from the gas valve

Mounting
bracket

**Figure 8-3:**
Replacing
filters
(A) and
checking
tension on
the blower
belt (B)

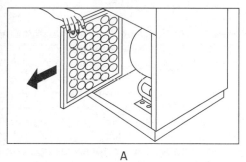

A

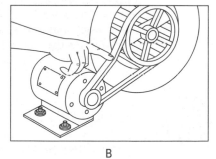

B

### Working on blowers

Most furnaces made after about 1990 have direct-drive blowers that do not have belts or need lubrication. To avoid problems with them, clean the blower at the beginning of each heating season. Older furnaces also need to be cleaned annually, but they probably also have a belt and a blower that should be oiled. You can tell if your furnace blower needs oil by looking for an oil cup on either end of the motor. It's funnel shaped and no larger than a new pencil eraser, with a spring-loaded cap or door on top. While you're looking for that, also see if there's a belt on your furnace. If it's worn or broken, or if the fan squeals when the blower's on, the belt needs replacing. We explain how to do that below.

To oil blowers that have oil cups — open the top and pour in two to three drops of 3-in-1 or another lightweight oil. Then close the top. To adjust the belt on the blower, follow the steps below:

1. **If the belt is loose, loosen the motor mounting bolts and slide the motor.** See Figure 8-3B. To run properly, there should be only ½ inch of slack when you push down on the belt.

2. **If the belt looks worn, put a new one on.**

## Fuel system furnaces

Regular maintenance, a must for oil and other fuel systems, will probably keep you from having to call for service. See Figure 8-4 for the anatomy of an oil furnace.

To keep your furnace running:

✔ Clean the pump strainer and the filter once a year (we give you a step-by-step guide on how to do that later in this section).

✔ Clean the fan blades each month during the heating season.

✔ Keep the burner motor well lubricated — do that every couple months.

✔ Inspect the flue connections.

✔ Get the furnace tuned up by a trained professional each year. If you do this, then the chance that anything else will be needed is extremely rare.

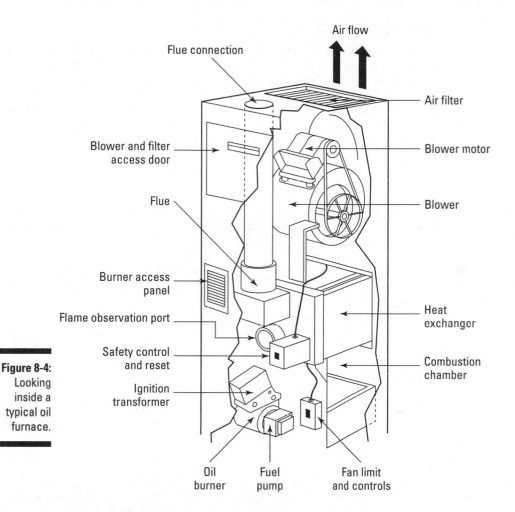

Air flow

Flue connection

Air filter

Blower and filter
access door

Blower motor

Flue

Blower

Burner access
panel

Heat
exchanger

Flame observation port

Safety control
and reset

Combustion
chamber

**Figure 8-4:**
Looking
inside a
typical oil
furnace.

Ignition
transformer

Oil
burner

Fuel
pump

Fan limit
and controls

If the burner stops running, raise the thermostat setting, and then check circuit breakers, switches, and fuses to make certain they're on. (See Figure 8-5.) Finally, oil the motor and push the reset button to restart the furnace. Now it should work properly.

To find out whether the switches are on or off, look for the burner disconnect switch located on the outside wall of the furnace — you may have another located nearby in a hallway or room — the safety reset button on top of the blower unit, and a reset button for the blower motor on the side of the combustion blower motor. It prevents overloads. See Figure 8-5.

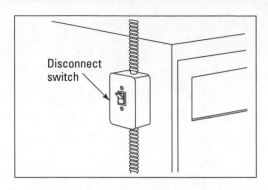

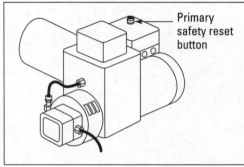

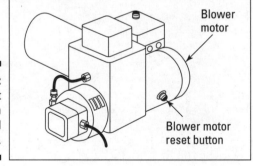

**Figure 8-5:**
Looking at
switches in
an oil
furnace.

Here's how to clean a pump strainer (refer to Figure 8-6):

1. **Turn off the valve at the fuel tank or coming from the tank.**

2. **Take the bolt out of the center of the filter.**

3. **Dump the oil into your waste oil recycle container.**

4. **Remove the filter and clean out any sediment that's left in the bowl.**

5. **Install a new filter, bowl gasket, and bolt gasket.** Screw the bowl back onto the base. No need to fill the bowl; it will gravity fill. (You can get these parts at a furnace parts and supply store. Look in the Yellow Pages.)

6. **Look for the pump screen, located in the line where it enters the pump.**

7. **Unscrew the line.**

8. **Remove the screen with a pick, clean it, and put it back in.**

9. **Turn the valve back on and check for leaks.**

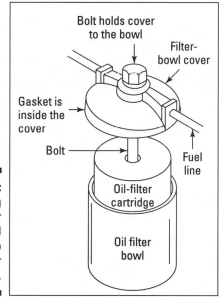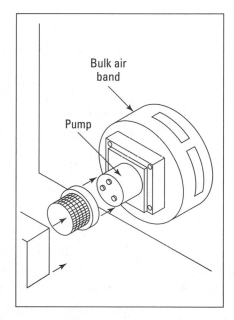

**Figure 8-6:** Changing the oil filter (left) and pump strainer (right).

# Working on hot water heating systems

Gravity and hot water furnaces are not often installed in new homes today, but similar systems with the old cast-iron radiators throughout the house were fixtures in homes built around 1900. And some of them are still working. Clanking, popping, and gurgling as they swing into action whenever the thermostat detects room temperatures dropping, they provide a relatively steady flow of heat without the drafts you get in forced-air furnaces.

Hot water systems are closed, meaning that the water constantly circulates through the pipes and into the boiler. Newer units have many zones with two water pipes linked to each zone: one circulating heated water to the rooms and the other returning the much cooler water back to the boiler to get reheated. In the older one-pipe series systems, hot water flowed from room to room, and then back again to the boiler in the same pipe. The last room on the circuit never got as warm as the first.

Instead of the old cast-iron radiators, today's units have free-standing or baseboard convectors. They're less bulky, more efficient, and look much nicer than their ancestors and they provide the same amount of heat to all the rooms. The disadvantage of hydronic or hot water heat is that because there is no duct work, you can't have central air.

To maintain a system, you should lubricate the circulating pump motor. Use a lightweight oil such as 3-in-1, and pour it in the oil cup like the ones described in the section "Working on blowers."

You also need to vent or purge radiators that don't have an automatic purge system in the fall and throughout the heating season. To vent the radiator, follow these directions:

1. **Open the valves on radiators and convectors to let out air.** Keep them open until water starts coming out. Be ready to catch the water in a bucket or container.

2. **Close the valve.**

3. **Don't forget to drain the boiler to get rid of rust and mineral deposits.** Read the manufacturer's instructions, and then follow the steps below:

   1. **Turn off the power and water.**

   2. **Flush the boiler drain cock.** To do this, stick the end of a garden hose into the drain cock.

   3. **Open the vent valves on a radiator located on the top floor of your house.** This lets air into the pipes which, in turn, makes the water bleed through the system.

   4. **Turn on the water supply valve so fresh water will flush through the system.** The valve is located on the water pipe going into the furnace.

   5. **When the water stops running, close the drain cock and vents.** Even though they're closed, the water will continue flowing into the boiler and through the system.

Systems with a pressure regulating valve automatically turns off the water when the boiler is full. With other systems, you must watch the pressure gauge. Refer to the owner's operating manual to find out what level is recommended by the manufacturer, and then let out the air in each convector, if needed, until the pressure is at the operating level.

# Fine-Tuning Furnace Humidifiers

With most furnaces, the humidity is always too low in the winter. Low humidity increases static electricity in the house, and can cause bloody noses or contribute to bronchitis and other lung complaints. Some people merely get dry, itchy skin. The only recourse we have is to get a humidifier.

Furnace and portable humidifiers are relatively simple machines. They have a source of water that's released as a fine mist or that evaporates and adds moisture to the air. Furnace models are connected to a water line, but they can be used only if you have a forced air furnace with heat ducts running through the house. To see what the innards of typical humidifiers look like, take a look at Figure 8-7.

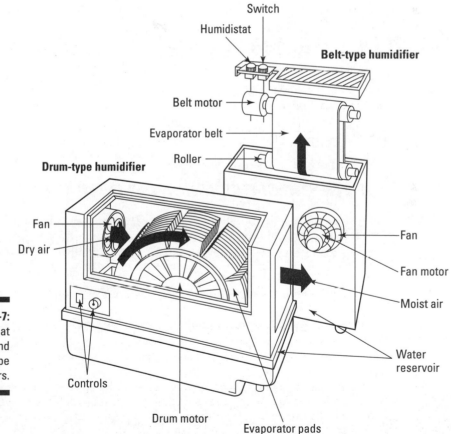

**Figure 8-7:**
Looking at belt- and drum-type humidifiers.

To humidify homes without ductwork, it's necessary to get a portable model that sits on the floor or table top. For more on these items, see the section "Getting portable humidifiers to work."

Check the manufacturer's directions for maintaining and cleaning your furnace humidifier. Use vinegar or a humidifier cleaner and antibacterial solution. If filters or pads start getting stiff with built-up minerals, replace them; otherwise, replace them once a year. Never scrub or brush the pads because you will remove the protective coating.

Some humidifiers have float assemblies and they should be taken out and cleaned when the furnace is turned off and put back into the humidifier in the fall. Humidity levels should be 35 to 40 percent year round. If the windows sweat in the winter, reduce the humidity in 5-percent increments until the problem stops.

# Improving Air Conditioner Efficiency

In the summer, we want air conditioning so we can sleep at night and work comfortably, leaving the hot, humid weather to a few hardy souls. Like everything else in a home, air conditioners have to be maintained if we want them to operate at peak performance, cooling and dehumidifying the dwelling and filtering dust from the air.

## Central air conditioner performance

Split-system central air conditioners, used with forced air furnaces, take hot air from the house and blow it through an evaporator coil located in the top of the furnace to cool the air. The cooled air circulates throughout the house via the heat ducts then returns to the furnace as warm air to be cooled again.

Central air conditioners can work for years without problems if properly maintained and serviced annually. If they aren't working properly, call a trained technician. But before you phone, see if the problem is caused by something else.

### What to do when the unit stops working

If you have your system inspected and cleaned annually, it should run without any trouble. However, if it stops working completely and you aren't sure why, here's something you can do to troubleshoot before calling a pro:

1. **Check the circuit breaker or fuse box to find out whether the unit has power.**

2. **Check the fuses in the disconnect box located outside, near the condenser to make sure there's power.**

3. **Replace or clean the furnace filter.**

4. **If the condenser coils are coated with dust or debris, use a garden hose to wash them off.**

5. **If the air conditioner still won't work, make the call.** A technician may have to recharge the refrigerant.

### What to do when the unit won't quit running

If the air conditioner runs constantly, here's what to do:

1. **Turn up the thermostat.**

   If you set the thermostat a few degrees higher, you will save energy and a lot of money when it comes time to pay your electric bill. And your significant other won't have to complain about wearing a sweater indoors.

2. **Take the cover off the condenser and find out whether anything is blocking the air flow.**

3. **Vacuum the interior of the condenser, and then flush it with a garden hose.**

4. **If the fan blades are bent or dirty, straighten them out and/or clean them.**

5. **While the cover is off, oil the motor on older air conditioners.** (Newer units are sealed and cannot be oiled.) Take off the plastic covers — there should be two — and put a couple drops of lightweight oil, such as 3-in-1, into each.

6. **Replace the cover.**

7. **Check the furnace filter and blower to see whether they're blocked.** Use a vacuum cleaner to clean dust and dirt on or around the blower.

8. **Replace the filter if necessary.**

### What to do when the unit freezes up

If the high pressure lines from the condenser to the furnace or the evaporator coil in the top of the furnace are iced up, then shut the system down:

1. **Either turn off the breaker in the panel or pull the disconnect switch outside at the condenser.**

2. **Call for service.** Your system is probably low on Freon and needs to be recharged.

### What to do when water pools under the evaporator

When there's water under the evaporator at the base of your furnace, the drain is probably clogged. You can clear it, but it's probably easier just to replace the whole thing. If you *want* to try clearing it, however, here's what to do.

1. **Take off the trap, and if it's PVC (plastic) you can cut the pipe to remove it.**

2. **Pour a vinegar-water or bleach-water solution (1 to 10 parts) into the drain.** That will help remove debris and algae.

3. **If you have flexible tubes, take them off and clean them by pouring the solution through them.** You can also run a wire through the tube to scrape the walls. Do it gently so you don't poke a hole.

4. **Reassemble the tubes and trap.**

## Window air conditioner performance

Window air conditioners contain the evaporator, condenser, and blower in one unit and are designed to cool one or more rooms. To get peak performance, you should clean the filter every couple weeks. Some have to be vacuumed; others are washable.

If the air conditioner stops working, make sure the power is on at the control box and that the cord and plug are plugged in and undamaged. (See Chapter 11 for more on cords and plugs.) Vacuum the filter at the front, just behind the control panel and cover. The condenser coils are located on the back, where the air conditioner hangs out of the window. Brush and clean them.

If you clean the air conditioner thoroughly in the spring, before it's set into the window, you shouldn't have a problem during hot weather. You won't have the hassle of pulling the unit out if you do the work then.

If your air conditioner stops working, always give it at least five minutes before you turn it back on. That gives the unit time to cool off.

When a window unit stops and starts for no apparent reason, you may have a problem with the thermostat. Check to see whether the sensor is out of position. You can readjust it by bending it so that it's near, but not on, the evaporator coil. It's usually held in place by a clip. See Figure 8-8. Also clean out the drain, hanging outside the unit. Clear it with a vinegar solution.

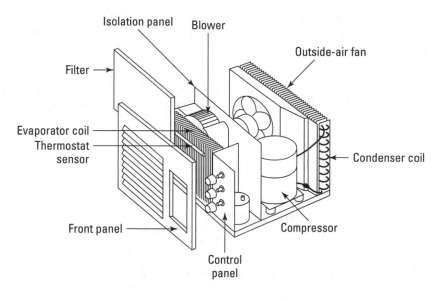

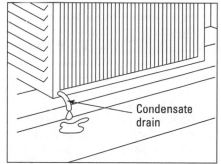

**Figure 8-8:** Looking at a window air conditioner and the condensate drain.

# Tending to Heat Registers and Cold Air Returns

Like everything else in the house, heat registers and cold air returns have to be cleaned periodically if they are to operate efficiently. Take the covers off and vacuum as far into the ducts as you can with your brush attachment. You'll be amazed at what you find in floor ducts along with dirt, fur, and dust, including small toys and pills you couldn't find after they dropped on the floor.

Even though you clean ducts every year, at five-year intervals call in for service. Professionals have the equipment to get to places that homeowners can't reach.

Never block the cold air returns or the heat registers with large furniture. They need to be uncovered to circulate the air through the heating system. The cold air returns usually are placed opposite the heat register on an inside wall.

# Troubleshooting Thermostats

A thermostat is a type of switch. But instead of controlling lights, it switches the furnace and air conditioner on and off, keeping rooms at the temperature you want. Some switches also control humidity levels in a home.

In addition to sensing changes in room temperature, automatic thermostats can be programmed to raise and lower temperatures at predetermined times during the day or night. For instance, while everyone's working or at school, the furnace can be turned down for most of the day and just before everyone gets home, start warming up the rooms to a more comfortable temperature. Some thermostats can do this twice in a 24-hour cycle, keeping rooms cooler while people are sleeping and warming them up just before everyone gets up. With the older mechanical models, you have to fiddle with the temperature setting by hand.

Thermostats don't work accurately forever and you can't purchase parts for them. So if the sensor control becomes faulty or stops working, buy a new thermostat. They're not expensive. And if you have to replace one, consider getting a digitally programmed thermostat. They're easier to use and in some states will increase the value of your home by making it more energy efficient. Such a thermostat will pay for itself in no time at all, considering the rising cost of energy.

Don't break apart your old thermostat or throw it in the trash! Older models often contain mercury, which like asbestos, is a lethal substance that can easily contaminate surrounding areas, including your own home. If you need to get rid of an old thermostat, check with your local hardware store to see if it recycles thermostats, or ask them where you can safely dispose of it.

# Getting Fans to Work: Floor to Ceiling

Attic fans often cool homes enough that air conditioning isn't needed. And ceiling, table, and floor fans make a room more comfortable by circulating

---

## Having humidistat heartaches?

Some furnaces have a humidistat to control room moisture. If the air gets too dry, it activates the humidifier, which adds humidity back into the air. If you're not sure the humidistat is working properly, turn it up and then listen to see if it comes on. If it doesn't, call a licensed HVAC (heating, ventilating, and air conditioning) professional to repair or replace it (see Chapter 18). A humidistat is one of those things that you really shouldn't tackle yourself unless you really know what you're doing.

---

the air. Attic and whole house fans should be cleaned and inspected each year. Here's what to do:

1. **Turn off the power to the fan.**

2. **Wipe the blades.**

3. **Put oil on the motor bearings.** You get at them through the oil cups. Some fans don't have them, so if you can't find them, don't worry.

4. **With a screwdriver or small wrench, tighten all screws and bolts.**

5. **If the belt looks cracked or worn, replace it.**

6. **Check the tension on the belt.** If the middle of the belt depresses more than ½ to ¾ inch, the belt has to be adjusted. Loosen the bolts and slide the motor, if it doesn't slide by itself. Then retighten the bolts. If the belt has no slack, loosen the mounting bolts and then retighten them.

7. **Clean the louvers on the shutters.**

8. **If you have screens on any vents in the attic, clean them too.** This is very important.

You can follow these same steps for table and floor fans. But carefully inspect the plugs and cords as well as the fan.

# Maintaining Portable Air Quality Appliances

A breath of fresh air isn't necessarily clean, at least not anymore. You read and hear plenty of news about air pollution, its causes, and how the number of children with asthma is going up. No wonder many households have turned to portable air purifiers, humidifiers, and dehumidifiers to improve the environment in their homes.

## Getting portable humidifiers to work

You can easily move a portable humidifier from one room to another, a convenience if you can't or don't want to humidify your whole home. Humidifiers or vaporizers are especially useful when someone in the family is sick, especially with chest congestion, colds, and allergies. But they do require more upkeep than a furnace-mounted humidifier because you have to fill the water reservoir regularly and clean it more frequently to avoid buildups of bacteria and mineral deposits. You also have to change the filter periodically.

The amount of moisture released in most humidifiers is controlled by a humidistat. It senses the moisture level in the air and turns the humidifier on when humidity drops below or goes above a certain range — usually 35 to 40 percent in the winter. However, vaporizers that are used when someone is sick can be turned up to a higher setting in that room.

If you clean your humidifier regularly and change the filter when it gets stiff with built-up mineral deposits, you probably won't have to deal with additional maintenance. What goes wrong? The float switch gets calcium and mineral deposits on it making it stick. The fan sucks in dirt that clogs the humidistat, and the fan and motor need to be cleaned and/or oiled. If cleaning doesn't get the humidifier or vaporizer working, buy a new one.

If you use a cleaning compound or chemicals when you clean the tank, make sure they're thoroughly rinsed off before you reuse the humidifier. You want to make your air better, not pollute it.

Your portable humidifier may not run if any of the following are dirty or defective:

- ✔ Float switches. Clean them with a calcium-lime-rust remover used in bathrooms. Follow the manufacturer's directions.

- ✔ Humidistats (the devices that regulate humidity). They have switches that can be replaced, if defective. We explain how to do it on small appliances in Chapter 11.

- ✔ On-off switches, cords, and plugs can also be replaced as described in Chapter 11.

- ✔ Fan motors.

## Tuning up dehumidifiers

In the summer, we complain about excessive humidity. It saps our energy, robs us of sleep, causes health and safety problems — especially in the elderly — and makes basements smell damp and musty. So if we don't have air conditioning to help dry out our homes, the next best thing to do is to buy a dehumidifier. They also come in handy in the spring or fall when there's a lot of rain but the outside temperature doesn't justify air conditioning. Equipped with an evaporator coil, compressor, fan, and humidistat, dehumidifiers wring moisture from the air. A comfortable moisture level during the summer is 35 to 40 percent.

For the most part dehumidifiers are trouble free, but they do require maintenance — emptying the tank, cleaning it periodically to keep bacteria and mildew in check, vacuuming the dirt from the coils, and replacing the power cord and plug if they get worn.

If it gets cool outdoors and you keep the dehumidifier in the basement, the coils will freeze up if the dehumidifier is switched on. Fortunately, all you have to do is turn it off manually and when you need it again, turn it back on.

When humidity is high, a portable dehumidifier with a 4-gallon tank needs to be emptied at least once a day. After the tank is full, the dehumidifier switches off and doesn't start working again until you empty it.

You can tell when a dehumidifier needs to be fixed — when the weather is hot and muggy, but there's not much water in the tank. We explain what to do:

1. **Clean and vacuum the coils.** Dirty coils also cause freezes. So whenever they accumulate a lot of dust, clean them.

2. **Tighten the screw on the fan shaft.** It may have slipped.

3. **Replace the fan motor if it's barely turning (low revolutions per minute).**

4. **Take it to a service technician if Steps 1 through 3 don't fix it.** The compressor may not be working or the dehumidifier may need recharging.

If you notice one or more fan blades are bent, they will have to be replaced before they damage the motor. Buy new ones, getting the manufacturer's name and the model number off the unit or from your instruction book. Then head to the nearest appliance parts store. When the fan blades need to be replaced, here's what to do:

1. **Take the front panel off to get at the motor.**

2. **Take the motor out, if necessary, to get at the fan blade.**

3. **Loosen the set screw in the blade hub and pull the blade off.**

4. **When installing new blades, be sure to tighten them on the shaft exactly where the old one was so they don't hit the fins or the motor.**

Sometimes a dehumidifier won't run because the humidistat is faulty. We explain how to replace it:

1. **Unplug it from the wall.**
2. **Pull off the knob.**
3. **Take off the nut holding the switch in.**
4. **Disconnect the wires.**
5. **Take the humidistat to an appliance parts store along with the numbers off the data plate.**

## Unclogging air cleaners and purifiers

Air purifiers filter pollutants and dust out of the air. These minute particles — a source of allergens for many people — are too tiny to be trapped by furnace and air conditioning filters. Electronic air purifiers *ionize* (magnetize) them by giving them a positive charge. Then the particles are drawn toward negative plates in the purifier and trapped.

You can get purifiers that sit on a table or floor and filter 90 percent of the dust mites, smoke, pollen, and bacteria from a room or whole-house models mounted on furnaces.

To keep them working efficiently, follow the manufacturer's directions for cleaning the plates and in some models, replacing charcoal filters. Purifiers should not be shoved against walls or anything else that may restrict the air flow. Typically, they filter the air three times an hour. If you get one, you'll be amazed at how little dusting your room or home needs.

# Chapter 9

# Sailing Through the Waterworks: Plumbing Repairs

As you probably know, plumbing problems cause a lot of stress on a household. Water leaks can turn from a minor annoyance to a major tragedy in a matter of days — or hours. Some repairs really need a professional plumber to handle them. But you don't have to be licensed to handle typical problems in bathrooms and kitchens. In this chapter, we tell you how to handle the most common problems — from unblocking pipes to putting in washers and getting rid of leaks.

## Before You Do Anything, Shut Off the Water!

Well, okay — you don't have to turn off the water when you unclog drains. But if you plan to take apart any pipes, the water must be shut off. Most homes have shut-off valves located below sinks, tubs, and toilets. Ours didn't. So whenever we wanted to do any plumbing, we had to shut off the main valve which meant there was no running water in the house until the water was turned back on. Figure 9-1A shows a typical main shut-off valve. Yours may be located under your kitchen sink or near your water meter where the pipes enter the house. No problem, you think. But once while trying to twist a rusted nut under a bathroom sink, someone (deliberately nameless) got a bit of dirt in an eye. Howling in pain, cursing a blue streak, and racing from faucet to faucet to find water — which obviously wasn't flowing anywhere — that novice do-it-yourselfer finally tore the lid off the toilet tank. It broke, but there was plenty of water to flush dirt out of an eye and once again we had peace.

You can find individual shut-off valves under most sinks (Figure 9-1B) and toilets (Figure 9-1C). If they aren't there, have them installed next time you have to call a plumber. They save you a lot of grief and you won't have to buy a new lid for your toilet tank.

Any valve that hasn't been used in a long time may be stubborn or may leak when you try to turn it off or on. Before shutting off the water, spray the valve stem with a bit of WD-40 or put a few drops of oil on it before turning the nut or handle.

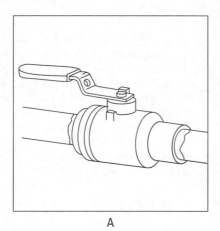

A

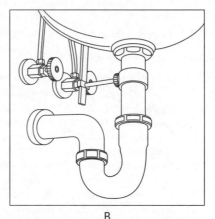

B

**Figure 9-1:**
Finding and using shut-off valves for the main water line (A), a sink (B), and a toilet (C).

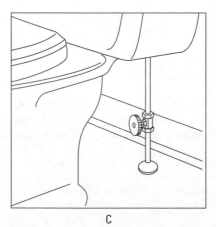

C

# Unclogging Drains

If water were the only thing that flowed into drains, we'd never have problems with them stopping up. But sadly, that isn't the case. Most shower drains are filled with a tangled mass of hair. Lint blocks up wash tubs. Food, grease, bristles, corn cobs, onion skins, chicken bones, bits of paper, small toys, and just about everything else goes down the kitchen sink.

When water won't flow freely, we pour common household bleach, about a cup of it, into the drain, and let it sit there for a couple of hours. When we flush out the bleach with water, the drain usually flows freely. If it still isn't totally clear, we repeat the process.

If you want to use this remedy, make sure the bleach fumes won't bother anyone with allergies. Also *never* pour ammonia or other strong chemicals into the drain when there's bleach in it. Together, ammonia and bleach create toxic fumes that are extremely dangerous.

The easiest way to keep sinks from clogging is to use strainers. Available for all sinks in a home, they keep food, hair, and other debris from entering drains. When you run a disposal, turn on the cold water, full force, while the food is being chopped up, and then run it a minute longer after the disposal is off. That totally flushes the drain. (If you use hot water, it dissolves grease, which then clings to the pipes, a magnet for trapping food particles and clogging the drain even sooner.)

Run a bit of bleach or cleaner through your drains once a month. Preventive maintenance is the easiest way to combat this problem.

## Plunging sinks

When the sink's plugged up, your second line of defense is the good old plunger. All you have to do is take out the stopper, stand the plunger upright over the drain, and then push it up and down to create enough suction to dislodge the mass. See Figure 9-2. After some of the mess comes up, pull out the rest by hand. Undoubtedly, most of it will be hair.

If you used bleach first, don't plunge the drain without wearing safety glasses. Preferably flush the bleach out of the pipes. Even if it trickles away slowly, that's better than risking splashing bleach everywhere.

To get better suction on the drain, put a wet washcloth or clean rag against the overflow hole to block off that source of air.

If you have children, you can try teaching them to use a bit of tissue or toilet paper to wipe the sink after they use it. That would keep most bathroom sinks clear. But good luck. It never worked in our house.

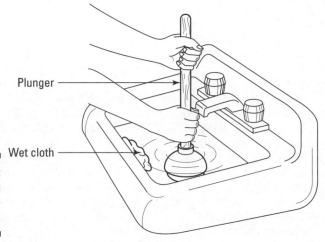

Plunger

Wet cloth

**Figure 9-2:**
Plunging
a stopped-
up sink.

## Using a plumber's snake

When bleach and plunging don't work, get out your snake, the one that you can work through drains to try to unclog them. These tightly coiled wires, attached to a handle, slither down the pipes, scraping against the pipe, and clearing blockages that are farther below the surface of the drain. See Figure 9-3.

The flexible snake, really an *auger,* is manually operated. You don't have to be Goliath to manually push the cable through the pipes. And for the most part, this inexpensive piece of equipment is all that most householders need. Motor-driven snakes, standard equipment for professional plumbers and are rarely needed. They have longer and thicker cables, can get deeper into pipes than a hand-operated snake, and can damage pipes if you don't know what you're doing. If the flexible snake doesn't work and you really want to clear the drain yourself, rent a motor-driven snake. But your best bet may be calling a plumber.

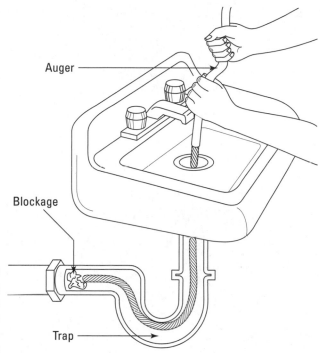

Auger

Blockage

**Figure 9-3:**
Using a
plumber's
snake.

Trap

## Removing the drain trap

If all else fails — or if someone dropped a valuable ring down the drain — you can remove the U-shaped pipe under your sink. That's the *trap,* and that's where you'll find the ring because its weight keeps it from flushing farther. (And from that location you can get at the pipe farther down the line to remove debris and clear blockages.) Some sinks have a plug on the pipe that can be removed to clean out the line. See Figure 9-4.

Some experts advise removing the trap first, and then plunging a drain. They say a plunger drives the blockage farther down the pipe, making it harder to get at. If you dropped a ring down the drain, definitely remove the trap first and clear the U-pipe. Then plunge the drain to remove hair just below the surface. You need an adjustable wrench or pliers, gloves, and a bucket because drain traps are gooey with a collection of rotting vegetable matter. Here's what to do:

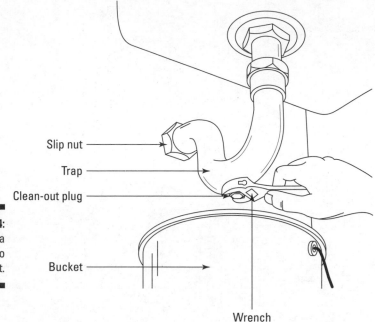

Slip nut

Trap

Clean-out plug

**Figure 9-4:**
Removing a
sink trap to
clear it.

Bucket

Wrench

1. **Put the bucket directly under the pipe to catch the water in the U-pipe.**

2. **Using an adjustable wrench or the pliers, give the nuts a half turn to loosen them.**

3. **Unscrew them the rest of the way by hand.**

   To avoid marring the finish on the nuts, put a piece of duct tape over the jaws of the wrench or pliers so they won't scratch.

4. **Take off the pipe.**

5. **Remove all debris trapped in the pipe.** If you suspect there's some other blockage, this is your chance to get even farther down the pipe. Use the snake again. See Figure 9-5.

6. **Put the pipe back in and tighten the nuts.**

## Unblocking tub drains

Hair gums up tubs, as well as sinks and showers. First try pouring bleach or a commercial drain cleaner down the drain and wait to see if it clears the blockage. A commercial drain cleaner contains chemicals that dissolve proteins, which include hair. It may take a few applications; in between, flush the drain with clear water, and then try again.

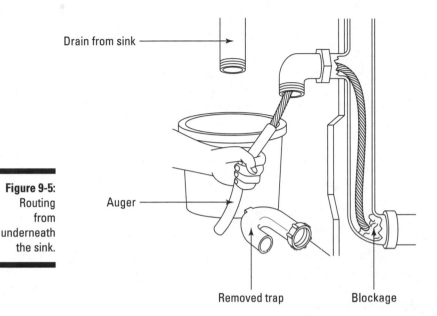

**Figure 9-5:**
Routing
from
underneath
the sink.

Drain from sink

Auger

Removed trap          Blockage

A plunger works on the drain in a tub, too. Follow the steps for clearing sinks with bleach or commercial drain cleaners, a plunger, or a plumber's snake.

Sometimes, it's a lot of work to get a snake through the blockage. You know you've gotten there when it won't go any farther even though there's plenty of coil left. You have to keep trying to force the auger through the mass. If you suspect the blockage is under the tub, remove the snake and push it through the overflow drain instead. On many tubs, the overflow drain is located at one end just under the faucets. Here's what to do:

1. **Take the cover off the overflow drain.** Some overflow drains open and shut by means of a lever attached to the cover. If that's what you have, pull the cover up and out to detach the mechanism, too. Also be careful not to drop any screws into the drain.

2. **Put the snake into the drain and work it through the blockage.** See Figure 9-6.

3. **When the drain seems to be clear, pull out the snake and flush the drain with water.** If it doesn't drain freely, repeat Steps 1 and 2 above.

Don't get discouraged if you have to do this several times. We once had to hire a plumber to clear a blockage that had taken years to build up. To our satisfaction, he really had to work to earn the flat-rate walk-in fee — almost $200. Even though he was using a motor-driven auger, he still had to go into the drain several times. When he thought the drain was clear, he'd flush it with water and except for a trickle, water still backed up.

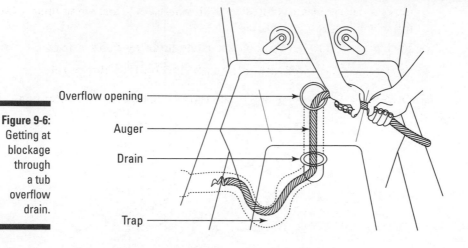

**Figure 9-6:**
Getting at
blockage
through
a tub
overflow
drain.

Overflow opening

Auger

Drain

Trap

# Doctoring Faucets

We use them when we take a shower, wash our hands, brush our teeth, scrub the floor. We go to them when we're thirsty, cleaning vegetables, and cooking. We turn them on to water our yards, clean the car, and do the laundry. And we hardly think about faucets until they start leaking or the water stops flowing freely. It doesn't, however, take a plumbing license to fix them. In the following sections, we explain how to clean aerators and stop leaks.

## Cleaning clogged aerators

Aerators are commonplace at the tip of most faucets. Located inside them are screens and a water restrictor that directs and conserves water. Without aerators, faucets would operate erratically, gushing and splashing water everywhere. Like all screens, aerators get clogged, but taking them apart and cleaning them is easy. We explain how to do it below. You need masking tape or a washcloth, a wrench or pliers, a brush, a safety or tailor's pin, and water. Here's what to do:

1. **To protect the end of the faucet, which has to be removed, wrap it with tape or the washcloth so it won't scratch.**

2. **Turn the end of the faucet counterclockwise with the wrench.**

3. **After the tip is off, take it apart.** See Figure 9-7. Sketch or take notes while you disassemble it so you can reassemble it the same way.

4. **Flush the screens and restrictor with water, and then clean them with the brush.**

5. **Stick the pin through the holes to clear anything that's stuck.**

6. **Put the aerator back together and screw it back on the faucet.**

Water should now flow freely and easily through the faucet no matter how much it's opened.

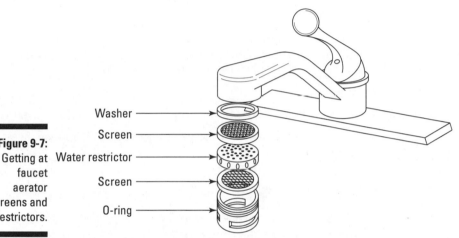

**Figure 9-7:** Getting at faucet aerator screens and restrictors.

Washer —

Screen —

Water restrictor —

Screen —

O-ring —

# Dealing with dripping faucets

When you're trying to sleep, a dripping faucet can just about drive you crazy. Instead of dropping off, you're listening for a drop to fall, wishing you could ignore it. But loss of sleep is nothing compared to the amount of water lost. If you let it drip into a gallon jug, you'd be amazed at how quickly it fills up. So think about your water bill, conserving water for your grandchildren to use, and most of all, getting a good night's sleep. Stop that leak right now.

There are four basic types of faucets: stem, ball-type, disc, and cartridge. And if you go into the plumbing display at any hardware or home improvement store, you find a myriad of parts, depending upon the manufacturer. We have to leave it up to you as to what parts to purchase. Just bring the manufacturer and faucet model number when you go for replacement parts.

If the faucet is more than 10 years old, consider a complete faucet replacement. The older the faucet, the more difficult it is to find parts for it.

We explain how to repair each type of faucet below. You need a wrench or pliers and the replacement parts.

### Fixing stem faucets

You can find stem faucets in old houses, particularly in the laundry area and outdoors. They haven't been refined — no aerators on them — and so there aren't as many pieces in them. They use packing (looks like string) to keep water from dripping out around the stem and the packing sometimes wears out or needs to be tightened. You need pliers or a wrench, a screwdriver, and packing. Here's what to do:

1. **Using the wrench or pliers, turn the packing nut clockwise to try to tighten it a little at a time.** If the leak stops, you're done, but if you have tightened it tight and it still leaks, then continue to Step 2.

2. **Turn off the water.**

3. **Unscrew the handle and take it off.**

4. **Use the pliers or wrench to turn the packing nut until it's loose.** See Figure 9-8.

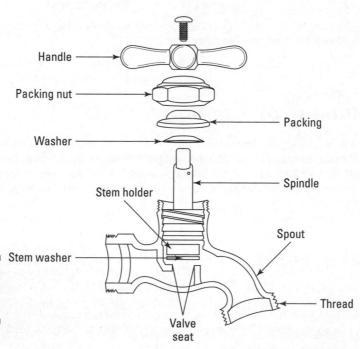

**Figure 9-8:**
Looking at a stem faucet.

5. **Take it all the way off.**

6. **Pull off the old packing.**

7. **Wind the new packing on the stem, but only enough to get the nut on.**

8. **Turn the water back on.**

9. **Put the handle on and tighten the nut enough to stop the water leak but not so much that the handle won't turn.**

### Replacing washer faucets

Washer faucets use compression of a rubber gasket to stop water from leaking out. Most common is a rubber *washer* that eventually becomes flat and worn; after that happens it no longer stops water from dripping out of the faucet. Washers also cushion the metal packing nut and the metal valve seat so they don't grind together. If the seat becomes worn, it must be replaced. You can easily put in new washers. You need a wrench or pliers and a washer the same size as the one you're replacing. Buy an assortment of washers so you can avoid going to the store the next time a faucet starts leaking. Here's what to do:

1. **Turn off the water under the sink or at the main intake.**

2. **Take the decorative cap off the handle to access the screw.** It might be fastened with a screw or simply pull off.

3. **Unfasten the handle and take it off.** Sometimes they stick; if so, use a screwdriver to edge it up. Wrap the tip of the screwdriver so you don't scratch the handle.

4. **Unscrew the packing nut.**

5. **Pull out the valve stem.**

   Some faucets have another cover over the valve that has to be removed. Under it is a packing nut. Turn it counterclockwise. Then twist the stem to take it out. It may take a little work. Just keep at it. See Figure 9-9.

6. **Take out the retaining screw and old washer.**

7. **Put in the new washer.**

   Buy a new washer after you have removed the stem and washer so you can take them with you when you go to the store and get an exact replacement. If you don't, you'll be making at least two trips because of all the different washers being sold. Keep extra washers in a labeled zip-lock plastic bag and write down what size the washers are and which sink they go to so you won't be confused the next time you have to replace one.

8. **Reassemble the faucet.**

9. **Turn the water back on.**

If the faucet still leaks, it may be because the metal seat is damaged. If it is, you have to buy a seat-grinding tool at a plumbing center or department, so it might be better to replace the faucet or to call a plumber. If you want to try to fix the damaged seat, take the faucet apart again and follow manufacturer's instructions on how to reshape the seat with the grinding tool.

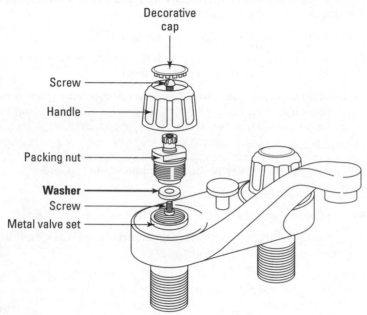

Decorative
cap

Screw

Handle

Packing nut

**Washer**

Screw

Metal valve set

**Figure 9-9:**
Replacing
washers.

### Rotating ball faucets

One-handled washerless faucets use balls, cartridges, or ceramic disks instead of washers. But even without a rubber gasket, they also wear down. With a ball-type faucet, you can move the handle up and down and to the side to select the water temperature. (If the handle moves both left and right, it has a cartridge or a disk mechanism.)

To repair a leaking ball-type faucet, you need an Allen wrench, needle-nose pliers, masking tape, and valve seat, spring, and O-ring. (They come in a repair kit. Shop for it after you remove the parts from the faucet so you can get exactly the right kind.) Here's what to do:

1. **Turn off the water.**

2. **Loosen the Allen screw that fastens the handle and take the handle off.** Find the screw recessed underneath the lever — you need an Allen wrench to unscrew it.

3. **Take off the cap and spout.** Turn the cap counterclockwise to remove it, and then pull off the spout.

4. **Pull out the cam, seal, ball, and stem.** See Figure 9-10.

Before you take out the ball, look at it carefully so that when you put it back in, you can place it precisely. There's a slot on one side of the ball that has to be aligned with an alignment pin. It sticks up from inside the housing.

5. **Inspect the O-ring.** If it looks worn, replace it.

6. **Take out the seals and springs; grab them with needle-nose pliers.** The repair kit has directions for replacing them.

The ball holding the seals, washers, and springs has a stem attached to it and the handle attaches to that. If it breaks off, the ball and stem can be replaced individually or when you replace any other part.

7. **Put the new parts in.**

8. **Reversing Steps 1 through 4, put the faucet back together.**

9. **Turn the water back on.**

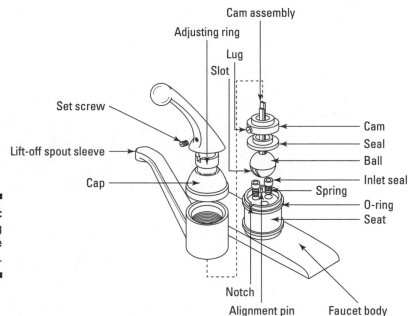

**Figure 9-10:**
Fixing
ball-type
faucets.

### Tackling cartridge faucets

When you work on a cartridge faucet, you find some of the parts are mounted in the cartridge assembly. The cartridge can be replaced when the faucet starts to leak. You need a screwdriver, pliers or a wrench, and a replacement cartridge. Here's how to fix it:

1. **Turn off the water.**

2. **Take off the handle cover so you can see the screw that holds the handle in place.** It may be necessary to pry it up, using the tip of a screwdriver underneath.

3. **Unscrew the screw by turning it counterclockwise, then remove it.**

4. **Pull the handle up so that it detaches from the valve unit and the unit stem is poking up from the cartridge.**

5. **First loosen, and then take off the pivot nut.** Again, turn it counter-clockwise with your pliers or a wrench. The nut keeps water from entering the top of the faucet. See Figure 9-11.

6. **Take off the spout unit by twisting it side to side while pulling it up.**

7. **Find the cartridge.** A U-shaped clip fastens it.

8. **Pull the clip up and out.** If you have difficulty moving the clip, put the head of a small screwdriver underneath the U-section and turn the screwdriver 45 degrees, lifting the clip high enough so that you can grab it with your pliers.

9. **Pull the clip all the way out.**

10. **Remove the cartridge by pulling it up at the same time you're twisting it.**

    If it won't come out easily, put the handle back on. That should allow you to grab the cartridge and pull it out.

11. **Get a replacement cartridge.** When you shop, be sure to take the old cartridge with you so you can get an exact replacement.

12. **Put the new cartridge in, making certain the cartridge slips into the notch on the body.** If you don't place it there, your cold position will give you hot water and vice versa.

13. **Reverse the steps above to put the faucet back together.**

### Troubleshooting ceramic disk faucets

Ceramic disk faucets need little repair and maintenance. But if your faucet develops a leak, you can get new seals and replacement cartridges to fix it. Take the faucet apart before you go shopping so you can get exactly what you need. You need an Allen wrench to take the faucet apart. Here's what to do:

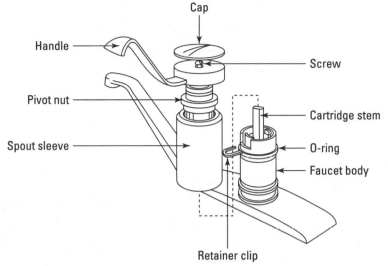

**Figure 9-11:**
Stopping leaks in cartridge faucets.

1. **Turn off the water.**

2. **Loosen the screw holding the control lever set with your Allen wrench.** See Figure 9-12. If you don't see the screws, lift the handle and look under it. The screws also might be mounted to the countertop.

If you can't find screws under the handle, look under the counter below the faucet. (When ceramic disk faucets first came out, that's how they were fastened.) After those screws are out, the cover and handle will come off.

3. **Pull the trim cap up and off the cartridge.**

4. **Loosen the cartridge screws.** Look for these long screws on top of the cartridge

5. **Take the cartridge off the faucet base.**

6. **Remove the seals under the cartridge and take them to the store so you can replace them.**

7. **Reassemble the faucet going from Steps 6 through 1.**

If this doesn't fix the leak, then take the faucet apart again, following Steps 1 through 5. When you take off the cartridge, take it to the store so you can get a kit with an exact replacement. Follow the manufacturer's instructions for putting the new cartridge on.

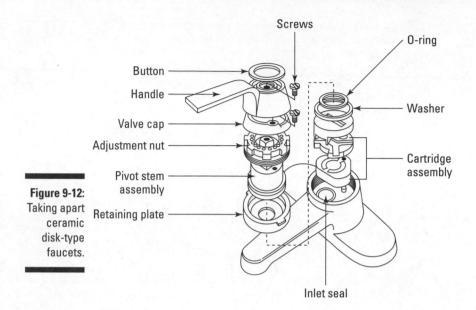

**Figure 9-12:** Taking apart ceramic disk-type faucets.

# Fixing Leaking Pipes

We don't expect you to become an expert plumber. But if a major water pipe is leaking, there are a few things you can try before calling in a professional. We explain what to do below.

## Putting a sleeve on the pipe

If you notice a leak somewhere along the water line, you can stop it up by purchasing a repair kit. They're designed for pipes of various sizes so be sure to get the right one. The kits contain a *sleeve* — a two-piece clamp — that you fasten around the leak and a rubber gasket. Here's how to use it:

1. **Put the gasket around the pipe where it's leaking.**

2. **Place both halves of the clamp on top of the gasket.** See Figure 9-13.

3. **Tighten the clamp.**

That's all you have to do. This fix won't last forever, but should keep the plumber away for a month or so. Just remember to check the clamp periodically to make sure it doesn't start leaking again.

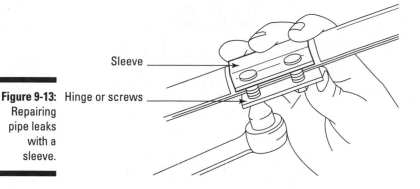

Sleeve

**Figure 9-13:**
Repairing
pipe leaks
with a
sleeve.

Hinge or screws

## Stopping up leaky pipe joints

For a quick fix on leaky joints, use two-part epoxy putty. Slather it on liberally. This fix may not last long on a water supply line that has a lot of pressure going through a galvanized pipe, especially if there's rust on the pipe. But drainpipe joints aren't subjected to force and this may be all you need to do to avoid a plumbing call.

The pipe must be dry for the putty to adhere, so turn off the water to the sink or tub, and then apply the putty following the manufacturer's instructions. Wrap the puttied joint with electrical tape before it dries, and then after it's dry, turn the water back on. If you still have a leak, get out the phone book. A plumber will have to repair the joint.

Be sure to keep an eye on the joint because it can fail again relatively quickly — especially if water is surging through the pipe. If another leak develops, you can try another application of putty, but resign yourself. You'll eventually have to call a plumber. The most you can hope for is to delay paying for one until you have a few more available resources.

Some leaky joints and pipes need a plumber immediately. If the problem is bigger than a slow leak when you first notice it, don't postpone the inevitable. If you're losing a fair amount of water through a pipe or joint, it won't take long before the water breaks through the line. Then you'll very likely have to replace everything that gets soaked — carpeting, furniture, appliances, drywall or plaster walls, and ceilings. It's not worth the risk to save a little money right now.

## Shoring Up Showerheads

Showerhead aerators are no different than those on sinks. They get clogged with mineral deposits. To clean them, follow the steps in the "Cleaning clogged aerators" section. And if the control knobs leak, they, too, can be repaired. See the steps for "Dealing with dripping faucets."

If certain members of your household use up a full tank of hot water every time they take a shower, consider putting in a low-flow restrictor. People will no longer be able to use 40 or more gallons of hot water every time they shower. In addition, it won't take long to recover the expense of installing a restrictor. Your utility bill savings will make up for it in a short time.

# Handling Typical Toilet Problems

Few things are as irritating as a backed-up toilet. It's bad enough when the kids throw a few toys in the bowl and then flush, not to mention the other most common reasons toilets get plugged. Now to add to the grief, we have to contend with saving resources — and a common way to participate in water conservation is to install low-flow toilets. The problem is, they don't always function as they should. You can handle most back-ups yourself. In the following sections, we explain how.

If you're planning to renovate a bathroom, by all means check *Consumer Reports* before buying a toilet. Periodically, this handy consumer's publication rates toilets as to how well they function even while saving water. They let you know what are the best buys. You'll get a good idea of what you should be thinking about when you look at features of the various brands and the different models made by manufacturers. You don't have to take out a subscription; your local library keeps the current year's copies on the shelf. You may have to ask for older issues kept behind the desk.

## When toilets back up

We have two classes of toilets in our home — one for serious business and the other, a liquid diet. Unfortunately that doesn't keep the water-saving toilet from getting clogged, so we keep a plunger available at all times. Water that doesn't swirl as it enters the toilet, a flush that only trickles into the drain, and water that backs up instead of flushing out are signs of clogged toilets. You may not want to, but you can fix it. Get out your plunger and hope for the best.

Before using the plunger, however, turn off the water or lift up on the float in the tank so that the toilet doesn't overflow. Then use the plunger.

### Using a plunger

By placing the plunger, a rubber cup mounted to a long handle, completely over the hole at the bottom of the toilet, most of the time you can suction up the blockage enough to let water flow freely through the drain. See Figure 9-14. After the rubber cup is in position, push the handle down gently — you don't need to exert yourself — and then quickly pull it up. Sometimes you have to do this repeatedly, but eventually you'll dislodge the mass. Then you're finished until the next time. Keep your cool. Nobody likes the job but it's one of the necessities of life — unless we want to dig a hole in the woods.

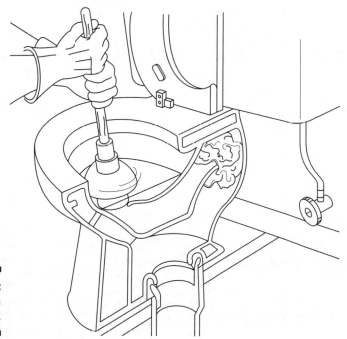

**Figure 9-14:**
Plunging a
toilet.

### Using an auger

When plungers fail, try a toilet auger. It has a stiff, hollow tube that you put far into the bowl. When you crank the handle, it works a flexible coil through the tube. When it reaches the blockage, very likely located in the trap under the toilet bowl, the coil pushes it out. See Figure 9-15. Augers are inexpensive, handy tools to keep in your home. Think of one as insurance — you have it in case you need it. But an auger is much more affordable than most insurance policies today.

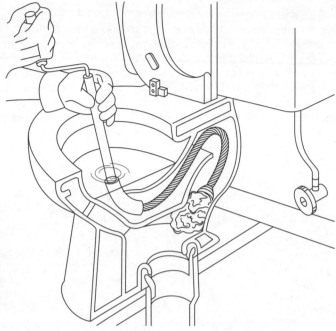

**Figure 9-15:**
Clearing
toilet
backups
with an
auger.

## When toilets keep on running

If your toilet is running, you're losing more gallons of water per hour than you think and no doubt you have to pay for usage. If your house has a septic tank, there's also a danger that the constantly-running toilet could cause backups and floods in your septic system. The only tool you need to fix the running toilet is a screwdriver, but you may have to buy replacement parts.

Here's what to look for after you take the lid off the toilet tank, flush the toilet, and watch what's going on:

✔ If the float ball is at least partially under water or you can easily push it under, buy a replacement. Unscrew the old float ball from the metal arm by turning it counterclockwise. Then go to the store for another and screw it on by turning clockwise. See Figure 9-16.

✔ If the float ball stays up, lift it higher. If that stops the water from running, bend the arm down to increase the pressure on the valve enough that it will force the valve closed. See Figure 9-17.

✔ If your tank won't fill up or the handle has to be wiggled to get the tank ball to seal over the outlet, try changing the length or position of the chain on the handle rod. If that doesn't work, replace the tank ball. Tank balls and chains should drop directly over the outlet pipe.

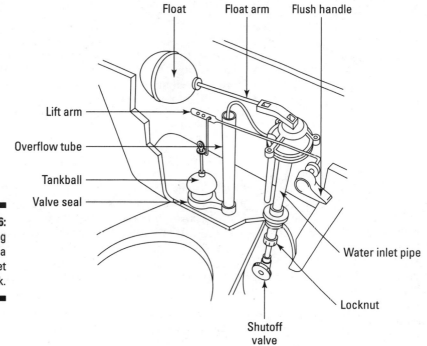

Float

Float arm

Flush handle

Lift arm

Overflow tube

Tankball

Valve seal

Water inlet pipe

Locknut

Shutoff valve

**Figure 9-16:**
Looking inside a typical toilet tank.

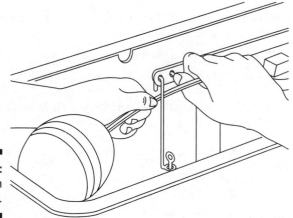

**Figure 9-17:**
Working on float balls.

## Fixing other toilet leaks

Toilets leak at the base when the wax gasket they sit on gets old or damaged. The first sign of warning is a toilet that rocks, then there's a puddle on the floor. Or if you're unlucky like we were, the drywall ceiling underneath the bathroom gets wet. (By the time the damage became obvious, after fixing the toilet, we had to cut out the wet patch, put in a drywall patch, and prime and paint it.) Another good indicator is a musty odor in the bathroom or the room beneath it. Don't ask.

Reseating toilets isn't expensive. Wax gaskets are cheap. But you have to unscrew (probably rusted) nuts and bolts, lift off the toilet, take out the old seal, replace it, and reinstall the toilet. Give yourself enough time to do the repair and plan on perhaps more than a little frustration. You need a wrench, a new wax gasket, a small cup or jar, a pan or small pail, and a commercial cleaner to use on the floor, base of the bowl, and top of the waste pipe. Here's what to do:

1. **Turn off the water at the shutoff valve at the toilet or to all of your plumbing.**

2. **Flush the toilet and use an old bottle or cup to remove whatever didn't flush from the tank.** Then sponge out the rest. You want to lift an empty tank. It's easier on your back.

3. **Now get the water out of the bowl, cupful by cupful.** Then wash your hands thoroughly with antiseptic soap!

4. **Put a pan or small bucket under the shut-off valve to catch water that will dribble out.**

5. **Disconnect the riser tube that comes up from the shut-off valve and brings water to the tank.** Take it off and set it aside where it won't get damaged.

   If you can take the tank and bowl off as one piece, it's heavier, but less work than if you take them off separately. But if you do have to separate them, follow Steps 6 and 7. Otherwise skip to Step 8.

6. **Remove the bolts that fasten the water tank to the toilet bowl using a screwdriver and a wrench.** The bolts on the bottom of the tank go through the back of the toilet bowl.

7. **Remove the tank from the bowl base.**

   If the tank fastens to the wall, it doesn't have to be removed. The only thing that comes out then is the pipe coming down from it and into the bowl. Look for two large nuts holding it in place.

8. **Using a wrench, take off the nuts at the bottom of the toilet that go into the floor.** They're usually under porcelain or plastic caps and rusted because of condensation that occurs in the summer. If they're rusty and won't loosen or break off, you can use a hacksaw blade to cut them off.

9. **After the nuts are off, rock the bowl gently to break the bond to the old wax seal and then lift the bowl off and set it aside.**

   Pounding on or hitting the bowl or trying to pry it up are sure paths to damage. Even if you don't break the porcelain, you can crack it — making another source for leaking water.

10. **After the bowl is off, clean the base, thoroughly removing all putty, wax, and dirt.** Now do the same to the floor and the toilet flange.

    You don't want to leave any putty, wax, or dirt under the new seal, because then you'll have problems with the new seal sealing.

11. **Let it dry before you lay down the replacement wax ring.** It should go all the way around the waste pipe.

12. **Carefully place the wax ring on the toilet bowl.**

13. **Push the toilet down hard, and then rock it in a circle to squeeze the wax and form a good seal.** Sitting on it helps to seat it.

14. **Put the nuts back on the base and reattach it to the floor.**

15. **Refasten the tank (or pipe) to the base.** Be sure to adjust the tank side to side so that it's straight up and down.

16. **Reconnect the water line.**

17. **Turn on the water.**

When you have the tank off the base, if you see any rubber seals or screw seals that are damaged, stiff, or dried out, go to the store and get replacements. Then you won't have to take the toilet apart again.

# Repairing Hot Water Tanks

Gas and electric water heaters usually don't require much attention, especially if you flush the tank once a year. But they do have a "faucet" (actually a drain valve), and it can develop leaks. The pressure relief valve and the anode rod may need to be replaced, but that doesn't happen very often. Please look at Figure 9-18 to familiarize yourself with the anatomy of a hot water tank before you proceed with making repairs.

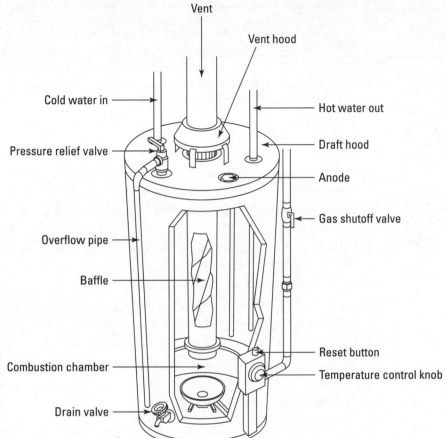

**Figure 9-18:**
The anatomy of a typical hot water tank.

## Fixing leaks in drain valves

If you spot water on the floor around the water tank or under the drain valve, you know something's leaking. Look first at the drain valve. Even though you use it infrequently to drain sediment out of the tank, it still can develop leaks. If the valve has a metal handle with a screw in the center, a *sillcock valve,* you can replace the washer. If it's a plastic drain valve, plan on buying a new valve. Keep in mind, though, that water under the water tank also indicates that the water heater is failing. Few will last much longer than 10 years.

You need an adjustable wrench, a screwdriver, Teflon pipe tape, and a washer or replacement drain valve. Your local hardware store should carry one that's right for your tank. Here's what to do if you're replacing a washer:

1. **Turn off the water supply.**

2. **Unscrew the handle of the metal drain valve, turning it counter-clockwise.**

3. **Pull out the stem assembly by turning the large nut counter clockwise.**

4. **Remove the washer and put the new one in.**

5. **Put the stem back in the valve.**

6. **Screw the handle back on.**

7. **Turn on the water.**

## Replacing pressure relief valves

A pressure relief (or safety) valve kicks in and relieves pressure should the controls on gas and electric water tanks fail. Without the relief valve, pressure would build up in the tank and the tank would eventually explode.

Located on the top or side of the tank, the valve should be tested once a year. You do this by putting a pail under the valve opening — there's a pipe screwed into the opening on some tanks — and lifting the handle.

Let about a cup of water drain out. Then open and close the lever on the valve several times to check for leaks. If it does leak or if there's a leak even before you test the valve, replace the unit. You need a cup, a medium-sized pail, a wrench, an exact replacement valve, and Teflon pipe tape. Here's what to do:

1. **Turn off the water supply and the power to the water tank if you have an electric hot water tank. If it's gas, turn off the water and the gas valve.**

2. **Put the pail under the drain valve and release as much water as it takes to get water level in the tank below the relief valve.** You should be there after collecting about two gallons of water.

3. **With a pipe wrench, remove the relief valve and discharge pipe.**

4. **Get a replacement valve at the hardware or home improvement store.**

   Your shopping will be easier if you take the old unit with you. Different manufacturers use different, yet similar, parts. Don't get into the guessing game; pointless trips back to the store waste a lot of your time.

5. **Wrap two turns of Teflon tape on the threads, screw the new pressure valve to the water tank, twisting it by hand and then tightening it with the wrench.**

6. **Put the discharge pipe back, connecting it to the new valve.**

7. **Turn on the water supply and fill the tank to the right level.**

8. **Turn on the power or ignite the pilot at the bottom of gas heaters.**

## Replacing anode rods

Anode rods — pipes that screw into the top of most electric and gas water tanks — keep the tanks from getting corroded. And if you replace the rod after the tank is about 10 years old, the water heater will last much longer. It's easy to put in a new anode rod, and your local hardware store should have the right one for your tank. You need a replacement rod, a bucket, an adjustable wrench (a socket wrench will do, too), and pipe tape. Here's what to do:

1. **Shut off the water to the house.**

2. **If it's an electric hot water tank, also turn off the power. On gas tanks, close the valve that supplies gas to the unit.**

3. **Place the bucket under the drain valve.**

4. **Open the valve and collect about 3 gallons of water.**

5. **Using a wrench, take off the hexagonal plug that's at the top of the water heater.**

6. **Pull the old rod out of the tank.**

7. **Put pipe tape on the threads at the end of the anode rod and put the rod into the hole.**

8. **Tighten the rod by hand, clockwise, and then use the wrench to tighten it.**

You'll find useful maintenance tips for gas hot water tanks, other appliances, and features in your home in *Home Improvement For Dummies* by James and Morris Carey (Wiley). It's available in most bookstores and some all-purpose stores. Maintaining your home is much easier than letting things wear out or down.

## Repairing Sump Pumps

Sump pumps usually live in holes in basements, although some sit on pedestals. They kick in when the water level reaches a certain height, connected to drainpipes that often lead to drainage ditches or drainage areas in your yard. Typical problems are bad switches, clogged pipes on the pump itself, and wearing out. You can take care of most repairs yourself.

When working on a sump pump, be sure to unplug the unit before messing with it. Otherwise, you could get a nasty shock!

If the pump stops working, check that a fuse or circuit breaker hasn't blown. If there's power and the pump still doesn't work, check the switch on the pump. You need a long stick (to raise the float switch), a circuit tester (for more on circuit testers, see Chapter 7), your owner's manual, and possibly a new switch. Here's what to do:

1. **Remove the power cord from the outlet.**

2. **Use the circuit tester to see whether there's power in the receptacle.** You can also plug in a small radio or lamp to see whether it will turn on.

3. **If the receptacle is faulty, replace it.** We explain how to do that in Chapter 7.

4. **If the receptacle works, plug the pump back in, then pull up the float switch using a long stick.** If the pump is on a pedestal, push the float up the rod until the rod lifts. Some sump pumps are under water. Lift the float to raise it.

5. **Turn the switch on and off.** If it doesn't work, buy a replacement.

## Unclogging sump pumps

Sump pumps get blocked at the base and in the pipes. To remove the blockage, you need a wrench and an old pail or bucket. Cleaning sump pumps is a dirty job. You may want to wear gloves. Here's what to do:

1. **Clean the pump base.** If there's a screen there make sure it's not clogged.

2. **Unscrew the cover, using the wrench that's on the check valve.** Most sump pumps have them. The check valve is on the discharge line leading from the pump to either the drainpipe or outdoors. It has a flap or valve that prevents water from backing up into the pump, but it can also prevent water from leaving the pump if anything blocks it.

3. **Clean the check valve and remove any blockage.**

4. **Put the cover back on.**

## *Replacing sump pumps*

Because sump pumps run off an electrical cord and hooks to a drain, replacing one that's burned out doesn't take much effort. You unplug it, unhook it, pull it out, get an exact replacement, and hook it back up.

If you don't have a sump pump and need to install one, have a professional do it. They have the equipment and know-how necessary to determine the best location, dig to the proper depth, install new electrical hookups, and ensure proper drainage among other things. See Chapter 18 for tips on how to hire a professional.

# Part IV
# Keeping Your Stuff in Good Shape

The 5th Wave    By Rich Tennant

"I think I found what's causing the holes in your laundry."

## In this part . . .

This part gives you common-sense advice about caring for major and minor appliances and electronic equipment. We tell you what kinds of things go wrong. These items most often stop working because the owner hasn't cleaned or maintained them regularly or because the power source or an easily fixable piece of hardware isn't working. We tell you when it's unsafe for novice do-it-yourselfers to make a repair, what parts are irreplaceable, and whether it's time to just toss it out and go to the store.

# Chapter 10

# Looming Large Over Major Appliances

*O*nly after a large appliance breaks down do we appreciate how much work and time they save us. Contrast our lives with those a hundred years ago. Laundry day then meant families hauled water and boiled it on a wood or coal-burning stove, poured the hot water into a tub, and scrubbed dirty clothes by hand. Now we have multicycle washers, and dryers — not outdoor clotheslines. Our refrigerators not only keep food fresh, but also dispense cold water and ice cubes on demand. We have automatic dishwashers, garbage disposals, trash compactors, and electric and gas ranges. And they operate for years without having major problems.

However, appliances do break down; and while we don't recommend that do-it-yourselfers make major repairs to these major appliances, we do have some help for the little things that go wrong: doors, hardware, belts, and gaskets. These repairs aren't costly, in and of themselves. But most repair services charge for service calls and who wants to pay a large fee for a quick fix?

This chapter is designed for do-it-yourselfers who aren't trained or certified in large appliance repairs. We concentrate on nuisances, fixing the little things that you'd otherwise put up with simply to avoid a service call.

# Working on Refrigerators and Icemakers

When it comes to refrigerators, most likely what you want to work on are odors, dried-out gaskets, water leaks, temperature extremes or uneven temperatures, doors that won't close, door handles that snap off, or plastic shelves that crack. Don't put up with any of it. You can take care of these small problems yourself. (With a little help from us!)

The first thing to remember about your refrigerator is that regular maintenance will do a lot toward keeping it running. Vacuum or pull out dirt and dust that's on the compressor and condenser coils at least twice a year. If you don't, the unit may not defrost or be cold enough to keep food safely. Dirty coils can also affect performance, turning the unit on and off or not letting it run at all. Use Figure 10-1 to familiarize yourself with the parts of a refrigerator.

 Dirt gets in the coils that are either beneath the refrigerator or in back. If underneath, use the crevice tool on your vacuum cleaner to get rid of the dirt; if the coils are on the back, pull the refrigerator away from the wall and use the brush attachment or a soft-bristled brush. You'll be amazed at how much dust and fur (if you have pets) accumulates.

## Dealing with funky-smelling fridges

Some foods have a pungent odor even when fresh and it lingers for days after it's been in the refrigerator. We forget about other food at the back of the fridge and it goes bad, forming mold. And the worst smell comes from refrigerators turned off and left to stand with the door closed. But you can get rid of bad odors. Here are several ways to refresh refrigerators:

✔ Turn off the power and remove all food. Wash the interior with 8 ounces of baking soda dissolved in ½ gallon of cold water. Leave the door open for several hours, and then turn the power back on. If, after it's running, the odor's still there, wash it again.

✔ Roll up several sheets of newspaper and put it in a compartment. Then do it again for the other compartments. The newspaper will absorb odors. After several days, throw them out.

✔ If you want to turn off an empty refrigerator, prop the door open and keep it that way until you turn it back on. You can hold the door open with a box or chair, rolled up newspapers, or a thick sponge. The door doesn't have to be wide open; a wide crack will do.

✔ An open box of baking soda absorbs odors. Some people keep a box of it at the back of the fridge all the time. Change the box once a month.

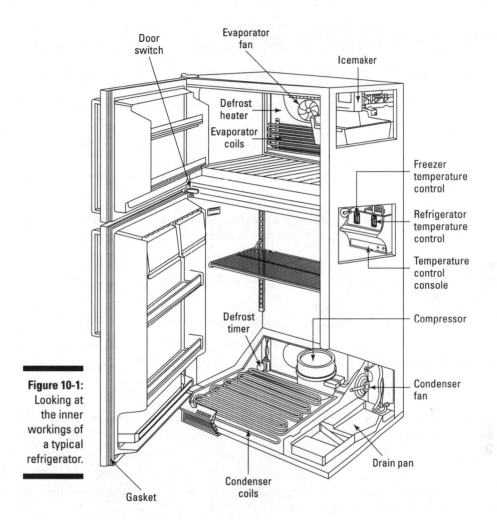

Door switch

Evaporator fan

Icemaker

Defrost heater

Evaporator coils

Freezer temperature control

Refrigerator temperature control

Temperature control console

Defrost timer

Compressor

**Figure 10-1:** Looking at the inner workings of a typical refrigerator.

Condenser fan

Drain pan

Gasket

Condenser coils

## Stopping water leaks

When you see water under a refrigerator, check the front legs and/or clean the drain hole. Water (actually condensation) is supposed to run from inside the refrigerator into a drain hole, and then into a drip pan underneath where it evaporates. If the refrigerator is completely level or tipped slightly forward, the water may not be able to flow into the drain. All you have to do to get it working is to adjust the front legs so that the refrigerator tips back slightly. That tilt also makes the door swing closed after you turn away from the refrigerator. Here's what to do:

1. **Have a helper tip the fridge slightly back so you can get under it.**

2. **Unscrew the front legs a couple turns to raise them.** (Don't take them off, though.)

3. **Put the refrigerator down.**

4. **Use a level on the front edge of the refrigerator to make sure the legs are even.**

5. **Partially open the door and walk away. It should close by itself now.**

Tip the refrigerator only slightly because it is designed to be (almost) level and tilting it too much might cause a problem somewhere else.

If you can't readjust the legs, put a shim under each of them, about ⅛ inch thick at the wide edge.

If adjusting the legs doesn't stop water from leaking, then you have to clear the drain hole. It gets clogged with food particles. See Figure 10-2. Here's what to do:

1. **Locate the drain tubes at the rear of the refrigerator or freezer.**

2. **Push a small plastic tube or a pipe cleaner through the tubes.**

3. **Pour a mild solution of soapy water and ammonia down the drain tube to kill bacteria.** If you have a turkey baster or syringe, use it to squeeze water into the hole.

4. **Check the drain pan under the refrigerator, on the left side, by removing the front grill.**

5. **If the soapy water hasn't drained into it, you still have a problem. Go to Step 6.**

6. **Working inside the refrigerator, push the tube or pipe cleaner into and through the drain tube.**

7. **Flush the hole with water again.**

8. **You should now find water in the pan.** If you do, don't worry; it evaporates.

You can also have water problems if you keep the refrigerator in an unheated garage, porch, or basement. As heat from the motor flows across the cold exterior, it condenses and water forms, dripping onto the floor. All you need to do is put a space heater nearby and if there's no more water, you know condensation's the problem. Solve the problem permanently by moving the refrigerator to a warmer place.

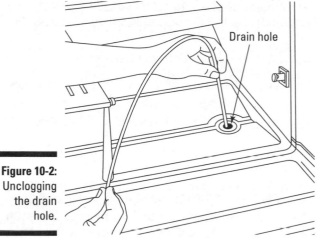

Drain hole

**Figure 10-2:**
Unclogging
the drain
hole.

## Tending to temperature problems

If the main compartment in your refrigerator is too warm or too cold and adjusting the temperature controls doesn't seem to help, first vacuum the compressor and condenser coils, as suggested at the beginning of this section. If they aren't cleaned a couple times a year, the refrigerator won't be efficient.

If you overstuff the food and freezer compartments, the refrigerator can't run efficiently. Don't do it.

If dirty coils aren't the problem, follow the steps below to check and reset the temperature in the food compartment. It should be between 35 and 40 degrees Fahrenheit. A freezer should be between 0 to 5 degrees Fahrenheit. Here's what to do:

1. **Put a refrigerator thermometer in the back of the food compartment to see whether the temperature is between 35 and 40 degrees.** If it's not, go to Step 2.

2. **Turn the control dial up or down, depending on the actual temperature.**

3. **Wait an hour to give the temperature time to readjust.**

4. **Write down what the dial says and what the temperature is on the thermometer.**

5. **Repeat this step several times, moving the dial to various settings until you get to a position that brings the temperature between 35 and 40 degrees.**

6. **Repeat these steps with the thermometer in the freezer.** Stop when the freezer temperature is between 0 and 5 degrees.

It really doesn't matter what the dial says if you know exactly where it should be to get the temperatures you need. You can try to readjust the dial controls by following the steps below, but it won't work for everyone.

### Fixing finicky temperature switches

Some do-it-yourselfers can fix the temperature control if it's accessible. To find out whether yours is, take the front panel off the control panel. You will see a small oval or cylindrical copper tube with a sensor bulb on one end. (The tube might be a few inches to a couple of feet long, depending on the model and make of the refrigerator.) If you can see all of tube, you can replace it and fix the control. If it leads into a side wall and hides there, forget it; there's nothing you can do. For those who have accessible controls, follow these steps:

1. **Unplug the refrigerator.**

2. **Mark the wires so you know where they go into the switch.**

3. **Take out the switch and tube.**

4. **Go to an appliance parts store with the switch and tube and the model and serial number of the refrigerator and get a new part.**

Do not kink, bend, or fold the new tube as you carry it home or install it. Doing so will permanently damage it because there's liquid inside the tube.

5. **Put the new tube into the refrigerator just as the old one was installed with either push-on clips or wires that have to be screwed together.**

6. **Screw the panel onto the control housing.**

The temperature switch and tube are preset by the manufacturer and you shouldn't try to change anything. If they quit altogether or else raise the temperature all the way up, they're bad and should be replaced. But also check to see whether the vents are plugged up or free. Like air conditioners, refrigerators must have air to operate and they won't self defrost if they're too full. Remember, too, to vacuum the coils and evaporator fan blades.

### Dealing with other temperature culprits

If the temperature switch appears to be fine and you think the food compartment is still too warm, check for gaps in the seal along the door. If the door isn't hanging right and the seal isn't working, warm air may be getting in.

The temperature can also go up if the light doesn't go off when you shut the door. You can find out by closing the door slowly while watching inside to see when and if the light goes off. If the light doesn't go on and off when you push the button manually, you know there's a problem. You may need a new door switch.

### Replacing door switches

It takes little more than a screwdriver and a new switch to replace faulty door switches. Here's how to do it:

1. **Unplug the refrigerator.**

2. **Pry up the ring beneath the push-button switch with a screwdriver.** If you wrap the tip with an old rag or masking tape, you won't scratch the finish on the refrigerator.

3. **After the switch and ring are loose, pull out the wires.**

4. **Detach them from the old switch.**

5. **Take the switch, model, and serial number to an appliance parts store and get an exact replacement.**

6. **Attach the new switch to the wires.**

7. **Insert the wires, ring, and switch into the hole.**

### Raising hanging doors

A bad hinge can cause a door to twist when the gasket's installed, just enough to produce a gap that keeps the door from closing tightly. If you suspect there's a problem, with the door closed, look at the seal. If you find a gap — usually on the opening side of the door — get out a screwdriver so you can tighten the hinges. Here's how to fix it:

1. **Open the door.**

2. **Loosen the hinge screws.**

3. **Push the door up or down, depending on where the gap is located.**

4. **Prop the door in that position with your foot or have a helper push it up and back to square it while you work on the hinge.**

5. **With a screwdriver, tighten the screws enough that the door will hang straight.**

6. **If the door still sags, back the screws out slightly and do it again.**
   That's all there is to the job.

### Changing the rubber gasket

If the food compartment is still too warm, look at the rubber gasket that runs around the door. It may be so worn or stretched out that it doesn't seal. Gaskets are fastened to the door with screws or metal or plastic retainers. See Figure 10-3. You need a screwdriver and a replacement gasket from an appliance supply store.

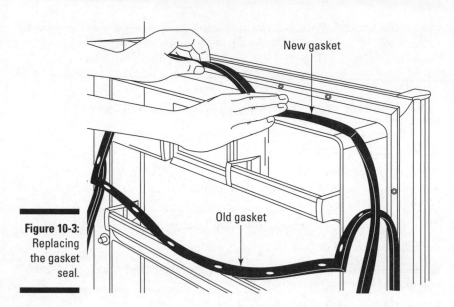

New gasket

Old gasket

**Figure 10-3:**
Replacing
the gasket
seal.

The new gasket will be folded when you get it. You can straighten the band by leaving it in the sun — on top of a car hood — or sticking it in a pan of boiling water. Obviously the first way will take some time; the other means you can install it right away. Here's what to do:

1. **To take off the old gasket, open the door.**

2. **Pull up the rubber at the top of the door.** You'll probably have to work a little to get the old gasket out. Don't be discouraged. You'll get the hang of it.

3. **Loosen, but don't take out, the screws at the top that hold the gasket in place.** You want to get them loose enough that they release the gasket, but don't fall out. See Figure 10-3.

4. **Go to the side of the door and loosen the screws there.** Don't go any lower than half way.

5. **Repeat Step 4 on the other side.**

6. **Go back to the top of the door to find the strip that holds the gasket in place. It's plastic or metal.**

7. **Pull up on the gasket first, and then out toward you.**

8. **Letting the old gasket hang, drape the new gasket on the door, matching its holes to the screws on the door.** If you put Crisco or some similar greasy substance on the belt, it will go in much easier.

The long ends of the new gasket will be dangling at the sides. You'll fasten them soon. Just make sure what's dangling is long enough to fit all the way around the door. If there are any gaps when you've finished, you'll have do this all over again. If it's not done right, warm air will get into the refrigerator and cold air will seep out.

9. **Going back to the top, shove the new gasket under the retainer.**

10. **Do the same thing on the side that opens.**

11. **Fasten the side screws if there are any or else put the gasket under the retaining strips.**

12. **Work your way down, first one side and then the other.** Keep checking that the dangling ends of the new gasket will meet at the bottom.

While you're working, don't fasten the screws tightly because you may have to repeat all the steps if you find there's a gap.

13. **When the side gaskets are loosely screwed in, work on getting the gasket around the corner after the old one is out.**

14. **Now do the other corner.**

15. **Working in the center bottom of the door, finish installing the gasket.**

16. **Inspect the gasket to make sure it fits tightly everywhere when the door's open and when it's closed.** Check to see if it twisted around the corners. If you find a gap or a twist, go back to it and reinstall the gasket.

17. **Tighten the screws.**

To clean the gasket when it gets moldy, use one part bleach to four parts water and scrub the gasket with an old toothbrush. You can keep the rubber supple if you rub it with lemon oil, mineral oil, or body lotion. Be sure, also, to wipe up drips and spills.

## *Stopping icemaker and water dispenser leaks*

Icemakers and water dispensers in refrigerator doors get water directly from the main water line. The filter (that should be on the bottom of the refrigerator) sometimes plugs up and should be replaced once a year. You may also need to replace the plastic tube that transports water from the main line. You can replace it by unhooking the tube at both ends, the refrigerator and the water line, and putting in a new line. It's easy to do and shouldn't take more than a trip to the appliance parts store. Be sure to take the model and serial number of the refrigerator with you when you get the replacement.

There's also a little valve that can be replaced if it leaks or doesn't shut off the water as it's supposed to. It's on the lever that you push in when you get water or ice. Just follow these steps:

1. **Unplug the refrigerator.**

2. **Turn off the water supply at the source.**

3. **Look for the valve.** The valve will have a plastic cover and should be outside the door or in it, depending on the year it was made, the manufacturer, and the model.

4. **Find the screws holding valve in.** If there's a panel in the center of the controls, take it off first.

5. **Look at the valve carefully before going any further.** You want to note how it's attached so you can put it back together.

6. **Detach the line.**

7. **Take the part, along with model and serial number of the refrigerator, to an appliance parts store and get a new one.**

8. **Replace the part and reassemble the refrigerator.** Plug it back in to the main line and electricity.

### Freeing stuck icemakers

Icemakers have a wire that, when raised, shuts off the action and the water. This device works like a sensor and keeps the tray from overfilling. Sometimes, that wire gets stuck in the off position. It should be hanging down into the ice cube tray from the switch. To release it, look in the compartment and pull the L-shaped wire free and down. The icemaker will quickly resume its job.

### Restoring your ice cubes to their former glory

If the cubes are not the proper size , the unit may not be getting enough water. You can unclog the filter. Here's what to do:

1. **Unplug the refrigerator and pull it away from the wall.**

2. **Turn off the water supply.**

3. **Find the water line that hooks into the refrigerator and disconnect it.**

4. **Take out the filter.**

5. **Buy a new disposable filter and put it in.**

6. **Reconnect the hose.**

7. **Turn on the water.**

8. **Plug in the refrigerator and push it back against the wall.**

If the ice isn't solid, the icemaker needs to be tipped back a little. Try raising the front legs of the refrigerator following the manufacturer's directions.

# Handling Stalled Garbage Disposals

When garbage overheats a disposal and it stops working, it doesn't take much to get it grinding again. Some brands and models have a reset button that trips when there's a blockage. Others also have a socket on the underside that has to be turned to get the disposal going again. Here's what to do:

1. **Check that you haven't blown a fuse or circuit breaker, and then switch off the power to the disposal.**

2. **If the disposal motor doesn't operate, check whether a piece of plastic or a bone shard is jamming the disposal.** If you find anything, pull it out and then clear most of the food out of the unit.

3. **Let the disposal cool off.**

4. **If the unit has a reset button, turn on the power to the disposal.**

5. **Push the reset button.** If you hear it roar in response, that's all you have to do.

If the disposal motor tries to run but keeps popping the reset or breaker, follow the steps below. You need an Allen wrench with a hexagonal-shaped head; you may have gotten one when you installed the disposal. Here's what to do:

1. **Make sure the disposal is turned off.**

2. **Find the hole on the bottom of the unit.** See Figure 10-4.

3. **Insert the wrench.**

4. **Push the wrench several times with a back-and-forth motion.** That allows the motor shaft to get cleared up.

5. **Turn the disposal back on.**

If you can't get the disposal unblocked with the reset button or the Allen wrench, stick a broom handle into the top, lodge it against one of the blades, and force it to move until it moves without restraint in that direction. Now push the blade the other way. When that clears and the disposal moves back and forth freely, you can turn it on and use it.

If you overload a disposal, it will jam and overheat. Feed garbage in a bit at a time. If you hear a lot of clunking, however, turn it off right away. You've probably just wrecked a spoon or fork. Don't worry. The disposal can take it if you get the utensil out right away.

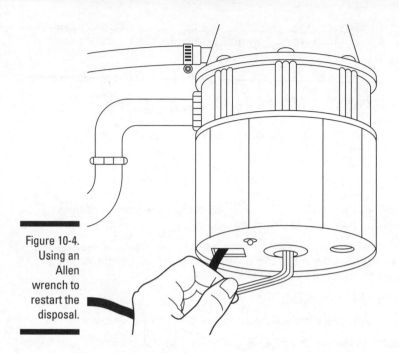

Figure 10-4. Using an Allen wrench to restart the disposal.

# Restoring Trash Compactors

As with all appliances, cleaning your trash compactor regularly is the best way to keep it running well. If you put dirty paper plates and cups into it, use an antibacterial cleaner; otherwise you'll eventually think you're living on the top of a garbage dump. Between cleanings, spray your compactor with a heavy-duty disinfectant that kills germs. You can also find spray deodorants for compactors that keep ants, roaches, and other insects from making a home there.

Periodically vacuum the inside of the bin to remove any debris. And follow the manufacturer's instructions about the type of bags to use, how to install them, and how often they should be changed.

# Doing Simple Range and Oven Repairs

The hardware on electric and gas ranges is likely to cause more trouble than anything inside. Electric coils on the range have to be replaced. Knobs, hinges, and handles may wear out. So save your money, buy the parts, and install them yourself at a fraction of the cost of calling for service. Figure 10-5 shows the anatomy of a typical electric oven. Refer to it when you need to know where something is.

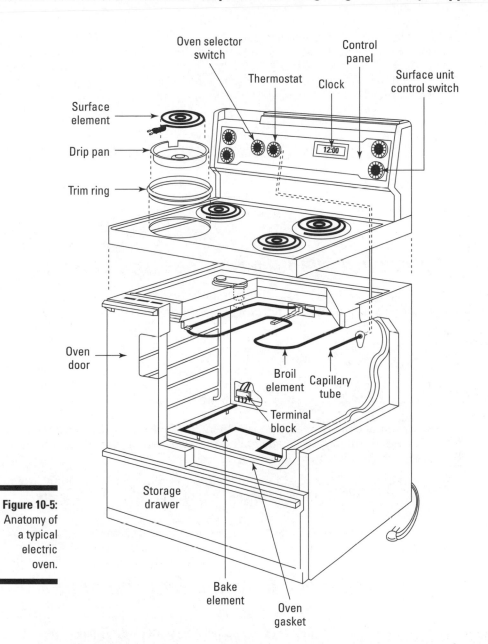

Oven selector switch

Control panel

Thermostat

Clock

Surface unit control switch

Surface element

Drip pan

Trim ring

Oven door

Broil element

Capillary tube

Terminal block

Storage drawer

**Figure 10-5:** Anatomy of a typical electric oven.

Bake element

Oven gasket

# Replacing oven coils

There are two heating coils in an oven — the one on top for the broiler and another for the oven. The oven coil is located under the oven floor. To release the top coils, take off the brackets holding it up and pull the coil out. It plugs in just the same as the burners on the range. To remove the bottom coils, first remove the tray (oven floor) that keeps food from dripping onto the coil. Then pull out the coil. Be sure to take the model and serial number — on the oven doorframe — with you when you go to the appliance parts store.

## Putting a new gasket around the oven door

When a gasket develops cracks, dries out, breaks, or doesn't seal tightly, replace it. You won't be able to maintain the heat you want if it escapes out the door. See the steps for replacing refrigerator gaskets.

## Replacing oven door hinges and springs

Most oven doors can be removed so that you can replace hinges or the spring that keeps the door from striking the floor. Here's how:

1. **Open the door partially.**

2. **Grab each side of the door.**

3. **Jerk up on the door.**

4. **Lift it off the hinges.**

5. **To replace the hinges, unscrew them, unhook the spring, and then install the new ones.** If you get exact replacements, you shouldn't have any problems with making them fit.

6. **To replace the springs, located behind but attached to the hinges, just pry them off the hinges, unhook the other ends, and buy replacements to match.**

7. **Slide the door back onto the hinges and push it down to install it.**

## Replacing electric range heating coils

If your range isn't working, make sure the power hasn't gone off. You can tell when the coils on the surface of the range start going bad because they no longer heat uniformly. Some parts may glow while other areas of the same coil may look dark, pitted, or burnt. Each coil on the stove operates independently, so if the others work well, just replace the faulty unit.

Coils have two long prongs on the end that plug into the stove. To get them out, remove the pan and support, and then pull the coil toward you. It should come right out. If the prongs also look pitted or burnt, that's another sign that they're faulty. When you go to the appliance parts store, be sure to have the model and serial number of the range with you, so you can get exactly the right part.

You can find new pans that will fit your stove at variety and food stores, but make sure you get an exact replacement for the coils so they fit in snugly as they should.

## Working on gas ranges

You can replace doors, handles, knobs, burners, grates, bulbs, springs, clocks, and timers on gas ranges. But if you have a timer-clock that isn't working, your hands are tied. They're difficult to replace.

Be sure to open windows and doors if you smell gas. Turn off the burners and check the pilots on the oven and burners to see if they've gone out. Don't try to relight the pilots until after the gas odor is gone. If you can't get rid of the odor with fresh air, turn off all the controls and call the gas company from a neighbor's house or outside from your cellphone. And stay out of the house until they arrive. If you know where the gas safety valve is for your home, shut it off until your gas is repaired. See Chapter 8 for more information on gas safety.

Burners need air to work efficiently. With too little air, a flame looks red or yellow and is weak, blackening the bottom of pots and further clogging the air vents with soot. If there's too much air, the flame looks uneven and you can hear it burning as it lifts off the burner.

You can easily get the optimum: an even blue flame with a yellow tip. We explain what to do below. You need a needle, soapy water, and a screwdriver. To readjust burner flames:

1. **Make sure the burners are off.**

2. **Look for the burner tube next to the pilot lines at the front of the stove.** There's an air shutter at the end of it. See Figure 10-6.

3. **Twist or slide the air shutter after loosening the screw on it.**

4. **Turn on the burner control knob.**

5. **Move the shutter around until the burner flame is blue with a yellow tip.**

6. **Hold the shutter there while you tighten the screw.**

7. **Now adjust the flames on the other burners if they need it.**

Air shutter

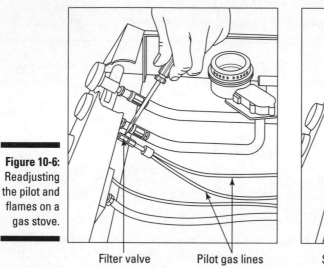
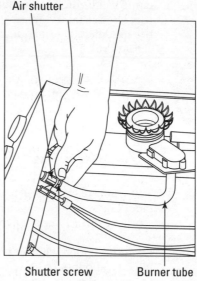

**Figure 10-6:**
Readjusting
the pilot and
flames on a
gas stove.

Filter valve        Pilot gas lines          Shutter screw          Burner tube

After you get the flames readjusted, find time at least once a year to maintain the burners. When we cook or a pot boils over, food particles and grease get trapped in burners and eventually plug up the air vents and pipes. It's easier to clean them periodically than wait until it's an absolute necessity. Here's how to clean the pilot:

1. **Turn off all the burners and the pilot light.**

2. **Take off the grids and drip pan on each burner.**

3. **Grab the front edges or the center of the lid, raise it, and tip it back.** Now you can get at the burners and pilot.

4. **Stick the needle down into the hole in the center of the pilot.** If there's a metal cap over the hole, just lift it up.

5. **Move the needle up and down several times to open up the hole.** Be careful that you don't damage the sides or make the hole larger.

6. **Relight the pilot by holding a match to it.** Then go to the next set of steps.

Here's how to clean out the air vents:

1. **Remove the screw that holds the burner and lift out the burner and tube.**

2. **Poke your needle or a pipe cleaner into each hole or slot, all the way around the burner.**

3. **Wash the burner in warm, soapy water.**

4. **Put the burner and tube back into the manifold tube.** The flash tube should be in alignment with the pilot.

5. **Repeat Steps 1 through 4 on each burner.** Then go to the next set of steps.

Any time you wash lines or other gas parts, make sure they're thoroughly dry before you put them back on the range. Water and gas don't mix.

## Replacing console panel features

You can replace clocks, timers, and lights on the console when the old ones stop working. Follow these steps:

1. **Unplug and pull out the stove.**

2. **Take off the back of the panel.**

3. **Unscrew the feature that you want to replace.**

4. **Take it to the parts store, along with the model and serial number of the stove, and get a replacement.**

5. **Screw the new one in.**

If the panel is solid-state and features are connected to a circuit board, call a service technician.

Don't bother trying to fix any of these parts. Replacements aren't expensive and are a whole lot easier to handle.

You can get at some parts to replace them by unscrewing the front panel, releasing the wires — draw a diagram so you'll know how to put them back together — and pulling them out.

# Reviving the Dishwasher

Dishwashers have hoses and after time, if the connection gets loose or becomes brittle or cracked, they can leak. The rubber gasket around the door also may become worn out and loose and then it has to be replaced. When there's a leak, first look at the rubber gasket. It could simply be out of place. If it's not, then make certain that all the hoses are clamped tightly and aren't damaged. If you find one that's brittle or cracked, replace it. Figure 10-7 shows you the anatomy of a typical dishwasher.

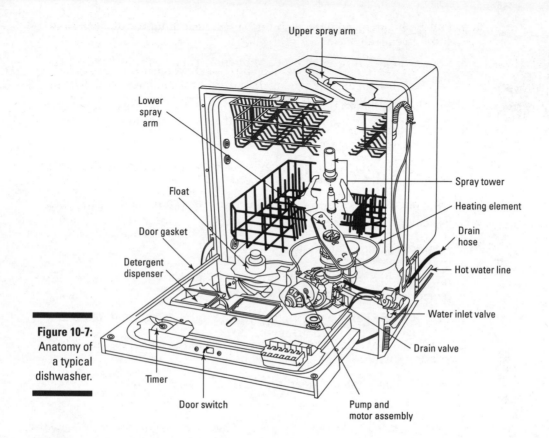

Upper spray arm

Lower spray arm

Float

Door gasket

Detergent dispenser

Spray tower

Heating element

Drain hose

Hot water line

Water inlet valve

Drain valve

**Figure 10-7:** Anatomy of a typical dishwasher.

Timer

Door switch

Pump and motor assembly

When you run the dishwasher, be sure to use hot water; otherwise you won't get clean dishes. Your water heater should be set at 120 degrees. And before starting the dishwasher, run the hot water faucet for a couple minutes. That will get hot water to the dishwasher right away.

Many dishwasher parts are replaceable, including the pump, hoses, and motor. But you have to pull out the dishwasher and tip it over to get at them, so call for service.

Pumps on older dishwashers require you to rinse and scrap plates and utensils before washing them; otherwise you'd gum up the pump. Pumps on some recently manufactured dishwashers *need* those scraps and grease to lubricate them. If you have one of these dishwashers and still clean everything before you load it, your pump will burn out. So read the manufacturer's instruction manual before you do great harm.

Some dishwashers have an air gap (a valve) on the drain line at the back of the sink between the faucet and dishwasher. It can get clogged and that affects the performance of the dishwasher. To clear it, you need a screwdriver and tweezers.

Air gaps aren't used much any more on new machines. Instead, most new dishwashers have an extremely long drain tube that's looped up under the counter as high as possible. Here's what to do:

1. **Pull off the drain tube air gap cover.** You can identify the air gap because it has a chrome cover.

2. **Unscrew the plastic cover underneath to get at the tube in the center of the air gap.**

3. **Use your tweezers to clean out the tube.** See Figure 10-8.

4. **Clean the cap and cover if they're dirty.**

5. **Replace the cap and cover.**

To clean the spray arm and filter screen in the dishwasher, you need a wire, a stiff brush, and soapy water. Here's what to do:

1. **Remove the lower rack by sliding it out.**

2. **If you see a plastic hubcap (cover) on top of the arm, unscrew it by hand.** If there isn't one, go to Step 3.

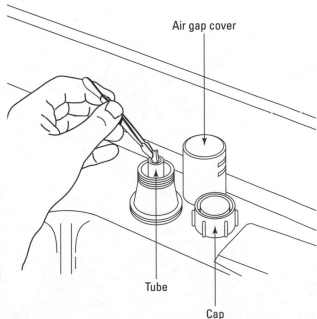

Air gap cover

Tube

Cap

**Figure 10-8:** Cleaning the air gap of a dishwasher.

3. **Take the arm off.**

4. **If your dishwasher has a removable strainer and filter, take it out.** See Figure 10-9. If it doesn't, go to Step 5.

5. **Poke the wire through the holes in the spray arm to clear them.**

6. **Wash the strainer and filter with the brush.**

7. **Rinse the arm strainer and filter.**

8. **Reinstall them.**

9. **Use the wire to remove debris from the holes in the spray arm at the top of the dishwasher.** This may call for a contortionist, but don't try to remove the arm.

If the dishwasher doesn't drain, the screen in the bottom, inside the dishwasher usually needs to be cleaned. If that doesn't end the problem, call for service.

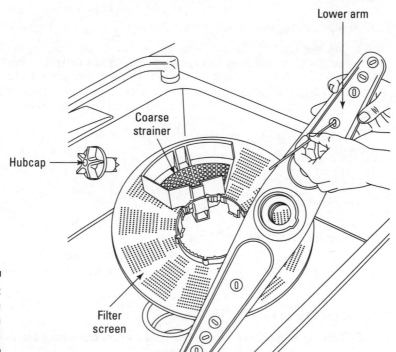

Lower arm

Coarse strainer

Hubcap

**Figure 10-9:**
Cleaning the spray arm and filter.

Filter screen

# Reconditioning Laundry Equipment

If you think your washing machine eats socks, you're right. You can retrieve them and do other simple repairs on laundry equipment. But it's impossible for us to get too detailed in this section: Washers and dryers come from different manufacturers and each has more than one model. And washers are complex machines with multiple wires running through them that operate all of the different features. You can replace damaged or worn parts in a washer, but it's not easy to sort out what belongs to what. So instead of getting specific, we're concentrating on general fixes; even then, you may have to adapt for your own machine.

## Restoring washers

In this section, we concentrate on less complicated fixes, such as replacing belts on older machines; getting lost socks, buttons, and pins out of the pump; cleaning out under the agitator; and working on hoses.

### Re-agitating agitators

Where can you find that long lost sock? Generally it's caught under the agitator. But even if nothing's missing, it's a good idea to occasionally take the agitator apart and clean under it. When an agitator's blocked, it may scrape and sound funny or not spin freely. To get the agitator off, just follow these steps:

1. **Take the cap off the agitator.**

2. **Pull it off the shaft.**

3. **Clean out the odds and ends underneath.**

4. **Reassemble the agitator.**

### Replacing belts and hoses

Older washers have a belt on the motor. If the belt breaks, you can pull it out and replace it. You need a screwdriver or pliers, a wrench and a new belt. Here's what to do:

1. **Turn off the power.**

2. **Pull the machine away from the wall so you can get at the back.**

3. **Remove the back panel by unscrewing it.**

4. **Loosen the motor and slide it enough to get the belt off.**

5. **Inspect the old belt.** If it's stretched out, cracked, or looks shiny on the inside, replace it.

6. **Get an exact replacement at an appliance parts store.**

7. **Slip the new belt on and tighten it.**

8. **Push down on it about halfway between both pulleys.**

9. **If it deflects more than ½ inch, tighten it some more; if it's too tight, loosen it.**

The hot and cold water and drain hoses can be disconnected and replaced. Get at them by following Steps 1 and 2 above. To clean them, follow the steps for cleaning showerheads in Chapter 9. If your water is especially hard, be sure to remove all the built-up lime on the screens of the water hoses. They're located just inside the end of the hoses.

It's a good idea to replace your hoses every 2 to 3 years to avoid repair problems.

### Putting in new motors and gear boxes

If you have an older machine with a belt, you can replace the motor. We don't recommend working on new machines because the motor and gearbox are one unit and difficult to work on. To replace an older motor, follow these steps:

1. **Unplug the machine and pull it out from the wall.**

2. **Remove the back panel.**

3. **Remove the motor mounting bolts.**

4. **Disconnect the wires.**

5. **Lift out the unit.**

6. **Get a replacement motor.** When you go for the part, be sure you have the model and serial number for the washer.

7. **Mount the new motor on the slide.**

8. **Hook up the wires.**

9. **Install and tighten the belt.**

10. **Screw on the back panel.**

11. **Turn the power back on.**

### Cleaning out the pump

The pump collects all sorts of things: pebbles, buttons, pins, paper, bits of plastic and cardboard. They disappear all the time in our house. You can get at the pump from the back panel and clean it out. Follow these steps:

1. **Unplug the machine and pull it out from the wall.**

2. **Remove the back panel.**

3. **Remove the motor mounting bolts.**

4. **Disconnect the wires.**

5. **Look for a clear plastic cylinder with hoses running into it.**

6. **Remove the pump or take it apart so you can dump out the garbage and rinse it off.**

### Cleaning the screen

Some washers have a lint filter or screen that should be cleaned every time you do a load of laundry, just as you clean the lint trap on a dryer. If your washer has one, you can find it on top of the agitator.

### Unkinking the inlet hose

Inlet hoses that are bent will sometimes kink for no apparent reason. If the washer fills slower than normal, check for kinked hoses.

### Fixing control panels

Because of the spaghetti wires in a washer, if you have a problem with the control panel, call for service. A trained technician can repair what might take you days within an hour or two.

### Replacing a solenoid

The mechanism that opens and shuts the water inlet and outlet hoses is a *solenoid*. It's accessible and can be replaced by do-it-yourselfers if the machine won't fill or if there's no hot or cold water when you select a warm setting. Just follow the steps below. You need a screwdriver and masking tape to mark the hoses before you detach them. Here's what to do:

1. **Turn off the power and water.**

2. **Take the back off the washer.**

3. **Take the two hoses off the machine.** They're screwed onto the back wall.

4. **Look for a square box in the machine with two tubes running into it and a round solenoid on top.** The solenoid looks like a coil of wire and is usually near the top of the washer.

5. **Unscrew the hose fittings on the solenoid.**

6. **Take the solenoid out.**

7. **Get an exact replacement at the appliance parts store.** Take the washer serial and model number with you.

8. **Put the new solenoid in.**

9. **Reassemble the hoses going from Steps 6 through 1.**

   If the hot and cold hose are not marked and look exactly the same, put a piece of tape on them to identify what they are and where they go. Left hose, right hose should be enough.

10. **Turn on the water and plug in the washer.**

Now you should get the right mix of hot and cold when you select cycles.

## Working on gas and electric dryers

In contrast to washers, dryers are relatively simple machines. Sometimes a strong wind will blow out the pilot on a gas dryer; other than that you can rely on having a constant source of gas. Small electric dryers (suitable for apartments) run off 110 volts and full-size ones run off 220 volts. If power is interrupted or a part goes bad, you have to wait for the problem to be fixed before you can use the dryer.

But the most typical problem comes from the belt that moves the drum. If the tension changes or the belt breaks, it needs to be replaced. You can do the work although it's not always easy getting the belt off and then back on. There's also an idler that maintains belt tension. It has a plastic wheel that sometimes breaks. You can replace it.

Again, be sure to open windows and doors if you smell gas. Call the gas company from a neighbor's house or your cellphone, and stay out of the house until they arrive. See Chapter 8 for more information on gas safety.

All dryers have lint baskets that should be emptied after every load. If you don't clean the lint basket, lint backs up into the vents and gets trapped there. You should inspect the vents once a year for the safety of your family. When blockages build up, the lint sometimes catches on fire and the fire transfers to the walls. By the time it's detected, the fire has almost totally engulfed the house and there's little that can be done to save it.

### Replacing the heating element

There are two heating elements in dryers and they are accessible and easy to replace. Here's what to do:

1. **Unplug the dryer.**

2. **Pull it away from the wall so you can get into the back of it.**

3. **Take the back off the dryer.**

4. **Look for the heating elements — they're circular.**

5. **Plug the dryer back in and turn it on.**

6. **Watch the heating elements to find out which one heats up and which doesn't.**

7. **Turn off the dryer and unplug it.**

8. **Remove the faulty element.** It's held in by brackets and has a couple wires on either end.

9. **After getting an exact replacement — remember to take the serial and model number — install the new element, reversing these steps.**

### Installing belts and pads

To get a belt off some dryers, you have to remove the drum and it takes a little work. Others are easier to remove. The thin belt winds around the drum, a pulley on the motor, and usually the idler. You need a screwdriver. Here's what to do:

1. **Unplug the dryer.**

2. **Unscrew the back panel and take it off.**

On some dryers you can remove the belt without taking out the drum. Look at your owner's manual and examine the belt before you go to Steps 3 and 4.

3. **Take off the bracket at the back of the drum that holds the drum up.**

4. **Slide the drum toward you so that it falls off the front lip.** Then you can get at the belt and remove it.

The front of the drum — which has a stationary outer shell and a moveable inner shell — rests on a lip that's visible if you open the front of the machine when the drum is pulled back. Take a look at it because you'll have to get the drum back over that lip after you've installed the belt.

5. **Draw a diagram showing how the belt is installed.**

6. **Take off the belt.**

7. **Examine the idler pulley to see if it looks damaged or worn.** You may as well replace it while you've got the back open and the belt off.

   While you're in there, also vacuum the built-up dust and dirt that accumulates in appliances. Everything will run much more smoothly when it's clean.

8. **Get an exact replacement from the appliance parts store.** Take the dryer model and serial number with you, as well as the belt.

9. **Install the new belt.**

10. **Push the drum back over the lip.**

11. **Hang it from the bracket.**

12. **Screw the back panel on.**

13. **Plug in the dryer.**

### Changing the idler pulley

If you hear squeaking or squawking when the dryer's on, the idler pulley wheel is going bad. The belt goes around the plastic wheel; so while you're replacing the belt, inspect the wheel. Take it from the housing by sliding it off the pin that it's mounted on. If you see any chips or cracks, you might as well replace it when you purchase the new belt. Then you can be assured that it won't give you a problem for a long time.

### Replacing the door switch

If the dryer won't start after you close the door or it doesn't stop running when you open it, the switch is probably faulty. You can replace it, as well as the plastic lever some switches have that are mounted where the door opens; they sometimes break off.

Most manufacturers make it easy to get at the switch; others have switches that are accessible only when the drum is backed out, or the top or front of the dryer is removed. Try the top first. They come off just the same as on a range: hold the sides at the front edges or the center, pull up the top, and lean it back to get it out of the way. You can replace the switch by following these steps:

1. **Unplug the dryer.**

2. **Mark the wires, and then unhook them.**

3. **Pry the switch from the hole.**

4. **Purchase a replacement.**

5. **Reverse the steps to install.**

### Fixing or replacing the control switch

If the control switch no longer works, most of them are easy to replace. Here's what to do:

1. **Unplug the dryer.**

2. **Take the panel off the console top.**

3. **Tape the wires leading into the switch or draw a picture of them to use as a reference guide.**

4. **Detach them.**

5. **Buy an exact replacement.** Take the serial and model number of the dryer with you to the appliance parts store.

6. **Put the new switch in.**

7. **Reattach the wires.**

8. **Put the panel cover back on.**

9. **Plug in the dryer.**

### Cleaning and/or replacing the air duct

The exhaust duct needs to be kept clean to prevent fires and to keep the dryer running efficiently. Remove the duct from the rear of the dryer and vacuum it out. If you can't get at the entire duct and it's still plugged, then replace it.

### Putting in a new motor

The motor can be replaced by simply removing the mounting bolts and the wires when replacing the idler.

# Chapter 11

# Getting Small Appliances to Work

. . . . . . . . . . . . . . . . . . . . . . . . . . . . . . . . . . . . . . . . . . . . . . . . . . .

## *In This Chapter*

▶ Checking out some easy fixes

▶ Looking at common appliances

. . . . . . . . . . . . . . . . . . . . . . . . . . . . . . . . . . . . . . . . . . . . . . . . . . .

*I*n this chapter, we give you step-by-step guidance on how to handle easy small-appliance repairs. We concentrate on easy repairs because it takes special tools and skills plus a lot of time to tackle anything harder, especially when you have to work in the tight, confined spaces of small appliances. To make working with small appliances even more difficult, most manufacturers don't bother making replacement parts. And although your neighbor may have sufficient experience and knowledge to rig up a substitute, that's not an option for most do-it-yourselfers.

Repairing table lamps is similar to repairing small appliances, but lamps aren't appliances. If you want to fix your lamp, refer to Chapter 7.

You're working with electricity, which can be very dangerous! Wires wrapped in black are *always* hot or power wires. It doesn't matter if you find them in a wall socket, power cord, appliance, lamp, or anywhere else. That's where the voltage comes from. The white wire you see is *always* the neutral and the green or bare wire is the ground. So be careful to differentiate between them. For more on working with electricity, turn to Chapter 7.

## *Looking at Some Quick Fixes*

All small appliances have a common denominator: They all need a source of power to operate. Not surprisingly, that's where a lot of things go wrong. So before you get out a hammer to demolish that blasted appliance, troubleshoot fixable problems — the power cords, plugs, sockets, and switches that frequently interfere with performance.

The first thing to check when an appliance isn't working is the outlet that it's plugged into. The simplest test is to plug a lamp or small working radio into the outlet. If the light or a radio station comes on, you know the problem doesn't originate in that outlet. Now test the other one. Sometimes one isn't working while the other works fine.

## Buying a tester

You should buy a power tester to fix small appliances, because then you can find out whether a plug, cord, switch, and other things are shot or just fine. Check with your local hardware store and ask a clerk about the right type of tester for your project and how to use it. We recommend two testers that are very inexpensive:

✔ The easiest way to test for power is with a *110-volt tester,* but you have to keep the electrical current on when you use it. So you have to be cautious while working. These testers have a glow light and are about 1 inch long with two 3-inch wires hanging out one end. The wires have probes on them. You can purchase a volt tester in a hardware or home supply store. If you decide to use a volt tester, don't touch a bare wire or the neutral as you're testing. If you do, you're in for a bit of a jolt.

✔ A *continuity light* allows you to test appliances with the power off. It has a light bulb, a battery, and two probes. If the bulb lights up when you connect the probes, you know that the cord, plug, or switch is working properly. A continuity light doesn't test for power. It tells you whether the power going into the appliance is making a complete circuit. You can get a continuity light at an auto supply store; they're a staple in auto repair shops. We assume that most people prefer to test with the power off, so our instructions in this chapter include using the continuity light.

Never connect a continuity light to a power source or you will fry the light and give yourself a shock.

## Checking appliance cords and plugs

After you make sure the outlet works, make sure the appliance's plug and cord aren't faulty. In this section, we go over the basics regarding plugs and cords and tell you how to test them.

All American plugs are made the same, with some minor variations. (See Figure 11-1). They have a narrow and a wide blade or prong. And if the appliance, such as the microwave, needs to be grounded, there also is a round prong below the two blades. The narrow prong *always* conducts the electricity and it fits into the narrow slot of an outlet, thus connecting to the black (hot) wiring in your home. The wide blade that fits only in the wide outlet slot is *always* neutral.

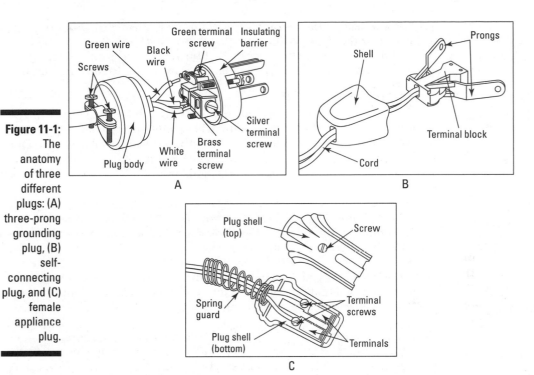

**Figure 11-1:**
The anatomy of three different plugs: (A) three-prong grounding plug, (B) self-connecting plug, and (C) female appliance plug.

When replacing the cord on an appliance, it must be as heavy a gauge as the one you're taking out, especially when an appliance heats up. These appliances must have cords that can resist fire; they have an Underwriters Laboratory (UL) fire rating. Think about the heavy, fabric-wrapped cord on an iron; it's made to withstand a lot of heat. Next in line come frying pans and electric griddles; they have medium-weight cords. Coffeepots and most appliances with motors have cords that are somewhat lighter because they operate at a much lower temperature. Now compare each of the three types of cords to a common extension cord and you'll see what we mean.

To use your continuity tester:

1. **Unplug the appliance and take out the four to six screws (or nuts) at the base of the appliance where the cord leads into it.** You have to expose the inside wiring and appliance switch or heating element.

2. **Using your continuity light, put one lead on the wide prong of the plug and the other lead on the white wire inside the appliance.** If the continuity light turns on, you know that that wire on the power cord and plug is working.

3. **Put one lead of the continuity light on the narrow prong of the plug and the other lead to the appliance's switch.** (It may be an on/off switch, a variable switch, or one that pushes down as on a toaster.) If the continuity light comes on, then the power wire to the cord and plug is good.

If you take the switch out of an appliance and find that it or the cord is bad, take it back to the appliance parts store where you purchased it and get a replacement, or order one from the manufacturer. Check your owner's manual or go to the company's Web site to order it. No matter where you get it, you need the model and serial number of the appliance.

With the exception of vacuum cleaner sales and repair shops, most appliance *repair* stores don't sell parts. Replacement parts usually have to be ordered from the manufacturer or purchased from an appliance *parts* store. It may seem silly, but there is a difference.

On most appliances, you can change the cord and switch or use a switch that doesn't exactly match the original. Just be careful the replacement you get has the same size fittings so that it can be put in the designated space.

A defective plug can be replaced without replacing the whole cord, although it won't look as nice as the original. You can purchase a variety of replacement plugs and cords at a hardware or home improvement store (See Figure 11-1). Here's what to remember about buying replacement cords and plugs:

✔ Make sure you correctly identify the polarity because if you reverse the polarity, you create a short and increase the potential for a fire.

 On flat two-wire cords, the wire with ribs on the outside is the neutral wire.

✔ If the appliance has a lighter cord (like on a coffeepot), you can simply use an extension cord; it's an economical replacement. Just cut off the plug-in end and you have a new cord and plug to use.

✔ Cords come in 20, 18, 16, and 14 gauge; gauge means the diameter of the wire, not the insulation size. The lower the number, the heavier the wire. Match the size to the old one.

## Replacing plugs and cords

If you decide to replace only the plug, follow the steps. Appliance cords have re-useable plastic outer insulators that hold the cord into the base (See Figure 11-2A). To remove the insulator, squeeze it on the inside with pliers until it pushes out of the hole. Take it off the wire and don't throw it away. Now follow these steps:

1. **Cut off the cord about 2 inches above the plug.** The wiring just above the plug can get damaged when you insert or take the plug out of wall sockets. By cutting the cord shorter, you avoid potential trouble spots.

2. **Squeeze the two prongs of the new plug together (like you squeeze tweezers) so you can pull them out of the casing.** The plastic insulator will come off with them. Now you have to attach the wires of the cord to the plug.

3. **Slip the cord through the plug casing.**

4. **If the prongs are on a single unit with crimp-style connectors, open the prongs by gently pulling them apart.** (If the wires connect to screws, skip to the directions for connecting cords to round and rectangular screw-type plugs.)

5. **Push the cord into the slot at the back of the unit.**

6. **Squeeze the prongs closed (together).**

7. **Slide the unit back into the casing.**

8. **Replace the plastic insulator.**

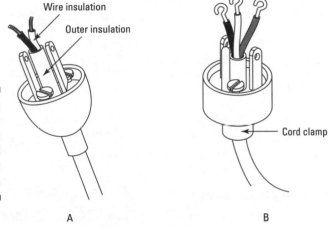

**Figure 11-2:**
Replacing a
two-prong
(A) and
three-prong
(B) plug.

A                                B

This describes only one type of two-prong replacement plugs. If you've got a three-prong plug (see Figure 11-2B) or another type, follow the package directions.

To connect cords to round and rectangular screw-type plugs, usually found on small appliances, refer to Figure 11-3 and follow these steps:

1. **Strip about ½ inch of the insulating wrap off the end of the cord to expose the wires.**

2. **Tie a security knot in the wires.** It takes the strain off the wires so they can't later be pulled off the screws if someone yanks the cord. See Figure 11-3B.

3. **Wrap each wire around one screw, turning the wire in a clockwise direction.** See figures 11-3C and 11-3D.

4. **Push the wires down into the plug and reinsert the plastic insulator.**

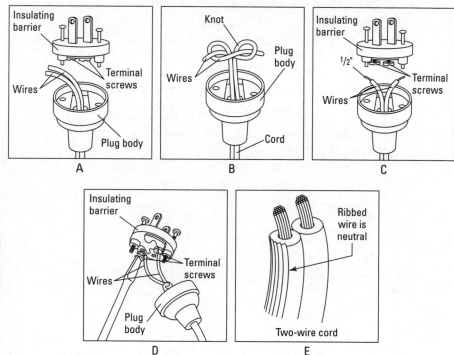

**Figure 11-3:**
Replacing a plug with terminal screws.

### Installing a new plug and cord

If you decide to buy both the cord and plug, you only have to attach the cord to the appliance. Buy the new cord before you take the old one off the base of the appliance. Then attach the new cord to the base in reverse order for taking it off.

In two-wire cords, the neutral wire is usually encased in ribbed cord. See Figure 11-3E.

## Checking and replacing defective appliance switches

Appliances have switches that can go bad. Test switches after you find there's nothing wrong with the cord, plug, or outlet. Here's how:

1. **Put one lead of the continuity light on the black wire or terminals where the cord enters the switch.** First, locate the switch on the appliance. The location of the switch isn't always obvious. (See Figure 11-4).

2. **Put the other lead on the other side of the switch where the power leads from the switch to the motor or heating element of the appliance.**

3. **With the two leads connected, turn the switch on and off.** If the light goes on and off as it's supposed to, you know the switch is okay.

The hot side of the switch is where the cord enters it. The other side of the switch is intermittently hot or cold, depending on whether the switch is on or off. Check the plug and cord as it enters the switch first. Then check the other side of the switch to make sure there's juice to the heating element or motor when the switch is engaged.

Heavy duty switches sometimes have screw terminals and lighter ones often have pigtails attached to them. A *pigtail* is two little pieces of wire that stick out of the switch. Before you start working, be sure the appliance cord is unplugged. And remember that most cords have a smooth cover over the hot wire and a ribbed cover over the neutral.

If the old switch won't work, you'll have to replace it. A local parts supplier should have a new switch, or check the manufacturer's Web site to order a new one. Once you have the new switch, follow these directions to install it:

1. **Remove the knob, usually by pulling it straight off.**

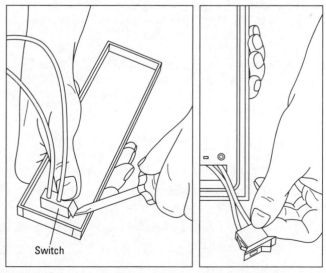

**Figure 11-4:**
Replacing a
switch on a
canister
vacuum

Switch

A                    B

2. **Take off the knot or whatever holds the switch and push it into the appliance.**

3. **Detach or cut the wires to the switch and remove them.**

4. **Reverse this procedure to install the new switch.** If you cut the wires, you can reconnect them with small wire nuts. Wire nuts are colored, cone-shaped plastic wire connectors. They screw onto the ends of two or more stripped-wire ends , connecting them together.

## Checking the heating element or motor

If the heating element or motor on an appliance is defective, and if the appliance was made relatively recently, you very likely will have to throw it out and get a new one. Parts are rarely available on recent appliances although you may find all the inner workings available as a total replacement unit. For the most part, manufacturers simply don't bother making parts. They expect you to replace the whole appliance.

So what's the point of checking the motor or heating element? Well, at least you'll know for certain whether you should trash the appliance. Plus, manufacturers used to make replacement parts for older appliances, but phased out production as newer appliances came out with more features. So, if you have an older appliance, you can fix it but you might have to dig to find the part still sitting on someone's shelf — or you can salvage the part from a similar product (as experienced do-it-yourselfers often do).

If you can put a new unit in the old housing, find out how much a new appliance costs compared to what you have to spend for the replacement unit. Then decide which option makes better sense.

When you test a heating element with a continuity light, if the light turns on, it isn't as bright as when you test the plug, cord, or switch. That's because the heating element is a resistor, and a resistor saps some of the applied power and turns it into heat and/or light.

Here's how to check whether the heating element is burned out:

1. **Put one end of the continuity light on one end of the heating element.**

2. **Put the other end of the continuity light on the other side of the element where the wires connect to it.**

3. **If the light goes on, the heating element works.** (See Figure 11-5.)

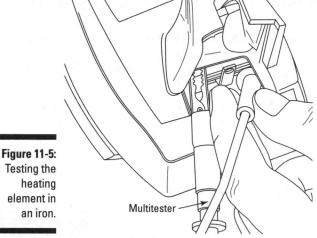

**Figure 11-5:**
Testing the
heating
element in
an iron.

Multitester

# Specific Repairs for Specific Appliances

Appliances are similar in that they have plugs, cords, and switches, and work either because of heating elements or motors. But they're not the quite the same when it comes to fine-tuning their functions. In this section we get more specific about common complaints.

## Mending toasters

Toasters are uncomplicated appliances with heating elements, a thermostat, switches, and plugs and cords. Most of the time when they malfunction, they haven't been cleaned thoroughly. Of course the heating elements can burn out after time, and plugs, cords, and switches get faulty, but if you maintain your toaster as suggested below, the toaster should give you years of service before the electrical parts wear out.

If you get a shock when you touch the toaster, it's not grounded. Get a replacement from the store or take it to a professional for repairs.

### Cleaning the toaster

Toasters tend to balk when the crumbs build up inside. If you don't clean them out several times a month, especially when you use the toaster daily, the crumbs interfere with heating elements and parts. To clean your toaster:

1. **When your toaster is cool, unplug it and slide out the tray (usually located in the base).** The tray catches most of the crumbs, so clean it up.

2. **Turn your toaster upside down and gently shake it.** More crumbs will dislodge and fall out the slots.

3. **Look at the heating elements on each side of the slots.** Make sure no crumbs are stuck behind or between the heating coils. Use an old toothbrush to clean them — not a knife or any other utensil that may damage the coil.

4. **After the toaster looks clean, plug it in and toast a slice of bread.** If it comes out fine, then you have nothing more to do.

### What to do when the toaster won't heat up

Check the plug, cord, switch, and heating element as described in the "Looking at Some Quick Fixes" section.

### What to do when your toast won't stay down

The latch that locks the carriage in place may still be blocked by crumbs. To clean them out, you need a screwdriver, canned air or a handheld pump, and lubricant — you can get a lubricant for appliances at an appliance service center. Now follow these steps:

1. **Remove the carriage lever and unscrew the front cover.**

2. **When the cover is off, blow any crumbs from the latch assembly.**

3. **Test the latch to make sure it moves up and down easily.** If it still sticks, apply a little lubricant.

4. **Look at the heating coils too to see whether all the crumbs have been removed.** If not, blow them out with the forced air.

5. **After cleaning and lubricating the toaster, put the cover back, plug it in, and fix yourself some toast.** If the toast still won't go up or down, buy yourself a new toaster.

### What to do when the toast won't pop up

Your toaster's thermostat may be set incorrectly. To reset it, follow these steps:

1. **Take off the carriage lever and front cover and look for a knob, screw, or nut located near the toast light-to-dark control on the outside of most toasters.**

2. **Turn the knob, screw, or switch to the left, as on the lighter-control position.**

3. **Replace the cover, plug in the toaster, and test it by toasting a piece of bread.**

If the toast still burns, then the thermostat has to be reset. This is controlled either by a dial or lever usually on the front of the toaster. You can reset the thermostat. Here's how.

1. **If you turn a dial to make the toast light-to-dark, take the dial knob off.**

2. **Readjust the screw behind it, turning it towards "lighter" on the toaster — or darker if the bread won't toast.** You'll probably have to turn the screw only slightly, not a full turn.

3. **Put the knob back on and test the toaster with a slice of bread.** If the toast is still dark, then adjust the screw a little again.

If your toaster has a lever controlling light and dark, bend it *slightly* up or down. For instance if you want your toast lighter, and the display for lighter is at the top of the lever channel, then you will bend the lever up.

### What if your toast won't stay down and the toaster buzzes?

This usually happens because the toaster hasn't cooled off. You can correct this problem by setting the control to dark or just depressing the lever again. If waiting or resetting the control doesn't work, then the solenoid switch needs to be replaced, a moderately difficult repair. Call for a service estimate and if it's too high, buy a new toaster.

### And if only one side of bread gets toasted . . .

One or both of the heating elements isn't working. The chassis needs to be replaced so it's probably wiser to get a new toaster.

## Adjusting stubborn blenders, mixers, and processors

When a blender, mixer, or food processor stops running completely, it usually means that the motor is bad. Refer to Figure 11-6 for the anatomy of a typical food processor. If you've tested the plug, cord, and switch and know the problem doesn't originate there, the motor is bad. Replace the appliance.

If you the motor runs, but the blades don't, the belt may need replacing. You can put in a new belt. Here's how:

1. **Unplug the appliance and take off all accessories.**

2. **Lay it sideways on the table or counter.**

3. **Take the top off by removing screws between it and the bottom.**

4. **Look for hidden screws in the middle of any of the legs and take them out too.** Sometimes there may be screws under a nameplate. Pry it up and remove them.

5. After you've exposed the base and the belt, loosen the bracket screw — do not take the screw off.

6. Take the belt off after loosening it by shifting the bracket.

7. Get an exact replacement from an appliance parts store and put it on your appliance.

8. Reassemble the appliance.

## Giving coffee makers new life

When your coffee maker stops making coffee, don't throw it away until you check that the cord and plug are not bad. Then give it a good cleaning. Coffee makers get clogged with mineral deposits in water, just like steam irons. If anything else goes wrong, there's little you can do. So inspect the plug and cord, and then follow the cleaning steps. Repeat them several times if necessary. And if the coffee maker doesn't work after several attempts to clean it (do it several times), get a new one.

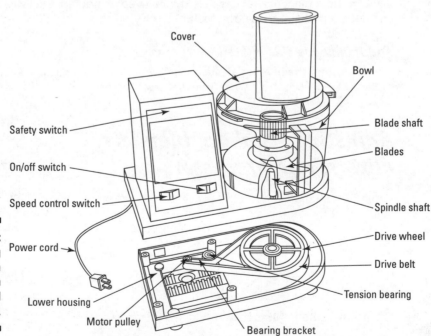

**Figure 11-6:** Looking inside a belt-driven food processor.

Cover

Bowl

Safety switch

Blade shaft

Blades

On/off switch

Speed control switch

Spindle shaft

Drive wheel

Power cord

Drive belt

Tension bearing

Lower housing

Motor pulley

Bearing bracket

If you know the coffee maker is getting the power it needs, and it still isn't working well, it may be clogged with mineral deposits from water. Here's how to clean it up:

1. **Pour full-strength white vinegar into the water reservoir.**

2. **Turn on the appliance and let it go through a full cycle.**

3. **Turn it off and rinse out the vinegar thoroughly.**

4. **Put some fresh water into the reservoir again.**

5. **Run through another full cycle.** You may have to do this two or three times. If the coffee maker is still clogged, go to Step 6.

6. **Turn the coffee maker upside down.**

7. **Remove the screws holding the base plate.** Check the legs, too, to see whether a screw is hidden in the middle of one or more. You'll sec a tube that goes from the base of the coffee maker up to the basket.

8. **Push a long, narrow wire through the tube.**

9. **Reassemble everything.**

10. **Use more vinegar for another cycle to clear out the debris you've loosened with the wire.** Don't forget to rinse with a cycle or two of water.

Enjoy your next cup of coffee!

## *Restoring microwaves*

In this section, we show you a few quick fixes for your microwave oven: you can replace a burned out bulb, put in a new turntable adapter, or clean the filter. If you've worked on other appliances, you can also replace a touch pad, but it's a little more complicated, and we don't recommend it for beginners. If your microwave needs more work than the repairs listed above, take it to a certified service center for repairs. They have been trained in electronics and have the special tools needed to work on microwaves. Get a cost estimate before it's fixed, however, so that you can judge whether your best bet (and cheapest) is to buy a new microwave.

Before talking about what you can do with your microwave, it's important to know that you should *never* take the cover off and try to work on the inside. Microwaves have electronic circuit boards, *magnetrons* (generators), transformers, and capacitors. The capacitor stores energy. So even if you unplug the microwave, you can encounter high levels of voltage that pack a powerful punch if you inadvertently touch the capacitor. For more information about using professionals, see Chapter 18.

### Replacing the light bulb

When the light bulb burns out, you can take it out and replace it. First you have to find the cover. Depending on the brand of microwave, it's either inside the cooking compartment under a cover-plate shielding the light, or it's accessible from the back of the appliance. Here's what to do:

1. **Unplug the microwave and examine the cooking area.** If you see a cover-plate, unscrew it to get at the bulb. Then go to Step 4.

2. **If you don't see a cover-plate on the interior wall, turn the microwave around and look for a cover on the back.**

3. **Unscrew that cover to get at the bulb.**

4. **When you see the bulb, turn it a quarter turn to the left and pull the base straight out.** The bulb has two prongs, just like many automotive bulbs.

5. **Push in the new bulb and turn it a quarter turn to the right.**

6. **Screw the cover-plate back on.**

### Putting in a new turntable adapter

Microwave turntables usually rest on a little plastic adaptor that sits on a gear and connects the gear to the plate. That little piece breaks when too much weight sits on the plate or the plate hits the side wall — it's meant to keep the motor from burning up. On some microwaves, this plastic piece is attached to the plate and you can break it off inadvertently when you're cleaning the plate.

The adaptor, usually a 1-inch-long square or triangular piece, is replaceable. Different brands are made differently. You can get a replacement at an appliance parts service center. Look in the Yellow Pages to find one in your vicinity. Now you're ready to fix the turntable. Here's what to do:

1. **Fish the broken pieces from the microwave.**

2. **Find the serial and model number for your microwave and for the part.** You'll need it when you go to the store. Look at the service booklet that came with the microwave. If you can't find the booklet, turn the microwave around and copy the numbers on the back panel.

3. **After you have the part, snap it into place and set the plate on top.** That engages the turntable motor so that it once again performs just like new.

### Replacing the touch pad

The all-digital LED lights on the microwave touch pad don't last forever. One or two will go out and then, perhaps, a few more. But you don't have to guess how many minutes or seconds are left when you're using the appliance. Nor do you need to panic if the protective plastic covering over the numeric display gets punctured. There are no moving parts on touch pads, so replacing them is easy if you can get the touchpad off. If you can't figure out how to remove it, have the microwave serviced. Here are the steps for removing and replacing the touch pad:

1. **Unplug the cord of the microwave.**

2. **Get the model and serial number from your instruction book or the data plate that the manufacturer installed on the back of the microwave.** You need that information when you go to the appliance parts service center near your home.

3. **Look at the touch pad to find out whether it snaps out or is screwed into place.** Take it out.

4. **If the reverse side of the touch pad is plugged into the wires of the microwave, unplug them from the wiring harness.** Don't worry, they're not hot.

5. **Plug the new touch pad to the wiring harness.**

6. **Reattach the touch pad to the front of the microwave the same way you took it apart.**

7. **Plug in the microwave and put it back on the shelf or counter.** You'll love having numbers to look at once again.

### Cleaning microwave filters

If your microwave isn't performing up to par, a dirty filter may be restricting the air flow. The filter traps grease and keeps it from blowing back into the kitchen, which is why it needs cleaning now and then. Here's how:

1. **To get at the filter, unscrew the vent and take it off the microwave.**

2. **Clean or replace the filter.** If the filter looks like metal wire or plastic mesh or if it's spongy, wash it in warm soapy water, dry it, and put it back in. If filter is a paper product, buy a new one. Get them at an appliance or appliance parts store.

## Heating up dead irons

When working with an iron, always start by checking the plug, cord, and switch, as explained in the "Looking at Some Quick Fixes" section earlier in the chapter. If these items aren't defective, you're iron may be plugged up. Minerals in water eventually clog up the small tubes and the vents. The main culprits are tap and well water; you can try to clean the iron. But if cleaning doesn't work, the heating element is bad and your only recourse is to get a new iron. Here's how to clean your iron:

1. **Pour white vinegar into the top and reservoir.**

2. **Turn on the iron.**

3. **As it heats up, give it a few shakes.** You want to break those calcium and sulfur deposits loose in both the tubes and reservoir.

4. **Hold the iron over the sink and push the steam button several times to get the vinegar all the way through the vents on the base of the iron.**

5. **Dump out the vinegar and pour water — preferably distilled — into the top.**

6. **Let the water heat up and steam to get all the vinegar out.**

If necessary, repeat these steps several times. After all, the mineral deposits didn't build up overnight; it may take some effort to get rid of them.

## Servicing vacuum cleaners

Vacuum cleaners take a beating. Who hasn't run over pennies and long pieces of string, ribbon, or rubber bands? Then there's the cord itself; it gets stepped on, twisted, wrapped around chairs, and the plug gets yanked out of the wall — sometimes sideways — when you pull the cord too tight. As you know, there are two main categories of vacuum cleaners: upright and canister. In this section, we give you some quick fixes for each.

### Upright vacuum cleaners

If an upright vacuum cleaner doesn't work turn it upside down and look at the base — before you test the plug, cord, or switch. (See Figure 11-7.) Is there anything wrapped around the beater brushes? If so, just pull those items off. The roller will turn both ways, so unwinding extraneous garbage is simple.

Next take off the base plate. Also on the bottom, the plate is usually held in place by two flat metal wings that rotate off. Under the plate, you'll see a rubber belt. Is it loose, off the roller, or broken? It should fit tightly onto the beater brush. If it doesn't or it won't stay in position, you have to get a new one. Sometimes, you'll find them hanging from a display rack at the grocery store, sold in packages of two, or you can get them at hardware and home improvement stores.

Before you head off to buy a new belt, write down the brand and model of your vacuum cleaner and for good measure take the old belt along. Belts come in several different widths and lengths and you want to be sure to get the right one.

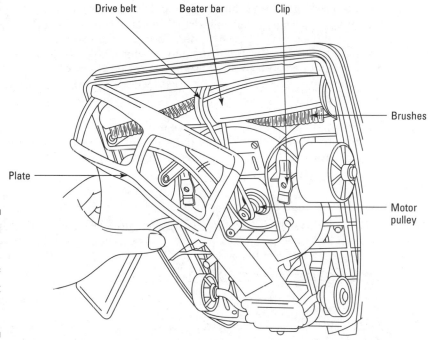

Drive belt    Beater bar    Clip

Brushes

Plate

Motor pulley

**Figure 11-7:**
Looking into the underside of an upright vacuum cleaner.

Replacing the belt is easy, just follow the directions on the package you just bought (see Figure 11-8). After you put the new belt in place, make sure it's on correctly:

1. **Plug the vacuum cleaner into the wall and look at the direction in which the brushes are turning.** They should be rotating forward. That's where the vacuum sucks in trash, animal fur, and hair on your rugs and floors. This forward rotation is also why it's harder to push the vacuum cleaner forward than it is to pull it back.

2. **If the brushes are rotating toward the back, turn off the vacuum cleaner.**

3. **Unhook just one end of the belt.**

4. **Twist it in the opposite direction.**

5. **Hook it back in place.**

6. **Turn on the vacuum again to make sure the brushes are rotating forward.**

Before you close up the base and check the plug, cord, and switch, look at each end of the beater brush cylinder. Sometimes, the bushings or bearings get worn or too dirty and that stops the cylinder from rotating or causes the belt to burn out. With the belt off, the brush should spin freely by hand. Snap the brush cylinder out of the base of the vacuum cleaner and clean the bushings and/or bearings which support the ends of the brush. If that doesn't help, you have to buy a new cylinder. Go to a vacuum appliance store or a dealer that sells your brand of vacuum cleaner. They usually have a supply of replacements on hand. (A dealer selling several brands of vacuum cleaners, including yours, very likely will have replacement parts for all brands. Just be sure you know your brand and model before you head off to the store.)

After the bristles on the beater bar wear down, they won't be long enough to reach a hardwood floor. When that happens, the whole roller needs to be replaced. You don't want to waste your energy going through the motions of vacuuming without any results!

### Canister vacuum cleaners

The hose on a canister vacuum cleaner lasts about 5 years. After that, it becomes less effective in picking up dirt; or you may find holes or weak spots in the hose. If the vacuum is damaged at its base — where the hose connects to the canister — it can't be fixed.

Your best bet in replacing the hose is to take the machine to a vacuum cleaner appliance center and have someone figure out whether the hose or the base plate is defective. Let them do the work on replacing the hose because putting a new one on calls for special tools.

Be sure to check the plug, cord, and switch as described "Looking at Some Quick Fixes" section earlier in this chapter. If any of these are bad, they can be easily replaced in the same manner as most appliances. (Refer back to Figure 11-4.) Parts can be purchased from an appliance store or vacuum cleaner center.

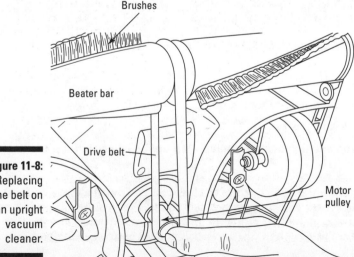

Brushes

Beater bar

Drive belt

Motor pulley

**Figure 11-8:**
Replacing
the belt on
an upright
vacuum
cleaner.

# Chapter 12

# Fine-Tuning Communication Equipment

................................................................

## In This Chapter

▶ Making minor computer adjustments

▶ Getting printers and copiers to work

▶ Tuning up fax machines and scanners

▶ Restoring TVs

▶ Giving satellite dishes first aid

▶ Making music with CD, DVD, and VCR players

▶ Fixing telephones

................................................................

*E*lectronic gadgets have come a long way in the last decade, and now seem to be an integral part of almost every home. As a rule, most of the electronic equipment we use today can work for years without problems — if people take care of it. Most glitches occur as a result of neglect — people failing to maintain their computers, fax machines, or CD and DVD players as manufacturers recommend. We eat or drink while surfing the Net, we don't clean the print head or the platen on our printers, and we don't wipe dust and fingerprints off disks. And who thinks about trackballs until the computer's mouse stops working?

In this chapter, we go over ways to clean keyboards and spills, unjam disk drives, and clean track balls and printers. We also include tips for keeping other electronic equipment up to snuff — fax machines, scanners, TVs, radios, telephones, and CD, DVD, and VCR players. We haven't included any tips for repairing cellphones; the technology is still advancing too rapidly. You have to rely on your owner's manual and service provider for that.

We all like to toss out the reams of manuals we get with every new communication system or appliance. But it's a mistake. Right now think about starting a central storage area: a drawer, file cabinet, or system for every single instruction sheet or manual that enters your home. They contain valuable advice about how to troubleshoot and what to do when something breaks down.

# Handling Minor Computer Repairs

Some people get new computers every two years or so. They hang around computer stores, buying this add-on or that plug-in. The rest of us are content or struggle with the dinosaurs, computer equipment more than 5 years old. Whatever category you fall in, we hope the information we provide about computers will be helpful. Refer to Figure 12-1 for the anatomy of a typical desktop computer.

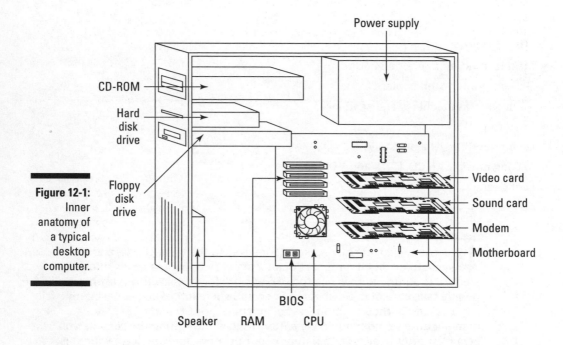

**Figure 12-1:** Inner anatomy of a typical desktop computer.

Power supply

CD-ROM

Hard disk drive

Floppy disk drive

Video card

Sound card

Modem

Motherboard

Speaker    RAM    CPU

BIOS

Lengthy books have been written about computers, computer equipment, software, and other communication devices; we won't try to compete with them because this is a general fix-it book. So if you yearn to get more computer-specific information, we recommend you get hold of the latest editions of *Upgrading and Fixing PCs For Dummies* by Andy Rathbone, *Fighting Spam For Dummies* by John R. Levine, Margaret Levine Young, and Ray Everett-Church, *Computer Viruses For Dummies* by Peter H. Gregory, or *Windows XP For Dummies* by Andy Rathbone (all published by Wiley). In this book, we stick to easy, do-it-yourself repairs.

If your mind draws a blank at computer jargon, the Web site for Sharpened.net has a glossary and other helpful information to help you become familiar with computer geek speak: www.sharpened.net.

## A couple of 'puter tools to keep around

If you want to fix and maintain your electrical equipment, keep a small supply of products on hand so you don't have shop every time you want to take something apart. Two standbys that you'll use over and over again are rubbing alcohol and canned air or a hair blower. You need air to blow dust and fur — it gravitates to electronic equipment — off electrical devices. Think how often a TV needs to be dusted. Because the television picture tube operates with very high voltage, a static charge develops and this attracts dust. Well, that dust isn't simply sticking to the exterior or casing of your equipment; it's finding a way inside. After it's there, it can gum up the works. A vacuum cleaner with a brush attachment also can remove dust from electronics. Isopropyl (rubbing) alcohol, lens cleaners for cameras, cotton and foam swabs, and clean, soft, lint-free cloths will come in handy. Also keep some small bottles of lubricant such as silicone spray to lubricate, waterproof, and clean corroded parts, and lithium grease, a petroleum grease with lithium powder, to improve lubrication, and a silicone lubricant.

## *Checking cable connections*

You've probably heard it before but here we say it again: If your computer is not behaving up to par, start out by looking at the cable connections. Make sure the cat or a curious kid didn't pull on them and loosen something. Inspect the cables to make sure they aren't defective. When you put a cable into the computer or monitor, reconnect it a couple times, making certain that all pins and holes match up. Don't try jamming a plug in. Those tiny pins bend and break off easily if they aren't in the right slot. Also look at the pins in the receptacle to see whether any one of them is bent. You can try straightening bent pins but do it carefully. Don't use too much force or a pin can snap off.

If the fittings appear to be corroded, use an electrical contact cleaner to clean them up. Follow the manufacturer's instructions. If a cable still doesn't work, have it tested at a computer repair shop where you can get an exact replacement if necessary.

Sometimes, a keyboard doesn't work because the cable connecting it to the computer is loose. Before you go to the store or tear out your hair, push the cable in firmly. Then restart the computer so it recognizes that the keyboard is available now.

If your computer is hooked up to an Internet service provided through your phone lines, and you're having trouble accessing the Internet, check your phone connections before calling your Internet service provider. We tell you what to look for in the "Troubleshooting Phones and Phone Lines" section later in this chapter.

# Cleaning up spills and keyboard sticks

We all get hungry and thirsty while we're working on the computer. Even when you think you're being careful, you can spill something in a flash. In the following sections, we tell you how to clean up dirty keyboards.

### Getting rid of the crud

You need screwdrivers; a blow dryer, vacuum cleaner with a brush attachment, or canned air (available at a hardware or home improvement stores); a soft brush; and electrical contact cleaner. If you can't find the cleaner at the store, go to a store that specializes in computer sales and parts. Now follow these steps:

1. **Disconnect the cable from the computer to the keyboard.**

2. **Turn your keyboard upside down.**

3. **Unscrew the screws in the base.** After they're off, you'll notice that there are two halves, the top with the keys and the bottom.

4. **Pry the halves apart.**

5. **Lift up the top of the keyboard.**

6. **Shake and blow out any debris with a blow dryer, canned air, or vacuum cleaner attachment.**

7. **Remove residue and corrosion with the electrical contact cleaner.**

8. **Reassemble your keyboard.**

If the keyboard is balky or won't work after you clean it, just get a new one. Luckily, it's one of the less expensive computer components.

### Mopping up spills

Keyboards usually don't sit flat on the desk, so anything spilled on the surface very likely won't destroy the keyboard. But if you spill a drink directly onto the keyboard, follow Steps 1 through 4 in the "Getting rid of the crud" section to take the keyboard apart. Then mop up moisture with a soft cloth or sponge. The keyboard has to dry out before you use it again. You can wait a day or blow dry the two halves, using canned air, a vacuum cleaner attachment, or a hair dryer. Just don't use the hottest setting; low will work better.

Sugary spills do a lot of damage. The sugar coats the keys and in turn, that works like a magnet to attract dust. So even if the mopped-up keyboard works initially, it might not be long before you have to shop for a replacement. If you want to ensure you've gotten every bit of the sticky stuff off, you can take the covers off each key in turn to get at moisture that may have seeped inside. Use a small screwdriver to pry off the covers.

## A note about wireless keyboards

Wireless keyboards depend on power, just as much as wired ones do. If your wireless seems lazy, it's probably the batteries. Get some new ones at a computer store. And get real. You can't drive off with it in the car and then expect to use it; it has to be fairly close to the computer to keep working

# Troubleshooting disk drives

Disk drives often freeze, but you can't do anything about it because they're sealed tight. You can try a new disk to find out whether the disk is at fault. To test the disk, put another disk into the drive — computer or CD/DVD player. If the second disk works, you know the first disk is faulty, and not the computer or player. If it's the disk drive that failed, try blowing dust out, as best you can, with canned air because dust will gum up the works. Then if the drive still doesn't work, buy a new one at a computer store. They aren't expensive, usually under $50, and you can install the new drive yourself. It comes with detailed instructions and software for clearing it up. If you're nervous about taking out and installing a new disk drive, you can take your computer/CD/DVD to the repair department at a computer store and they'll do it for you for a small fee.

# Rolling, rolling, rolling: Trackballs and roller balls

If you still have a trackball on your computer keyboard or a roller ball under the mouse, they may start performing erratically. That's usually because they and the rollers beneath the balls need cleaning. We explain what to do below. You need a lint-free cloth, rubbing alcohol, a sponge swab, and compressed air or a hair dryer to blow dirt out of the housing. Here's how to clean a roller ball:

1. **Unplug the mouse from the back of the computer.**

2. **Turn the mouse upside down.**

3. **Remove the bottom panel.** It will either rotate clockwise or push forward. Look for instructions on the bottom of the mouse.

4. **Take out the roller ball.**

5. **Dampen the lint-free cloth with the alcohol.**

6. **Wipe the roller ball clean and let it dry.**

7. **Scrape off accumulated crud (don't use anything sharp because you'll damage the spongy ball) and wipe the rollers underneath it clean with rubbing alcohol.**

8. **Blow out any loose dirt and dust.** If you have great lung capacity, marvelous; otherwise, use the canned air or a hair blower.

9. **Put the roller ball back in, and then reassemble the mouse.**

Never use a knife or any other sharp tool to clean the roller or any other plastic parts. If you scratch them, they'll pick up dirt faster. If doesn't come off with a cotton swab the first time, keep swabbing with the rubbing alcohol, gently.

Here's how to clean a trackball:

1. **Pop the trackball, made of hard plastic, glass, or marble, out.**

2. **Clean it with alcohol as described in steps 5 through 9 of the steps for cleaning roller balls.**

3. **Roll it around in your hand to lubricate it with the oil in your skin. If your hands are dry, rub in some lotion. Then lubricate the trackball.**

4. **Pop the trackball back into the keyboard.**

# Maintaining Cathode Ray Monitors

Your computer monitor is a lot like a television (see Figure 12-2). When it stops working, there's not much you can do except get a new one. But before you head for the store, make sure the cables are plugged into the computer and that a circuit breaker hasn't shut off the power. Also don't forget to look at the on/off button on any power strips that the computer uses. Little fingers may enjoy flipping the red switch off and on. We've even had heavy books topple over and close the switch.

If you can't find anything wrong with the power supply, inspect the cables to make sure they aren't damaged. If one of them looks suspicious, put in a replacement. Make sure it's exactly like the original cable. If the second cable works, you know the first is faulty.

The new flat monitors have enclosed parts that you can't get into. The only "fix" possible is to check the connections to your computer and any other equipment used in tandem with computer.

Most tabletop monitors have buttons on the front or side of the screen that you can adjust. Before going too far, play with them a while to find out whether all that's need is to readjust them. If that hasn't helped, head to the store. The flat-screen monitors require very little space and the prices are down. You know you've been yearning to get one. Now's your chance.

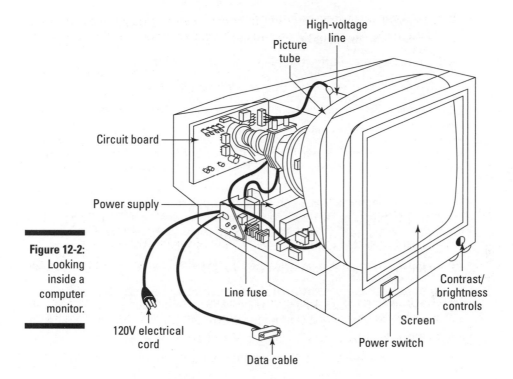

High-voltage
line

Picture
tube

Circuit board

Power supply

**Figure 12-2:**
Looking
inside a
computer
monitor.

Line fuse

120V electrical
cord

Data cable

Contrast/
brightness
controls

Screen

Power switch

# Readjusting Printers

Computers have specific software pertaining to the printer or printers that
they use. Whenever you encounter problems, make sure the printer is still
connected to the computer and that the cables are working properly. In the
following sections, we tell you how to restore communications between the
computer and printer. There's also information about cleaning and unjamming printers.

## Restoring communication capabilities

Sometimes computers stop talking to printers or the printer "freezes." You
may have overloaded the printer by giving it repeated commands because
you weren't sure the first, and second, registered or you expected an instan-
taneous response. When the printer freezes, start off by rebooting (restarting
the computer.) You may then get a pop-up that says there are print jobs waiting and asks if you wish to delete or continue. Select delete to erase the repe-
titious commands. That will clear the print memory. Now ask it to print just
once. Here's what to do when your printer doesn't work:

1. **Look for a loose connection or damaged cable.**

2. **Check inside the printer for a paper jam.**

3. **If you see paper under the platen or roller, unplug the printer.** Refer to Figure 12-3.

4. **Pull the paper towards you.** Some printers have a manually operated paper release; check the manual to locate it. In addition, there may be more than one sheet jammed, so make sure you get every single page.

5. **Look at the configurations in the printer software and the drivers.** If anything has changed, change it back to the original configurations.

6. **Clean and lubricate the printer, according to instructions in the manufacturer's manual.** If you can't find the booklets, take the printer to the computer store or go there yourself and ask questions. Usually, you'll find knowledgeable staff, or someone in the service department will help you out.

7. **Delete your most recent print commands.**

8. **Reboot the computer or turn it off for 10 to 15 seconds, and then restart it.** After restarting you might get a pop-up that asks whether you want to cancel the jobs waiting to be printed or try again. Play it safe — cancel them.

9. **Try printing again.** Don't worry that the printer didn't receive the command; once is enough.

10. **Perform a self-test on the printer.** The computer doesn't even have to be powered on. You can do this with every printer. The self-test isolates the problem to the printer and forces a printout that provides a list of the printer's current settings and options, showing all the print density and quality features.

 Ink-jet and bubble-jet printers have printer heads that move back and forth as jets of ink produce rows of dots that build images on the paper. Laser printers, top-of-the-line technology, have a light-emitting diode (LED) that flashes rows of lights on and off to the print drum; like copiers, there's no ink involved, just toner.

 Don't use recycled paper in a printer because it sheds particles. If you use a high quality paper that doesn't shed, such as conventional 20 pound xerographic paper, you'll get better results and have fewer maintenance problems.

 If you don't already have a cover for your printer, get one and put it on when you're not using the computer. That will keep it free of dust and anything else floating around in your home.

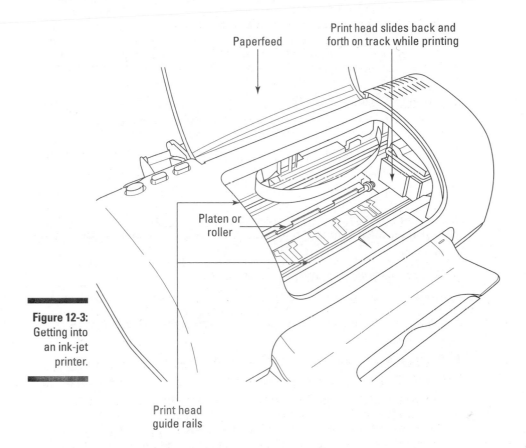

Paperfeed

Print head slides back and
forth on track while printing

Platen or
roller

**Figure 12-3:**
Getting into
an ink-jet
printer.

Print head
guide rails

# Cleaning printers

If your printer suddenly starts spitting out distorted print or smeared pages,
try cleaning it. To clean your printer, you need rubbing alcohol, a cotton
swab, a vacuum cleaner or canned air, and a clean cloth.

If you see streaks or the paper is smeared, clean the platen or roller to
remove built-up ink. Then use the vacuum cleaner or canned air to remove
any remaining ink or dust particles from the printer.

### Cleaning an ink jet printer

If an ink jet printer is giving you problems, here's what to do:

1. **Take out the ink-head or cartridge.**

2. **Gently clean the print head contacts.** Ink builds up on them because
   the ink runs out to them. Pour a little rubbing alcohol on a sponge swab.

Or you can put a little alcohol on a stiff bristle brush and brush the contacts. After brushing, run a little of the alcohol over the print head to rinse off broken bristles. Don't worry. It evaporates very quickly

3. **Wipe excess ink off the nozzles.**

4. **Put the cartridge back in.**

5. **Start a print test to make sure you've gotten rid of excess ink.**

If this doesn't work, put in a new ink cartridge. That should take care of the problem.

### Cleaning a laser printer

Laser printers have corona wires that distribute toner. Use the illustrations in your printer manual to find out where it is. Here's how to clean the corona wire:

1. **Unplug the printer and turn it off.**

2. **Let it cool down.**

3. **Blow out dust from around the drum and corona wire.** Use canned air, a vacuum cleaner nozzle, or a blow dryer.

4. **Dampen a cotton swab with rubbing alcohol.**

5. **Gently rub the swab along corona wire to remove built-up toner and dust that still is on the wire.**

# Working on Fax Machines and Scanners

Fax machines are usually trouble free. The best way to keep your fax machine in top condition is to service it periodically, as recommended by the manufacturer. Use good paper that doesn't leave a residue or film and the appropriate ink cartridges. A fax scans paper images, and then transmits them to another machine via a modem linked to your telephone. The receiving fax decodes and translates the light and dark images and reproduces them on thermal or plain paper. There are so many different models and manufacturers of fax machines that it's not possible to explain how to fix them. But you can troubleshoot your machine as explained below.

## Troubleshooting fax machines

All fax machines have phone receivers. If the fax doesn't work, then call a friend or neighbor to see if there's a problem with the phone. If it's not the phone, get your owner's manual and check the settings. Also review all setup instructions. You can check how your fax machine works by putting a document into the fax and copying it. If the copy looks like the original, your machine is trouble free. If you have two phone lines and a computer, send yourself a fax. If it doesn't arrive, take the machine for service, or service it yourself by following the manufacturer's instructions.

If you get a fax that's hard to read, it's not your machine: the sender's machine has a problem. Let that person or company know the fax was unreadable.

The best way to avoid problems is to use rubbing alcohol periodically to clean the machine; also blow out accumulated dust and fuzz with canned air, your vacuum cleaner, or blow dryer. See Figure 12-4.

Spray nozzle

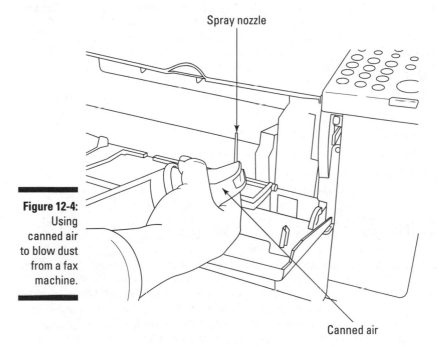

**Figure 12-4:**
Using
canned air
to blow dust
from a fax
machine.

Canned air

## *Scanning scanners for problems*

We once had three or four different machines in our offices and homes. Now we can connect our computers to a combination printer that also scans, faxes, and copies documents. When a scanner scans a document or picture, it converts the image into a file that can be stored on your computer. Then you can send that image anywhere using the modem. It's also possible to make a quality reproduction of the original page on the printer. Dust, lint, fur, fingerprints, and other culprits can cause smudges or mar the glass. Keep the glass bed on scanners clean by wiping it periodically with a good glass cleaner and soft paper towel. Here's how:

1. **Turn the scanner off and unplug it.**

2. **Raise the cover.**

3. **Dampen the cloth or paper towel slightly with a non-abrasive glass cleaner.** Don't spray the glass directly and don't use too much liquid. You don't want it to seep into the scanner.

   Avoid cleaners with abrasives in them because these chemicals may permanently damage the glass. We recommend Windex or a similar product.

4. **Keep the lid open until the glass dries.**

If you recently bought your scanner and you have an older computer, it's possible the USB ports aren't compatible. Check the ratings. A USB 2.0 scanner should plug into a USB 2.0 port; anything less means that the scanner will send information faster than the computer port can accept it. What can you do, short of buying a new computer? Ask the service department or a knowledgeable sales person what you should do.

# Tuning Up TVs

Television technology leaped from vacuum tubes (that could be replaced) to digital models with solid-state electronic components, hand-held remote controls, on-screen commands, enormous flat screens, picture-upon-picture capabilities, and the capability of projecting surround sound through multiple speakers. Now viewing a movie at home is almost as good as going to a top-of-the-line theater. And often better because you don't have to pay for wallet-shrinking tickets and those price-gouging snacks.

The downside: TVs are so high tech nowadays that most problems need to be addressed by a trained technician. A TV set will give you years of trouble-free service. Nevertheless, you might find yourself shopping for a new TV in a couple of years, just to keep up with technology. And if you're thinking of getting a 42-inch (the most popular size) flat-screen TV, put it off. The prices are expected to drop drastically.

In this section, we give you a few tips to try before you haul that TV in to the service center or plunk down the money for a new one. To troubleshoot your TV:

✔ Start out by making sure the power is on.

✔ Check for loose connections and damaged cords.

✔ Get out your owner's manual and make certain the controls are set properly. Reset them just to be sure.

- If you have cable or satellite service, turn on the other televisions in your home to find out whether they are working or have a similar problem.

- Change channels; it may be the TV station that's having trouble, not your TV.

- Go next door. If the cable provider has a problem, you can almost bet that it's affecting your neighbors too, unless they have a satellite dish. If the cable line from the street to your house is faulty, however, that will affect only you. If it's a line problem, call the cable company for service.

- If a heavy storm provided fireworks recently, a power surge may have caused a component to fail. Surges, however, usually fry the whole set — as well as the other TVs and computers in your home. Shock, vibration, and heat can burn out electronic devices that were plugged in during the storm. If a power surge is the culprit, plan on getting a new TV.

- Adjust the controls to reset the color, brightness, and sound. Also see if the remote is set for surround sound. Our minimally equipped TV mutilates voices when surround sound is set.

- If you see colored blotches within an image it could be that one of your loudspeakers is too close to the TV. If you see distortion, move the speakers. Even though TVs do have a built-in degaussing coil to remove distortion caused by a magnetized picture tube, this applies to cathode ray tube only, not flat screens. The metal parts in the set or the picture tube can be magnetized by the speaker. To demagnetize the set, turn it on and off several times within a 30-minute period. Also, move the speakers.

---

# Dissecting digital television

If you really want flat or plasma screen digital television (and so many of us do these days), think twice. The technology is still so new that the prices are high. Even worse, some blow out after only a few months of operation because the manufacturing bugs haven't yet been worked out. We recommend that you wait until prices drop by nearly 50 percent of what they were when this was first published. Even if you aren't in the market for a flat-screen TV, you'll eventually be tempted to get one because we're on the verge of a quantum leap forward technologically. The transition to DTV "digital television" service with all-digital channels is currently scheduled for the end of 2006, subject to periodic review and depending on DTV availability. When the conversion takes place, the analog TVs in your home today won't be able to receive any of the digital channels unless you purchase a converter for each set. With a converter you'll see clear pictures without the "ghosts" and interference characteristic of analog transmission. But they won't have the higher DTV picture quality. To receive that benefit you'll need a new digital television set. It will be just like the early days of television when everyone who wanted to see all the new ultra-high frequency (UHF) channels had to purchase a special antenna. Only now the magic letters are HDTV, not UHF.

To be able to isolate problems — such as a blank screen — not being caused by external controlling devices, first check all the controls. That means on the CD/DVD/VCR players and anything else hooked up to your TV.

A television set typically lasts from 5 to 8 years. Just hope that your set lasts long enough that the prices on flat-screen, HDTV-quality sets come down enough that you don't have to break the bank account to get one.

## Using Satellite Dishes

You get hundreds of channels with a satellite dish, but there are problems, too. Satellite servers are sensitive to heavy weather — rain, ice, and snow. The best way to make sure your signals and favorite programs aren't interrupted or interfered with is to get a cover for the dish. Then snow and ice won't affect reception. The cover also reduces rain fade, but you'll still have to put up with rain interference. If you suspect that something else's signal is affecting the quality of your programs, call the satellite company for service.

## Adjusting CD, DVD, and VCR Players

CD, DVD, and VCR players let you know right away when they need attention. Although relatively trouble free, when these electronic devices get dirty, they won't play at all or the picture on the television screen looks fuzzy. On rare occasions, a power cord, belt, or tray must be replaced. Here are a few quick fixes:

- ✓ **If the device doesn't work, make sure that the power cord is plugged in and that the fuse or circuit breaker hasn't tripped.** If devices are also plugged into a remote power strip that has a circuit breaker, check the reset control. Look at the connections between the device and the speakers or television set. Then inspect the cord and on-off switch for damage and if you see any, replace them following the directions in Chapter 11. Also look at Chapter 7 for minor electrical repairs.

- ✓ **If the DVD player gives you a picture but you can't hear anything, check connections and settings on your TV set.**

- ✓ **If the disk skips or sounds scratchy, it needs to be cleaned.**

- ✓ **If the slide-out tray doesn't work, clean the disk.** Then get out your owner's manual and follow instructions. Replacement parts are usually available from the manufacturer or at an electronics center. If you have a multi-disk player, see if one of the disks is jammed. If the tray attempts to eject but doesn't, remove the cover and see that the disk is in place and not blocking the tray.

If you're getting constant dirty disk errors on your DVD player, put in a different disk. If that one works, the first disk is the problem. Clean it with a soft, lint-free cloth slightly dampened with a few drops of isopropyl (rubbing) alcohol. You particularly need to clean the disk if you borrowed it from a library or video store. They don't have time to inspect each disk when it's returned and clean it if needed.

If the drive still doesn't work, you may have a faulty player or the drive may need cleaning. Always try cleaning the disk first before you focus on the player.

## Unjamming drives and trays

Unless your home has air purifiers, the dust raised by you and your children and pets gravitates to everything that's plugged in. Look at the TV a few days after you dust it; it's coated again. CD and DVD players attract just as much dust as televisions, which can affect the trays and rails that move disks back and forth. Once the cover is off, you can blow air into the player to remove the dust. Follow the steps below. You need a screwdriver and canned air, a blow dryer, or a vacuum cleaner attachment. Here's what to do:

1. **Unplug the disk player.**

2. **Take out the screws securing the cover and remove it.** If it won't come off, look for clips or more screws along the cover's rear and bottom perimeter and take them out. Be careful here. You may see some screws on the underside, but they may be securing working parts of the mechanism. Don't unscrew them.

3. **Blow air into the mechanism to remove dust.**

4. **Plug the player back in.**

5. **Try ejecting the tray.**

6. **If it doesn't eject, look for something jamming the tray.** Most of time you'll find a foreign object in it, such as a paper clip or pin.

7. **Also see if the belt is damaged or broken, or fell off.** You can try to put the belt back on if it fell off, but if it's damaged or broken, it has to be replaced. Take the player in for service.

8. **If the tray chatters as it tries to come out, look it over to see if there's anything obvious blocking it.** But most of time you'll have to take it in for service.

   Always wash your hands to remove oils before wiping a belt or the drive. An oily fingerprint will affect how well the player works. If you touch the parts accidentally, leaving a fingerprint, clean it off with rubbing alcohol.

9. **Reassemble the player.**

## Cleaning the laser lens

CD and DVD players need to be cleaned periodically, just as VCRs do. And the disk you want to play needs to be cleaned more frequently, too. See the section "Keeping your DVDs and CDs squeaky clean." In this section, we tell you what you have to do when the laser lens gets dirty. Occasionally unscrew the case of your DVD or CD player so you can get at the lens to clean it. You need a screwdriver, canned air or a soft brush, a foam swab or camera-lens cleaner, and lens cleaning fluid from a camera store. Here's what to do:

1. **Remove the top cover screws. (Follow the steps in "Unjamming drives and trays.")** If the cover wraps around the unit, there may be more screws to take off. See Figure 12-5.

2. **Blow off the dust with canned air or a hair dryer set on cool.**

3. **Dampen a foam or lint-free swab with a few drops of lens cleaner.** You don't need a lot, just a couple drops.

4. **Reassemble the cover and put the screws back in.**

Laser lens

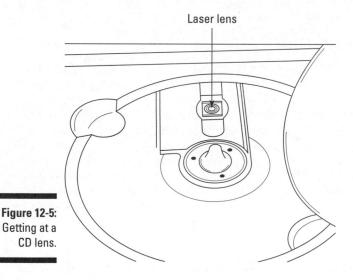

**Figure 12-5:**
Getting at a
CD lens.

## Keeping your DVDs and CDs squeaky clean

Don't blame your CD or DVD player every time your music or favorite movie starts skipping or refuses to play. The disk may be dirty or scratched. You can purchase a cleaning kit at an electronics store, but rubbing alcohol is a lot cheaper and you can get it at the grocery store or pharmacy. If the problem is dirt or dust, here are some tips for keeping your disks in top condition:

- ✔ When you select a disk to play, the first thing you should do — every single time — is blow dust off even if you faithfully keep your disks in their sleeves.

- ✔ Next wipe your disks with a lint-free cloth dampened slightly in rubbing alcohol *every time you use them.* They not only accumulate dust, but also oily fingerprints that make dust stick.

- ✔ Put your fingers only on the edge and through the center hole.

And if your favorite disk is scratched, before throwing it out, try polishing it to remove the scratch. Disk repair kits are sold at electronics stores and some video stores.

It's the bottom of the disk, the unadorned side, that the laser reads. That's the side you need to clean.

## Cleaning VCRs

Video cassette recorders don't like dirt and dust. You should keep a head-cleaning tape right next to your old movies. Not long ago, our VCR seemed to be totally dead and it was some time before we realized we hadn't cleaned it for a long time. Because we had nothing to lose, we gave cleaning a try. And to our amazement, one swish was all it took to rejuvenate the old device. If you get interference on a VCR and you *have* cleaned it recently, it may be coming from an appliance or power tool being used. Transformers in doorbells also cause interference. If that's the cause, refer to Chapter 7. Another culprit to focus on is the signal from your cable company. Put on your sleuth's hat. And don't forget, Sherlock, el-cheapo dimmer switches introduce noise on the power lines too. The trick is to buy dimmers that have noise suppressers.

# Troubleshooting Phones and Phone Lines

If you still have wired telephone service, you know that very little goes wrong with house phones. It takes a storm or ice on the lines to cause most problems, unless you spill a drink on the jack and short it out. You probably also know that telephone companies no longer come into your home for repairs. They're responsible for the outside lines and service to the house. Indoors, like it or not, repairs are up to you. Or you can call for service. Look in the Yellow Pages under "Telephone Equipment and Systems — Services and Repair."

## Fixing house lines

When the house phone is out of service, you can think of a dozen calls that have to be made right now — phoning for a doctor or dentist appointment, getting online (when you have a dial-up Internet provider), calling the school or a member of the family. But you're stuck because you're not quite sure who to call and if they will do anything.

The quickest and easiest way to figure out why your phone is giving you trouble and where the problem is, is to go outdoors to the telephone access service box. It's usually a gray plastic box mounted on the side of the house. You'll see two doors on the box, one of them labeled "customer access door." The other door is locked and used only by service providers. You can't fix outside lines, and finding a problem indoors isn't easy. But you can figure out where the problem is located. Take a flat blade and a Phillips screwdriver, just so you don't have to make another trip if you brought the wrong one, and two house phones. Here's what to do:

1. **Depending on the type of screw, remove it with one of the screwdrivers.**

2. **Open the door.**

3. **Inside you'll see a cord with a modular plug that looks just like the plug you put into a jack in various rooms in the house. It's on the line connected to the receiver.**

4. **Unplug that small cord.**

5. **Plug one of the phones you brought with you into the jack.**

6. **If you don't hear anything, plug the other phone into the jack.**

If you now hear a dial tone on one phone, but not the other, it means something is wrong with the phone. If you hear a dial tone on either or both of the phones, that means that the trouble is inside the house, not outdoors. It could be in the wiring, a faulty jack, a broken wire at a connection point, wiring in the wall that a mouse may have chewed, a water problem, or something else.

It won't be easy for you to find the problem. But if you pay monthly for "Linebacker Service" (check your phone bill), call the company that sends you the bill. They'll send someone out to find and fix the problem. Otherwise you have to schedule an independent contractor to come in.

If you don't hear a dial tone on either telephone, then the problem originates outdoors. There may be something wrong with the phone line to your house or on the street, downed wires at a nearby intersection, or a tree on a line. You should call your service provider, anyway. Although they won't send someone out, because telephone lines are not their problem, they'll contact the company that fixes and maintains them. That work is entirely outdoors on the lines or at the telephone access service box.

You should always be able to hear a dial tone in the telephone access service box. If you do, you know you've got an in-house problem.

When you want to clean your phone use rubbing alcohol or spray some electrical contact cleaner on it. Go to an electronics store to get the contact cleaner. Not long ago you could dismantle receivers to clean them. Now they're sealed. If you have recurring problems with the phone itself, from crackling to cracking, get a new phone. They're inexpensive.

## Fixing cordless phones

Cordless phones also connect to the house phone lines. The base plugs into the wall jack and an electrical outlet. The phone receives signals transmitted through the line, and then turns them into radio waves that are picked up by the freestanding handset. Handset batteries are recharged whenever the handset rests on the base.

If the cordless phone doesn't work right the batteries are probably bad. Sometimes the phone's not plugged in completely. So check the connections. If you replace the battery, be sure the one you buy is an exact match. When you plug the new battery into the receiver, make sure it snaps in. If you don't hear a snap, it's probably not in all the way. Also make sure the charger or base is working. It should have a constant light on when it is. Check the outlet you have the phone plugged into. Someone might have pulled it out, or if it's in a power strip, shut it off. Clean the contacts on the bottom of the phone and on the charger. Use an electronic contact cleaner or rubbing alcohol. And if you always hear crackles and noise, get another phone from a discount store. You can get one for less than $20.

# Chapter 13

# Rescuing Your Favorite Furnishings

*W*hen chair legs wiggle, expensive storage units and tables exhibit nicks, scratches, dents, or stains, or a thin layer of veneer lifts or cracks, you don't have to throw it out and replace it. Nor do you always have to find someone to handle the repairs. Before searching the Yellow Pages, use this chapter to find out whether the repair is a job that you can handle yourself.

In this chapter, we go over some simple ways to restore your furniture, even those things that you never dreamed you could fix. We tell you what the typical problems are and how to repair them.

This chapter also tells you what tools and supplies you need in order to work on the piece. Have them handy before you start the repair. That way, you can work without interruptions — assuming the telephone or doorbell doesn't ring or your children don't come up to you saying, "I'm hungry!"

## Tightening Loose Chair and Table Legs

When a chair or table starts wiggling, the first thing you need to do is figure out why the leg is loose. Think about what happens to a chair when we want to sit at the table. First, we pull out the chair, and then we sit and slide the chair closer to the table. Inevitably, we shift our weight trying to get a little more comfortable. All this moving around wreaks havoc on chairs. And remember that all furniture gets stressed when you rearrange a room or move into a new apartment or home.

The most common reasons for wobbly legs are loose or stripped screws and loose wing nuts in corner braces. In some cases, a dowel rod may be loose. Dowels are also used to stabilize furniture legs. They're fitted into holes in the legs and glued in place. But over time, the glue loses its grip because of stress or because it dries out and cracks.

The easiest repair is to refasten the screws and wing nuts on braced corners, but you can also fix loose dowel rods. We show you how in the following sections.

When repairing furniture, you can often come up with several approaches. Always start with the method that is totally reversible so that if it doesn't work you can go right back to where you started. If the first remedy doesn't work, then progress to another method of repairing your furnishings. In some instances, you may even find a third method of repair, but save it for last when it involves a bit more work, different supplies, or a little more risk if you aren't careful about what you're doing.

## Troubleshooting wood and metal corner bracings

Furniture made today is often braced (to stabilize it). If the piece has wood panels (aprons) between each leg, you'll find corner bracings on the underside. The braces form a triangle in each corner where the aprons join the legs. Screws are inserted through the brace and into the panels. For additional security, a metal brace might be bolted to the leg itself. See Figure 13-1 for examples.

**Figure 13-1:**
Two different corner braces: (A) wood brace (B) metal brace fastened with a wing nut.

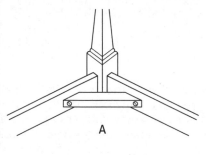
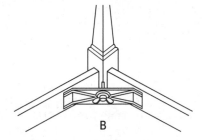

A          B

### Adjusting loose screws

Don't be intimidated by a loose leg. When you realize a chair or table has a loose leg, follow Steps 1 and 2 in the following numbered list. Usually that's all you have to do, so don't procrastinate. The faster you get to the repair, the better, because if you wait, the loose fastener can cause more damage. So get out your Phillips screwdrivers. (Phillips screws are widely used on furniture with the exception of furniture in build-it-yourself kits.)

When tightening the screws doesn't fix the problem, it's very likely the loose screw has gouged a bigger hole in the wood or the metal threads are stripped. Don't fret. It's still fixable. You just have a little more work.

To refasten screws or wing nuts, you need a screwdriver or small pliers. If you find the hole is larger than it should be, you also need toothpicks or wooden kitchen matches, carpenter's glue, and a utility knife. Here's how to fix the fastener:

1. **Take the chair and turn it upside down.**

2. **Using a screwdriver or small pliers, tighten the screw or wing nut.** If the leg still feels loose, go to Steps 3 through 7. If not, you're done already!

3. **Fill the hole with glue.**

4. **Insert toothpicks into the hole until no more will go in.**

5. **Cut off the protruding tips of the toothpicks with a utility knife.**

6. **Drill a pilot hole into the toothpicks using a bit smaller than the screw.** It doesn't matter whether the glue is wet or dry.

7. **Reinsert the screw and tighten it with a screwdriver.**

### Replacing wood braces

Occasionally, you may need to replace a wood brace. Over time, wood dries out and shrinks, and the fittings no longer match up as they did originally. When that happens, the stress of people sitting on the chair and shifting their weight can cause the screws to gouge holes in the brace. You need a block of wood for each brace that has a gouged-out hole, a saw, a drill and bit, and the original or similar replacement screws. Here's how to put in a new wood brace:

1. **Get a block of oak or maple hardwood (not pine) that's similar in size to the old brace, but slightly larger.** You can find scrap hardwood at lumberyards or home improvement stores. (You may need to purchase a bag of scraps, but the cost will be miniscule compared to the price of a new chair.)

2. **Using the original brace as a pattern and making certain the grain of the wood runs horizontally across the wedge, cut off the two top corners at an angle.** Refer to Figure 13-1 for an example.

3. **Cut the rest of the brace, making it slightly larger than the original piece of wood.**

The original brace has long dried out and is probably smaller than it should be.

When you're finished, the new block should look like a trapezoid and fit snugly into the corner.

4. **Drill pilot holes in the wood block where you will later screw the block into the frame.**

5. **Glue the new wood brace to the wood frame of the chair or table.**

6. **When the glue dries, drill holes through the brace using a drill bit slightly smaller than the screws.**

7. **Screw each end of the brace into the frame.**

## Regluing dowel rods

Some chairs and tables are fitted together with a piece of wood (dowel rod) that runs from one leg to another. The dowels are glued into holes cut into the legs. (See Figure 13-2 for an example.) When a dowel rod becomes loose, you can't simply take it out and reglue it. If you remove just one dowel, you risk splitting or cracking the others. It's better to take all the joints apart and glue them at the same time. You need clear furniture glue and clamps. You can use C-clamps, a length of rope or clothesline, or ratchet straps. We like ratchet straps because the 1-inch wide band made of nylon webbing doesn't damage furniture. For more information about clamps, go to Chapter 2. Here's how to repair a dowel rod:

1. **Disassemble the legs by gently twisting the dowel back and forth to break the bond of the old glue.** Make sure you carefully inspect each joint first, looking for nails and screws that may have been used to reinforce the joint. They may be hidden on the underside or backside of the piece. Sometimes they're deliberately hidden by being countersunk below the surface of the leg. When a nail or screw is countersunk, the assembler usually fills the hole with a wood or plastic patch matched to the finish of the piece. Look for a slight roughness in the finish where the hole has been patched.

If the dowel shows any damage at all, replace it.

2. **Using hot water or vinegar, remove the old glue.** Yes, all of the glue must be removed before you reglue the pieces in place. If any residue is left, it will weaken the bonding qualities and effectiveness of the new glue.

You can use a wood *rasp* (a coarse metal file) or medium grade sandpaper to remove glue, but that is more risky because it's easy to scratch the wood finish. Then you end up with a second repair job on your hands.

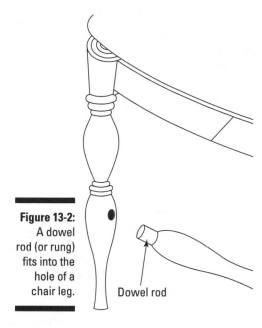

**Figure 13-2:**
A dowel rod (or rung) fits into the hole of a chair leg.

Dowel rod

Vinegar and hot water soften old glue so either can be used to take the legs and dowels apart and to remove all traces of glue on individual pieces and in the holes.

3. **When you're ready to reglue, squirt the glue into the hole and spread it around to make sure it coats all surfaces.**

When you're purchasing glue, look for one that is clear or invisible after it dries. Two-part epoxy glue is exceptionally strong and the best product for gluing dowels. However, it sets up unexpectedly and sometimes exceptionally fast. And after it sets, you can't break it loose because the glue is stronger than the wood. Beginners who want to use epoxy should purchase only "extended-working-time" epoxy. For more information on glue, see the sidebar "Sticky business: Choosing the right glue."

4. **Place more glue on the tips of the dowels, again making sure that all surfaces are well coated.** You get a stronger bond if both the tip of the dowel and the hole you place it in are completely coated with glue. Use a toothpick or small screwdriver to spread it around. Another way to make sure everything's evenly coated is to insert the dowel into the hole and rotate it gently.

5. **Push the dowel securely into place.**

6. **Repeat the process as necessary until all the dowels have been glued.**

7. **Apply pressure to the joints until the glue dries.** You can do this with bar or C-clamps if you have them, but you can achieve the same result with inexpensive ratchet straps or by wrapping a length of clothesline or

rope around the legs and tying the parts together. For more information on bars and C-clamps, see Chapter 2.

8. **Wrap the clothesline twice around and between each pair of legs and then tie a knot in the rope.** (See Figure 13-3 for an example.)

9. **Insert a stick between the two pieces of rope that stretch from one leg to another.**

10. **Twist the stick to tighten the ropes, gently increasing the pressure until the ropes are taut.**

Before you twist the rope, put a piece of cardboard under it and around each leg to avoid damaging the wood finish.

**Figure 13-3:** Using a rope (A) or ratchet strap (B) to maintain pressure while the glue dries.

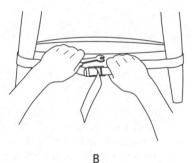

A                                                    B

## *Filling enlarged holes*

Wood dries out and shrinks with age. If your dowel is now too small for its hole, wind cotton or linen thread around the tip of the dowel to make it thicker. Then coat the wood and thread with glue, and finish reassembling by following Steps 4 through 9 in the previous section.

Another way to fit a shrunken dowel into the hole is with a shim. A *shim* is a tapered piece of wood that carpenters and woodworkers use to fill spaces. Shims can be purchased where wood is sold. If you want to use a shim, look for a small shim no wider than the tip of the dowel. Now follow these steps:

1. **Cut a small slit in the end of the dowel with a sharp utility knife.** Try to center the cut so that each side will be equal in size and strength.

## Sticky business: Choosing the right glue

Many glue products are available today, each stronger than the glue you find on old furniture and each with its own qualities. Read the labels to find out which glue is right for your project. A rule of thumb to guide you is that if wood joints are snug fitting, carpenter's glue will work. If they're loose, use epoxy.

✔ White glue (polyvinyl acetate), usually available in squeeze bottles, forms moderately strong bonds that can be washed away. It dries in one hour and takes three to six to cure.

✔ Carpenter's glue is an all-purpose yellow glue — it also comes in "dark" for older or darker stained furniture. It has more strength than white glue, but can be reversed with warm water. It dries in one hour and takes three to six to cure.

✔ Hide glue is water-soluble, sets up slowly, and is extremely strong, but reversible. It's good for veneering and can be reactivated with steam. Takes 24 hours to cure.

✔ Resorcinol, a two-part glue, forms excellent bonds. It requires ten hours and at least 70-degree heat to cure.

✔ Epoxy comes with two parts to mix. Excellent bonding on nonporous materials and for wood that has wobbled out, such as dowels; resists water and chemicals, but sets up extremely fast. Beginners should only use epoxy that has an extended working time.

✔ Contact adhesive is good for laminated materials. Applied to both pieces, they must dry before fastening. Accuracy is essential — there are no second chances.

2. **Carefully slip the small shim into the slit, the pointed edge first.**

3. **Gently push it in so that it expands both sides of the tip.** Don't worry if a little of the thick edge of the shim protrudes from the dowel. (Too much wedge sticking out, however, will prevent the dowel from fitting in all the way.) When you insert the dowel into the leg, the shim will continue to work its way down into the tip.

Toothpicks and wooden matches with the heads broken off can also be used as shims.

4. **Insert the dowel tip into the hole in the leg and tap it gently into place.** See Figure 13-4 for an example. The dowel should now fit tightly.

Never use too much force in getting the shim into the end of the dowel and don't use a shim that is too large. If you do, you can easily crack the wooden tip. Yes, you can glue the pieces back together, but the joint will be weak unless you use epoxy glue.

5. **Remove the dowel and shim.** If the dowel isn't tight when tapped in (step 4), that means the shim is sticking out too far and bottoming in the hole before the dowel gets tight. If that happens you can trim a little off the blunt end of the shim.

6. **Glue all surfaces of the tip and the hole, and then follow Steps 2 through 9 under "Regluing dowel rods."**

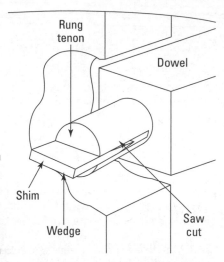

**Figure 13-4:**
Using a
shim to
enlarge the
dowel tip.

Putting pressure on the joint strengthens the glued bond. But don't apply too much pressure, because you don't want all the glue to seep out. That weakens the joint. Too little pressure also results in a weak joint, because the glue isn't as effective. If you wind up with a weak joint, you may have to disassemble the pieces and reglue everything. Read the package directions to determine just how much force to use.

## Adding screws and nails

If, after you've glued the dowels into place, you're still uncomfortable about the joint's strength, you can use small nails or screws to reinforce it. The trick here is to place them through the dowel and leg joint in an inconspicuous position; the backside or underside of the furniture works best. For an example, see Figure 13-5. You need a drill, screwdriver, and/or a hammer. Here's how to add screws and nails:

1. **After the glue has dried, drill a small hole at an angle through the dowel and into the leg.** The glue must be dry so the pieces don't move around; if they do, the wood may crack or split.

2. **After the nail or screw is flush with the surface of the leg, *countersink* it (which means driving the head of the screw below the surface of the leg).**

    Place a nail or screw that's the same size as the head of the nail on it and tap it with a hammer. That will drive the nail further down.

3. **Fill in the indentation with plastic wood or a wood patch in the same color and shade as the chair's finish to make the depression undetectable.**

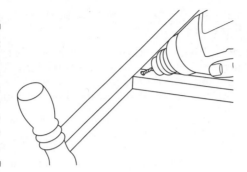

**Figure 13-5:**
Inserting a
screw at an
angle
through the
dowel rod to
secure the
chair leg.

## What to do with wicker

Wicker gets brittle after time and pieces may break and split. But they can be glued and tucked underneath wrapped sections of the frame to prevent further damage. When the wrapping itself starts drooping, spread glue all around the leg or frame, and then rewrap the flat wicker around it. The glue will not, however, hold the end down. You have to tuck that edge under the last bit of wrapping and if any excess protrudes, cut it off with scissors or a utility knife.

Don't try to nail or staple wicker to the frame. Because of its brittleness, wicker will only split and crack more, causing more damage.

Recaning wicker mesh in wood-framed furniture requires a special approach. For information on how to repair this type of furniture, see the section "Recaning Chairs" at the end of this chapter.

# Mending Furniture Boo-Boos: Nicks, Scratches, and Burns

Accidents happen even when you think you're being careful. It's inevitable that some of your furnishings and decorative objects will be marred by a scratch, bump, or scrape. Or perhaps you have a family heirloom that's in beautiful shape, except for a cigarette burn. People like antique and distressed furniture, but that doesn't mean you have to put up with eye-catching flaws — especially when they can easily be made invisible.

## Removing cigarette burns in wood

Getting rid of unsightly cigarette burns is a snap. All you need is nail polish remover, clear nail polish, a cotton swab, and a small knife. Here's what to do:

1. **Place a little nail polish remover on the swab and rub it into the burn mark until the discoloration disappears.**

2. **If you still have a dark residue around the edges, scrape it gently with a small knife until it's gone. You can stop here if it is.** If the burn is deeper than you thought and has actually gone into the surface of the furniture, you need to fill it. We show you how in Steps 3 through 5.

3. **Mix ¼ teaspoon each of nail polisher remover and clear nail polish in a shallow container.** Use a tuna or cat-food can, or a frozen potpie dish. Or make a container with a 2- or 3-inch strip of aluminum foil. Fold it in half. Next fold or roll the edges to create a shallow depression in the center. When you finish the repairs, just throw it out.

4. **Test the mixture on a finished underside of the piece.** Nail polish will curdle some lacquer or enamel finishes making them rough or milky, especially old varnished pieces. If that happens, use polyurethane instead.

   If you have polyurethane in the house, you can substitute it for nail polish to fill burns on any wood furniture. Apply it with a small brush or put a drop on your finger and transfer it to the hole. We've also used medical syringes to add drops of polyurethane. They're also great for getting glue into tight spaces.

5. **Apply coats of the mixture with a nail polish brush one at a time to the damaged area.** Let each coat dry before applying another layer. You may have to repeat this step eight or ten times before you've filled in the hole.

## Concealing dents, scratches, and gouges

The easiest way to hide a short or narrow scratch is to purchase a furniture touch-up stick at your hardware, paint, or home supply store. (They look like fat felt-tip markers and can usually be found hanging on a display rack.) Get a shade that matches or is darker than your furniture, and follow package directions. One or two swipes of the cover-up, rubbed across the scratch, not along the length, should hide the scratch. Let one coat dry before you apply another.

When faced with deeper scratches, you can fill the area with melted crayon wax. Select a crayon close to or slightly darker than the finish of your furniture. Or purchase a product such as Formby's Furniture Repair Kit, which has 20 hot-melt sticks in various colors that can be matched to the wood. Here's what you do:

1. **Melt the wax with a safety match and let it drip into the marred area.** Don't worry about dripping wax outside the scratched area. You'll scrape it off in the next step.

2. **When the wax is dry, smooth the surface by scraping off the excess with a stiff plastic card: Membership cards and credit cards are perfect for this.**

The imperfection should now be undetectable.

## Hiding chipped edges

You can treat chipped edges on furniture and decorative objects with melted crayon wax. For this project, you need masking tape, a crayon that matches the finish on your furniture, a candle, matches, and a smooth-shanked nail or screwdriver. Here's what to do:

1. **Tape around and underneath the edges of the chipped area with masking tape.**

2. **Tilt the piece up if you can, so that the chip is facing up. This keeps the melted wax from spreading too far.**

3. **Melt a brown crayon that matches the finish of the wood onto the chipped edge.** Heat the wax with a long safety match or a small candle.

4. **After the wax hardens thoroughly, remove the tape.**

5. **Using another safety match, heat a small, round piece of metal such as the shank of a small screwdriver or a nail.**

6. **Roll the screwdriver or nail around on the patch to make it smooth and round off the edges, or use the head of a common nail to form and shape.**

If necessary, repeat Steps 5 and 6 several times.

Don't worry about making mistakes. You can always scrape off all the wax and go through the whole process again.

If you use a nail, be sure to hold the shank with a potholder or thick cloth, so you don't burn yourself. Metal is a good conductor of heat and the nail shank will get just as hot as the head.

## Removing stains and water marks

You don't have to panic when a steaming cup of coffee, sloshed water, or some other liquid leaves a mark on your wood furniture. Most of the time, getting the piece back to its original condition is fairly easy. The first thing you have to do is determine how deep the damage is. You can tell that by the color of the stain or water mark.

Stains and marks made by liquid or steam are usually white or light-colored. That means that they haven't penetrated much more deeply than through the waxed or polished surface. When the stain is dark, however, it indicates that the liquid has penetrated through the finish on the wood and possibly through to the wood itself. If this is the case, you have more of a fix on your hands.

### Hiding light-colored stains and rings

Here are some ways to treat light-colored stains. Start with the first and if it doesn't work, then try the next step:

1. **Rub the area with an oily furniture polish, mayonnaise, or petroleum jelly.** The goal is to displace the water mark with the oil. If the stain disappears, good. Skip to Step 6. If the stain is still there, try Step 2.

2. **If rubbing the area with an oily substance doesn't work, put a little toothpaste on a wet cloth and rub the stain gently until the spot disappears.** Toothpaste sometimes contains a mild abrasive that will help get rid of the stain. If toothpaste does the job, skip to Step 6.

3. **If the stain is still there, mix equal amounts of baking soda and toothpaste together to make a slightly stronger, yet still mild, abrasive and rub that mixture on the stain.** Depending on the size of the stain, ¼ or ½ teaspoon of each should do the trick. Apply a little more pressure than you did in Step 2. If the stain is gone, go to Step 6; otherwise proceed with Steps 4 and 5 for stubborn water marks.

4. **Thoroughly clean the area.**

5. **Rub a mild solvent on the stain like so:** Dip a soft cloth — an old T-shirt will do — into a mild solvent such as mineral spirits or paint thinner (odorless). Squeeze excess moisture from the cloth, and then rub gently until the stain is gone.

   To make sure you won't harm the surface, pretest the solvent on a finished underside of the furniture first. If the solvent doesn't dissolve your finish, then it's safe to work on the stain itself. If it does dissolve the finish, you'll have to try another product.

6. **After the water mark is gone, wax your table, chest, or chair.** Use a thin layer of paste wax and a clean, soft cloth. Although paste wax takes a little more work to apply, it leaves a nicer, longer-lasting finish than a liquid or cream wax.

7. **After the paste wax thoroughly dries — give it half an hour — buff the piece with another soft, clean cloth until you have a rich, smooth patina.**

You'll love how it looks.

### Removing dark or black stains

When liquid penetrates through wax and polish and gets into the finish (varnish, lacquer, or shellac) or even down to the wood itself, there may be tiny cracks in the wood. To reach them, you must strip the stained area of finish by using furniture stripper, oxalic acid crystals, or a two-step wood bleach or liquid laundry bleach. You also need to refinish the piece with varnish, lacquer, shellac, or urethane. (See the "Refinishing that furniture when you're finished" sidebar.) And if, when you strip off the finish, you get down to bare wood, so you need to restain it with a matching wood stain.

Oxalic acid comes in crystals and can be purchased at paint stores and some pharmacies. Here's what you have to do to remove the stain with oxalic acid:

1. **Melt the oxalic crystals in hot water.**

2. **While the water is still hot, place the oxalic acid on the surface of the furniture.**

3. **Let the liquid dry until it looks powdery.**

4. **Rinse the area thoroughly with clear water.**

5. **Repeat Steps 2 and 3 if the dark stain hasn't disappeared. If it has, go to Step 6.** Just be sure to rinse the area thoroughly between applications to get all of the dried crystals off the surface.

6. **Apply the finishing coat: varnish, lacquer, shellac, or polyurethane.**

A two-step wood bleach or liquid laundry bleach will also remove the stain. (Laundry bleach is weaker than either oxalic acid or a two-step wood bleach and, therefore, may have to be applied several times. It can be effective, however, if you only want to work only in a small area.)

If you got down to bare wood when you tried to remove the finish, you must restain the piece after removing the original stain. Here's how to do it:

1. **Lightly sand the surface with fine sandpaper.**

2. **Wipe the surface with a tack-cloth to clean up all loose particles.** You can purchase tack-cloths at stores that sell paint, hardware, or do-it-yourself supplies.

3. **Apply a light coat of stain that matches the stain on your furniture.** Let it dry. If the color doesn't match the furniture, repeat the steps until the color looks right.

Be sure to use the tacky cloth every time you sand the piece and before applying another coat of stain or finish. If all small particles haven't been removed, the surface will be marred and you'll be able to feel small bumps after the finish dries.

## Refinishing that furniture when you're finished

Varnish, lacquer, shellac, or impenetrable polyurethane can be used to finish furniture. With polyurethane, however, you won't have to worry about future stains or water marks marring the piece. That's a plus when you have children who rarely think twice about setting wet cloths, towels, and clothes on wood surfaces or wiping up spills and splashes. And polyurethane is a good choice in heavy-duty areas such as a family or great room where people watch TV and movies while snacking and drinking.

# Rejuvenating Veneer

Like icing on a cake, veneer is what makes furniture attractive. A thin sheet of wood applied to the frame and panels of most furniture, it comes from top quality hardwood that looks elegant when it's stained and finished. The framework or furniture casing and panels are usually made from inferior wood, plywood, laminated board, or fiberboard.

Veneer is glued onto the surface of furniture after the framework and panels have been built. Sometimes, the glue comes loose and the veneer blisters or the edges loosen and lift up. It's relatively easy to reattach the glued area, but you must work carefully so you don't split or crack the veneer. We go over how to do this in the following sections.

## Venerable veneer

Early Egyptians and Romans decorated objects with veneer, but the fashion waned by the early Middle Ages. Then in the seventeenth and eighteenth centuries, European cabinetmakers realized that the beautiful graining exposed by thin-cut veneer made furniture look elegant. Veneer exposes the most attractive qualities of hardwood, especially if it is cut crosswise, which displays the beautiful grain found in top quality hardwood. Veneer is sliced from the trunks of slow-growing trees that take decades to fully mature. Because the supply of hardwood is limited, especially in the United States and Western Europe where most of the primary growth forests have been fully harvested, the wood is expensive. Furniture makers get more use from a tree if it's sliced into veneer. By using veneer they also can make the furniture frame out of a more stable product than solid wood, which expands, contracts, and becomes brittle if exposed to excessive moisture. Veneer can be sawed, machine-cut, or peeled by machine. Saw-cut veneer is the best, but it's very expensive because much more wood is wasted. Most furniture sold today displays machine-cut veneer.

## Securing lifted edges

When an edge lifts, you can fix it by using a metal emery board and white glue that dries invisibly. You'll also need a thin-bladed knife, a piece of wire or a single-edge razor blade, clean soft cloths to wipe up excess glue, and weights. Heavy books will do. Here's what to do:

1. **Use a metal emery board or your fingernail to lift the veneer just enough so that you can get under it to scratch out as much of the old glue as possible.** See Figure 13-6 as an example. Be extremely careful not to pull the piece up too high or you may crack or break the veneer.

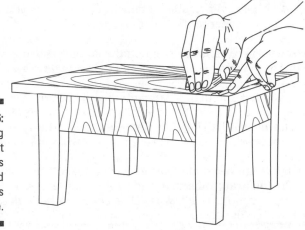

**Figure 13-6:** Regluing veneer that has separated from its frame.

2. **Blow between the surface of the frame and the veneer to remove dried glue dust or flakes.**

3. **Put some glue on a thin knife blade, a thin piece of wire, or the edge of a single-edge razor blade.**

4. **Lift the veneer again and slip the utensil and glue underneath it. Then smear it around.** You want to coat the underside of the veneer, as well as the furniture frame. If you use white glue, it will dry invisibly.

5. **Push down on the veneer to evenly coat the frame.**

6. **Lift and press the veneer down gently several times so the glue coats all surfaces.**

7. **Press the veneer down hard and weight it with a pile of books.**

Don't forget to wipe away excess glue that bleeds out from between the two surfaces. You want to clean it up before it dries. If you're not sure you got it all off, dampen a cloth and wash the surface, then wipe it dry.

## Squashing surface blisters in veneer

You may be able to squash a veneer blister simply by placing a damp cloth over it, and then holding a hot iron on the cloth for a minute or so until the cloth starts getting dry. The heat and moisture sometimes reactivate the glue. It may be necessary, however, to do this several times.

Unlike veneer that lifts at the edges, a blister can occur anywhere on the surface, maybe even in the center of a table or chest. A blister tells you that the glue no longer bonds the veneer to the frame.

Be careful that you don't keep a damp cloth on the surface too long without applying heat. Otherwise you may also have to repair a water mark.

To fix a blister that won't respond to a damp cloth and hot iron, you have to create a little more damage to fix it. You need a single-edge razor blade or sharp utility knife, a knife with a long thin blade, white furniture glue, a damp soft cloth, and several books to use as weights. This is what you have to do:

1. **With your single-edge razor blade or utility knife, slit the blister in half, going with the grain (fibers) in the veneer, not across it.** See Figure 13-7 for an example. Don't worry. The slit won't be noticeable after you've repaired the piece.

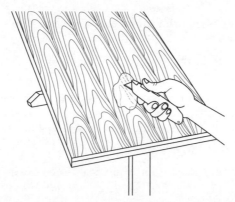

**Figure 13-7:**
Removing
bubbles
from veneer.

2. **Keeping one side flat, work the glue under the other side very carefully with a thin, long blade.** The more flexible the blade is, the easier the job will be.

It's easier to get glue to flow if thinned first with water. Also, syringes are now available for injecting glue in tight spots such as blisters. They work great.

3. **Smear the glue around to coat the underside of the veneer as well as the frame of the furniture.** You can do that by pushing the blistered edge up and down firmly several times.

4. **After gluing the first half, press it down.**

5. **Repeat Steps 2 through 4 on the other half of the veneer.**

6. **Press down hard on both edges to force excess glue out from under veneer.** You can use a rolling pin, roller, or cold iron, but if you use an iron, protect it by placing some wax paper between the iron and the repair to avoid scratching the finish or getting the steam vents clogged.

Be sure to wipe away any excess glue that seeps out of the split. Use a damp cloth to wash it off the surface and then wipe it dry.

7. **After you're certain all the excess glue is gone, weight the blistered area with several old books until the glue has dried.**

# Recaning Chairs

Cane woven by machine makes it easy to repair caning — if you have the right kind of chair. Look at the seat. Does a band of wood on all four sides frame the cane? And is there a "ribbon" between the cane and the wood? If so, you can fix the seat. That ribbon, actually called *spline*, conceals the raw edges of cane.

Cane sheets and spline are sold by the running inch or foot in various widths. (The sheets are from 12 to 24 inches wide.) Both are pressed into a groove carved on all four inner edges of the wood frame. Here's what you have to do to repair them, after you've identified that the caning fits into a groove:

1. **Look in the Yellow Pages under "caning supplies" to find a fabric or do-it-yourself supply store selling what you need.**

2. **Measure the width and length of the old cane seat.**

3. **Next measure the width and length of the groove.**

When you go to the store to purchase sheets of cane, you'll also have to purchase *spline*, the ribbon-like finishing piece. Spline comes in different widths, so you want to get exactly the right width and length that you need for the project.

Also purchase caning wedges. Ask the sales clerk how many you'll need. And have a screwdriver, hammer, utility knife, carpenter's glue, and fine sandpaper handy. Now here's what you have to do to replace the cane seat:

1. **Precut the new cane sheet so that it extends about 1 inch beyond the groove on all four sides of the chair.**

2. **Soak the sheet in warm water for an hour so that it's pliant and easy to work with.**

3. **While the cane is soaking, cut around both edges of the old spline on the chair with a utility knife.** Break the bond of the old glue so you can easily lift the spline out of the groove.

4. **Use a screwdriver to get under and lift up the edges of the old spline.**

5. **Pull out the old spline and then the old caning and set them aside.**

6. **Place the softened sheet of cane on top of the chair, overlapping the groove by about 1 inch on all sides.**

7. **Keeping the pattern square on all edges, stretch the caning slightly and hammer a caning wedge into the groove on each side.** See Figure 13-8A for an example.

When you put the new sheet down, be sure the woven pattern runs straight across and up and down the seat of the chair, not diagonal. Recheck the pattern as you push the first four caning wedges into the groove.

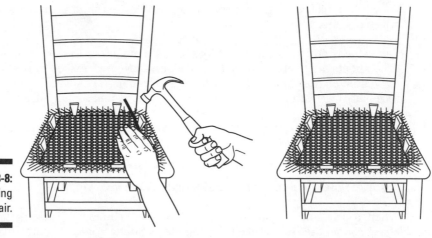

**Figure 13-8:**
Recaning
a chair.

A                                    B

8. **Now hammer a few more wedges into each side.** See Figure 13-8B.

9. **Push the cane into the groove.** Be sure to maintain the stretch and pattern so that it doesn't loosen or slip off square.

10. **Soak the spline in warm water for 15 minutes to soften it.**

11. **Take out the wedges one at a time as you squeeze carpenter's glue into the groove and press in the soft spline working your way around the chair.** To push it down more firmly, use one of the wedges and a hammer to tap the spline into place.

12. **Using a utility knife, trim off the excess cane.**

13. **Sand the cane seat gently with fine sandpaper.**

14. **Spray the cane with lacquer and let it set for a few days before sitting on the chair.**

If only one or two chairs in a set are damaged, match the pattern of the cane to the other chairs. So cut off a sizable piece of the damaged cane to use as a sample and take it to the store with you.

Prior to the Industrial Revolution and machine manufacturing, skilled craftsmen made cane chairs by threading individual strands of cane into holes located around the frame of the chair. They then wove the cane strands together. Unless you're willing to learn the trade, you probably won't be able to fix these handmade chairs by yourself. Look in your local Yellow Pages under the sections for furniture upholstery or furniture repair and refinishing and call each listing to see if someone there knows how to do it and if so, what it will cost.

# Part V
# Working Outside Your House

The 5th Wave    By Rich Tennant

# In this part . . .

Often there's as much or more work to do outdoors as there is indoors. In this part of the book, we tell you how to make repairs to your home's exterior, how to maintain those exciting outdoor leisure areas (including the grill!), and finally, we fill you in on the basics of working with asphalt and concrete.

At least you can take heart that most outside fix-its aren't ongoing. A fix gives you at least a year or two — and most often more — before you have to think about repeating it. And after the house, leisure areas, driveway, and sidewalks are repaired, they're a whole lot easier to maintain. That gives you the opportunity to put off more repairs even longer. You don't need major carpentry skills to do the repairs in this chapter, just a willingness to get things in shape!

# Chapter 14

# Sprucing Up Your Home's Exterior

*E*xposed to sun, inclement weather, and climate extremes, your house and garage can be damaged even when they're in good condition. A good example is what happens when roof shingles get loose or rip off during storms. If you don't notice the damage and repair it, eventually the tar paper and the boards underneath it get soaked. After that, water seeps through the insulation in the attic and onto the plaster or drywall, causing water marks on ceilings and walls. When the ceiling's soaked, it can collapse. So what started out as a minor problem on the outside of your house becomes a major repair entailing quite a bit of time and money to reverse the damage both inside and outside your house.

It pays to be vigilant. Examine your home after storms and keep an eye on things outdoors, as well as what's happening inside. In this chapter, we give you tips about what to look for and how to repair damage to framing, siding, roofing, and bricks. In this chapter, we give you information on how to repair the outside of your home. If you rent, you'll be able to alert your landlord to problems when they're minor. We also talk about siding and roofs, patching mortar, and replacing cracked bricks.

## Shedding the rust

Most of the repairs in this chapter can also be made to outdoor storage sheds and greenhouses. However, steel sheds can rust, and the rust needs to be removed or eventually the shed might collapse. Scrape and sand off the rust and then paint the cleaned surface with rust-resistant paint to protect it from further rusting. Keep in mind that steel can rust in any structure with a steel frame, even if the steel isn't exposed to the weather.

# Repairing Your Outside Walls

Most homes start off with lumber framing. Then we add walls and the roof to keep the frame sound and dry, to keep us warm and safe, and to make homes look appealing inside and out. You don't have to throw up your hands and live with dents in aluminum siding, a hole where the vinyl fell off or melted, or rotted wood shingles that look awful. In any case, all of these need to be fixed because they can lead to problems inside the house.

## Replacing missing or melted vinyl

Vinyl melts when it gets too hot, not only from the sun, but also from grills placed too near the house. You can replace the damaged panels if you have extras or you can try to find vinyl that will match the color on the rest of the house. Start out by calling the supplier that provided the originals. Vinyl panels interlock and are mounted from the bottom up. To get the damaged ones off, you have to lift the panel above the damaged area, unhook the damaged piece, and then hook the new one onto the undamaged panel. You need one or several pieces of vinyl, a zip tool (a tool with a handle and a metal hook which curves under on the other end), a pry bar to pull out nails, tin snips, a hammer, and nails. Here's what to do.

1. **Get replacement vinyl from the contractor or store that sold the siding.**

2. **Slip the curved edge of the zip tool under the undamaged panel just above the damaged area.**

3. **Hook the zip tool into the channel on the bottom edge of that panel, pulling it down.** The panels have lipped, curved edges on the bottom and top so that one piece hooks into the curved channel of another, securing them to each other. See Figure 14-1.

4. **Immediately twist the zip tool downwards.** That should unhook the good piece from the damaged one below it.

5. **With a pry bar, remove nails at the top of the damaged piece.**

6. **Repeat Steps 2 through 5 as many times as necessary.**

7. **Trim the new panels to fit the hole. They should overlap each end about an inch.**

8. **Starting at the bottom, hook a new panel into the channel of the vinyl strip below. Only install nails in the pre-punched slots and leave the nails loose to allow for expansion and contraction.** Now, if you have to replace more than one panel, repeat Step 8, as needed.

9. **When the last replacement panel is anchored, push down on the panel above it while you press it over the lower one.**

**Figure 14-1:**
Fitting replace-ment vinyl to an existing piece.

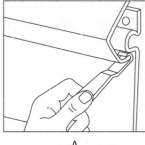 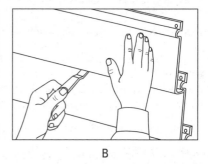

A                    B

Don't try to fix vinyl siding unless the outside temperature is moderate. Vinyl is flexible but becomes stiff and brittle in cold weather. You don't want to crack your replacement pieces.

## *Fixing dents and nicks in aluminum*

Large hail driving at a slant into aluminum siding leaves its mark. So do people. When your siding looks as though it's been knocked out, surprise, it can be fixed quite easily! You need a #6 self-tapping screw — it taps all by itself, no drilling hole first — 120-grit sandpaper, two-part auto body filler, pliers, a putty knife, and paint that matches the siding. Here's what to do:

1. **Screw the #6 self-tapping screw into the center of the dent.** You want it where it's deepest.

2. **Use pliers to pull the dent halfway up.**

3. **Using sandpaper, take off all the paint.**

4. **Fill the dent with the two-part auto body filler.**

5. **Use a putty knife to scrape the surface level with the siding.**

6. **Sand the patch to remove all roughness.**

7. **Paint it to match the siding.**

## Replacing damaged aluminum siding

You can remove a piece of aluminum siding and patch in a new one when it's so badly damaged that it's beyond repair. You need your utility knife, a piece of aluminum siding, a household cleaner, and a silicone sealant. Follow these steps:

1. **Draw a square around the damaged siding.**

2. **Cut the top and side edges, using your utility knife.** Bend the square down.

3. **Cut across the bottom.**

4. **Cut the replacement patch.** Make it 3 inches wider than the patch you removed so that it can overlap the panels on each side.

5. **Clean the area to be patched.**

6. **Take off the nailing strip at the top of the new piece.**

7. **Spread silicone on the back of the patch.** Use clear silicone, which is unnoticeable when it dries.

8. **Press the patch in place, locking the top edge under the piece above and overlapping adjacent panels.**

9. **Lock the bottom edge to the panel below.**

10. **Wipe off excess silicone and clean the patch and adjacent panels.**

Corner edges of aluminum siding, the end caps, get banged into a lot. You cut a corner too sharply and knock into them with ladders, the lawn mower, garden hose, bikes, you name it. End caps are very easy to replace. All you need are replacements, aluminum nails, a pry bar, a utility knife, silicone glue — preferably clear — and paint to match the siding. Follow these steps:

1. **Take off the damaged caps.**

2. **With a pry bar or pliers, remove all the nails underneath.** A screwdriver or cat's-paw can also slip under the heads, lifting them enough to grab with pliers or a claw hammer.

3. **Starting at the bottom and working your way up the corner, slip a replacement cap under the bottom edges of the panels above it.** See Figure 14-2.

4. **Nail the cap down.**

5. **Put the next cap on, repeating Steps 3 and 4.** Do it until all but the last end cap are fastened in place.

6. **Cut the nail strip off the last end cap with the utility knife.**

7. **Spread the silicone glue on the back of the cap.**

8. **Slide it in as you did the others.**

9. **Press down so the adhesive grips the wall.**

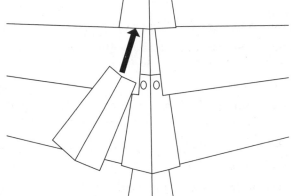

**Figure 14-2:**
Slipping an end cap under the panels above it.

# Repairing wood siding

Wood siding shrinks in cold weather and expands in the summer, especially in wet, humid weather. If it's nailed down so tightly that it can't "move," it will crack and split. You can fix damaged boards or replace them.

### Repairing split clapboard

*Clapboard* is made up of long strips of wood that usually overlap. If you fix a cracked board correctly, you probably won't have to replace the board. And by getting to it quickly, you reduce the risk of moisture damage in the house. You need a screwdriver, waterproof glue for outdoors, aluminum nails for roofing and siding, caulking, and the paint or stain you have on the rest of the house. Here's what to do:

1. **Use a screwdriver to open the crack a little wider.** Don't damage the wood by forcing it open.

2. **Fill the crack with waterproof glue.**

3. **Push the edges of the crack together.**

4. **Nail the edge down.**

5. **Clean the surface of excess glue.**

6. **Countersink the nails below the surface of the clapboard.**

7. **Caulk the nails.**

8. **When the glue dries, sand the crack.**

9. **Finish the clapboard with two coats of paint or stain.**

Cracks can also be caulked with a flexible all-weather caulk. Check with your local hardware store.

### Replacing clapboard strips

If you have to replace 3- or 12-inch-wide clapboard, you need a pry bar, a hammer, a small hacksaw, a keyhole saw, blunt-tipped thin-shank siding nails, and as many replacement boards as you need that are similar to what's on the house. Here's what to do:

1. **Carefully lift the panels above and below the damaged panel.** Place shims under the edges to keep the panels raised and so you can get at the damaged board. Notice where the nails securing the damaged piece are located because that's where you will nail the new panel. See Figure 14-3A.

2. **Use a small hacksaw to cut through existing nails.**

The hacksaw can make a coarse or finer cut, controlled by reversing the blade. When you're cutting wood siding, you want a more precise cut so you don't damage adjacent boards.

3. **Using a keyhole saw, cut the first board into pieces so you can take them out.** See Figure 14-3B. Cut the ends so that joints on the replacement board will not be directly above or below another joint. If they line up, the repair will be noticeable and less weather tight. If necessary, you can also cut through the center of a board and take it out in pieces.

4. **Pry up the split pieces.** Work carefully so you don't damage sound boards. Be sure to get everything out.

5. **If the saw cut into the underlayer, seal the damage with roofing cement.**

6. **Measure the space for the replacement panel, deducting ½ inch from the actual length of the space.** When the board is in, there has to be a ¼-inch gap on either side to allow for expansion.

7. **Cut the new panel to fit and seal the trimmed edges with paint or wood sealer.**

8. **Fit the replacement board in.** You can drive the replacement in without damaging it by placing a block of wood along the bottom edge and hammering on it instead of the panel.

If you're putting in several rows of replacement boards, start at the bottom and work your way up. Put the last board in following Step 8.

9. **Secure the panel with nails.** Place the new nails where the old ones were, and be sure the nails are set ⅛ inch below the surface of the board. Don't hammer nails through any adjacent clapboard or it may crack. See Figure 14-3C.

Never put nails directly into the boards below because doing so will impede expansion and contraction that occurs naturally throughout the year. If the boards can't move, they'll crack and moisture will get into the wood, causing even more damage.

10. **Caulk over the nails and along the joints between the new and old boards.**

Finish the boards with primer. And paint or stain matching the rest of the siding.

Figure 14-3:
Replacing
a section
of wood-
lap siding.

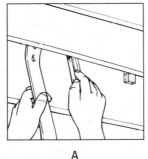 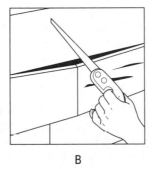 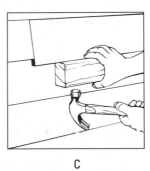

A      B      C

### Replacing shingle siding

Damaged shingle shakes should be replaced to keep the house weather tight and to prevent moisture damage. The process is similar to replacing roof shingles. In this section, we tell you how to do it. You need replacement shingles, a screwdriver, a wood chisel or small pry bar, a plane or sandpaper, a hacksaw, clear caulk, and galvanized or aluminum nails. Here's what to do:

1. **Take out the damaged shingle.** Split and crack it by inserting a small pry bar or screwdriver into the crack. Be careful not to damage adjacent shingles.

2. **With a hacksaw, cut through the nails that are under the shingle above.**

3. **Trim a new shingle to be slightly smaller — ½ inch — than the space it will fit.** There should be a ¼-inch gap between shingles, on each side.

4. **Straighten the sides with a plane or sandpaper.**

5. **Slide the new shingle under the one above.**

6. **Nail it to the frame of the house — not into another shingle — with galvanized or aluminum nails.**

7. **Put another nail into the gap on either side of the replacement shingle, as close to the shingle as possible.**

8. **Caulk under the edges and along the gap to seal it.**

## Patching stucco

You can fill small cracks with stucco caulk and patch larger areas with buckets of premixed patching material that you coat on twice. The first layer is scored with a stiff brush, and then the second applied with a steel trowel. It's similar to working with plaster or concrete — a lot of work, but it can be done by a do-it-yourselfer.

You can also make your own stucco mixture by adding water to dry-mix mortar or mortar cement and sand. And there are pigments available to color the mix, but matching the house isn't easy; when wet stucco dries, the color gets lighter.

### Filling small cracks

If you examine the stucco periodically you may be able to make it easier on yourself because you can fill cracks smaller than ¼ inch wide with stucco caulk. When they're ignored and get larger, you have a lot of work to do. You need a tube of stucco patching caulk, a hammer, a masonry cape chisel or cold chisel, a putty knife, a soft brush, and safety goggles. Here's what to do:

1. **If you're not using a tube of caulk, mix as much patching material as you need for the job.**

   Weather plays a big role in how successful your repair will be. Don't work if it's too humid or colder than 50 degrees Fahrenheit.

2. **Using the chisel and hammer, bevel the crack to make it wider underneath than it is on top.**

   The wedged tip on a masonry cape chisel easily cuts a groove under the surface of stucco.

3. **With a putty knife, carefully work out all loose and cracked stucco in the groove and brush out the pieces if needed.** You need the patch to adhere to a solid base.

4. **Spray water into the hole.**

5. **Squeeze more patching caulk than you need onto the crack.** You want enough to stuff it into the crack with a putty knife, and still have a mound on top of it.

6. **Let it stand for 15 minutes, and then try pushing more caulk into the crack.**

7. **Use your putty knife to smooth off the surface.**

### Filling large cracks and holes

When a patch of stucco falls out or a crack gets wider, you have to resurface the damaged area, as well as remove and repair any adjacent stucco that may be ready to fall out. You can tell when a section is unstable by pushing down on the stucco gently. It should feel solid; if it doesn't, you must remove it. You need one or more tubs of patching material (you have to put on three coats of stucco), wire mesh lath, a wire brush, a steel trowel, a wire comb or rake, water, and a *float* (a board with a handle that smoothes thick compounds such as concrete). Here's what to do:

1. **Remove damaged stucco.** Get all loose pieces off the wall. If the stucco is laid on a solid surface, such as concrete or brick, score the mortar joints or chip out pieces of the concrete to give it a rough surface to improve bonding.

   If wood studs are underneath, tear off the paper underlay except for the edges and replace it with new paper, overlapping the old.

2. **Cover the paper with wire mesh lath and nail it to the wall with galvanized roofing nails or another fastener that retards rust.** The wire mesh will hold the stucco in place.

3. **If you're using a tub of premixed stucco, use the trowel to apply the first coat.** Otherwise, mix the compound according to package directions and then apply it to the wall.

4. **After the stucco starts to stiffen, but isn't yet dry, use the toothed edge of the trowel or the wire rake to score it.**

5. **Use a spray bottle to mist the patch.** Don't soak the area. You should do this about every five hours if it's warm out. In cooler weather, the intervals can be longer.

6. **Wait 24 hours, and then put on a second coat of stucco patch.** It should be ⅜ inch thick.

7. **Level it smooth with the float.**

8. **For two days, spray the patch with a fine mist of water each morning and night.**

9. **Wait five more days for the second coat to finish curing.**

10. **Apply the final layer using the wire rake.** It should be ¼ inch thick.

If your house has stippled stucco, flip stucco onto the surface with the brush, then use the trowel to smooth it in areas.

## *Patching mortar on brick walls*

You'd think brick exteriors are indestructible but the mortar between the bricks isn't. And when it cracks or falls out, repairs are needed to keep moisture from entering into the crack and getting behind the bricks. When that happens, structural damage is a definite possibility. You can replace the mortar — called *tuckpointing* or *repointing*. We explain how to do it in this section. You need a chisel with a narrow blade, a stiff brush, mortar mix, a trowel or pointing tool, and a scrub brush for wiping off excess mortar.

You don't have to buy premixed mortar, although it's the best choice. To make it yourself, mix a small batch of mortar — 3 parts of sand and 1 part of Type N masonry cement. Slowly add water until the mix is stiff enough to form a ball. Then mound it up. The mix should stand without collapsing or slumping. Make only enough to use it within 30 minutes. Mortar sets up quickly and although you can add a little water at first, it soon becomes so stiff it has to be thrown out. At least you have a good excuse for working on the house a little at a time, as long as you do the worst areas first. Here's what to do:

1. **Use a chisel to take out any loose mortar.** Make sure the mortar underneath the area you are about to repair isn't damaged. See Figure 14-4.

2. **Brush out all loose particles.**

3. **Put new mortar into the hole.** While you work, put some mortar on the trowel, held upside down, and push it into the hole with a pointing tool. You can also push it in with your finger.

4. **After the hole is full and is stiff enough to feel hard when you push on it with your finger, pack it in some more.** A wheel rake or jointer does this effectively.

   Sometimes there are irregular or decorative shapes to mortar joints and some require different tools. When you buy your supplies, talk to the salesperson to find out what you need to make your repair. A rough sketch or photo of the surface will help you explain what you have.

5. **Scrub the area with a stiff brush to wipe away particles of mortar on the bricks.**

If you have bricks that are cracked or have fallen out, call masonry contractors to get estimates on repairs. If bricks have *spauled* — pieces pop out of the surface of bricks — most likely there's moisture getting into them.

If a brick building settles, it causes horizontal and/or step-shaped cracks (horizontal-vertical-horizontal) in the mortar between two or more layers of bricks. These start out as hairline cracks, which you don't have to worry about. But if they get larger, patch them with mortar. Far more common, however, are vertical cracks in the mortar caused by thermal expansion and contraction. Bricks shrink in cold weather and expand in hot weather. The problem occurs because the bricks don't go back to their original position if the bond to the mortar fails.

**Figure 14-4:** Chipping out damaged mortar.

Vertical cracks should *never* be patched with mortar, which would only restrict the movement of the bricks even more. When a vertical crack starts getting larger, patch it with a caulking-type compound because it never hardens and thus allows the bricks to move, and there's nothing you can do to stop thermal expansion.

When you see vertical cracks, patch them as soon as the weather permits; otherwise, you can get water damage behind the bricks. Get your patching material from a brick supply wholesaler. They sell materials to contractors and will know what to use to fill in the cracks and how to match the mortar color.

What if you don't use a flexible product? One homeowner diligently patched vertical cracks in the bricks with mortar every year. Eventually the bricks were pushed an inch or more past the ends of the wall and a mason had to redo the brick wall. This also happened at a school in the area and it was a much larger, more expensive project rebuilding the wall.

# Handling Paint Problems

Paint blisters, peels, stains, gets mildew, bleeds, chalks, and cracks, developing long cracks or an alligator-hide surface. These annoying problems are usually caused by moisture or building materials shrinking and expanding in different seasons. We explain some of the problems and what to do:

- **Peeling paint:** Paint peels when there's moisture underneath, coming from inside. Put in vents or new siding. Peeling paint also occurs when the primer was still wet when another layer of paint went on. Sand it down to the primer, or use stripper, and then repaint the primer. Let it dry thoroughly — read the manufacturer's instructions — and then put on the finish paint. And remember, if it's humid or raining, paint products take longer to dry.

- **Blisters:** You get blisters when paint is applied over a wet surface or wet paint. You can pop the blisters, but they'll come back. The best way to handle this is to scrape the paint off and repaint the area all over again.

- **Alligator cracks:** When wet primer is painted or when a paint thinner had too much oil in it, you may end up with alligator cracks. The surface has to be sanded, allowed to dry, and then repainted.

- **Long cracks:** These result from repeated shrinkage and expansion of building materials. Take the paint off, prime it, dry the wall, and then repaint.

- **Stains caused by uncoated nails:** Remove these by sanding, sealing the nail with shellac, and after it's dry, repainting.

- **Mildew:** Mildew forms when the weather's extremely moist or when there's not enough ventilation. You can get the mildew off by scrubbing the area with a bleach and water solution, letting it dry, and then using a mildew-resistant paint on the surface.

- **Chalking:** This occurs when the paint wasn't formulated correctly. Inexpensive paint may chalk, the end result of an inexpensive formula. Wash the area and then repaint it, using a quality product.

# Sealing Cracks with Caulk

If you think only the bathroom and kitchen need caulking, think again. Use that caulk gun everywhere, inside and out. Insert this practical compound in the joints around windows, doors, vents, between the foundation and building, and around chimneys and roof vents. You should seal all joints and cracks. Caulking cuts down on use of expensive utilities — electricity and fuel, barricades cold air, wind, moisture, and keeps heated and cooled air from leaking out, as well as (most) bugs. Even after your house is sealed, be vigilant and inspect the joints once a year. As caulking dries, it shrinks, cracks, and falls out. It may take a couple years, but eventually you'll have to go around the house all over again. When you do, remove the cracked pieces and fill in the holes with fresh caulk. As a reminder of where to put it, look at Figure 14-5.

## Caulk of the walk

You can find several different caulking compounds at the hardware or home improvement store. Don't grab one based on the price. Read the labels because each type is formulated for different things — they adhere best when you use them correctly. *Acrylic latex* is paintable and you can use it in many places, especially on small cracks and joints. *Vinyl latex* adheres to many things and is waterproof. Use it on your tubs and sinks. *Butyl,* which can be painted, should be used outdoors, especially on gutters, flashings around the chimney and other roof pipes, storm windows, and large joints. *Silicone,* the most expensive caulk, can be used around tubs and showers. It adheres well and lasts a long time, but paint doesn't stick to it.

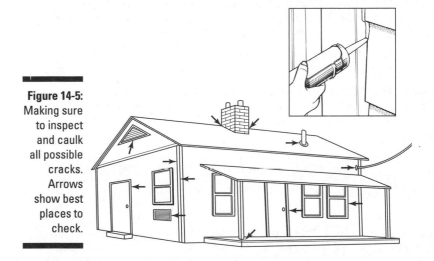

**Figure 14-5:**
Making sure to inspect and caulk all possible cracks. Arrows show best places to check.

# Restoring Your Roof

During a windstorm some roof shingles flutter off as the wind whips under them. Who knows where they land? The only thing we know for certain is that you have some work to do. Roofing shingles have to be replaced or re-anchored if they're to do their job — protecting the house. It's an easy fix-it if you don't mind climbing up on a roof. We explain what to do in the following sections. We also give you some pointers on finding elusive water leaks.

# Replacing and repairing asphalt shingles

When asphalt shingles are loose or missing, you can easily replace and refasten them. And as long as you're on the roof, inspect the others close up, as well as the flashing, to find out whether any shingles are damaged or likely to cause problems in the future. To fix the shingles, you need a pry bar, a hammer, galvanized roofing nails, a utility knife, roofing cement, a caulking gun, silicone caulk, a screwdriver or nail puller, and some matching shingles. If you don't have replacements, take a damaged shingle to the home improvement store and match it as best you can. One bundle isn't expensive and will probably be enough for current and future repairs.

### Adding replacement asphalt shingles

Before looking for loose and damaged shingles, replace the ones that blew away in case it rains before you finish the job. Also, plan to work when it's moderately warm outside; shingles get stiff and hard to handle when it's too cold. And on hot days, the shingles will be so hot that you will damage those on the roof just by walking on them. Here's what to do:

1. **Take off shingles just above the patch.** You should go two rows up and be careful that you don't damage others when you take them out. See Figure 14-6.

2. **Use the screwdriver or nail puller to raise the nails in the bare spot.**

3. **Starting at the bottom, put a new shingle onto the bottom row, overlapping the one below it.** Be sure to follow the line of the rest of the shingles in the row. Your patch will shout, "Look at me," if it angles up the roof.

4. **Nail the shingle to the roof, using the galvanized nails.** If you can't reuse the holes, fill them with roofing cement. You should also cover the nail head with cement. You don't want to leave holes in the roof because water will seep in and damage the wood underneath.

5. **When you get to the last shingle, cut off the nail strip on top with your utility knife.**

6. **Put roofing cement on the back of the shingle.**

7. **Slip the replacement under the shingle above it.**

8. **Press both shingles down firmly so the cement adheres to the roof.**

### Tarring torn and loose asphalt shingles

When a shingle is loose, it dries out, and after time, the bottom edge of the shingle begins to curl. Loose shingles are more likely to fly off in the next windstorm. So we explain how to find and fix loose and damaged shingles below. How do you know a shingle is damaged? Telltale signs are when the grit on top of the shingle starts coming off (you find the sandy substance accumulated in the gutter), tabs are missing, or you've got twigs, leaves, or something else wedged under a shingle. Here's what to do:

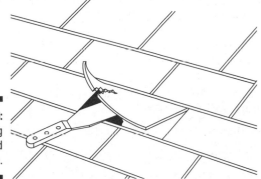

**Figure 14-6:**
Removing
damaged
shingles.

1. **If the shingle doesn't look bad and there's no grit collected in the gutter, lift the edge carefully, and pull out debris lodged under it.**

2. **Coat the underside of the shingle with roofing cement.**

3. **If a shingle is torn, glob roofing cement on top of the shingle to prevent leaks and rips from getting larger.**

## Fixing wooden shake shingles

You'd think wood shakes are trouble free. But they, too, get damaged. And because wood gets darker as it ages, a replacement shingle stands out from all the rest around it. If one on the street-side of the house is damaged, get your replacements from the back or side of your home. The new ones on the back will still stand out until they age, but the only people noticing it will be neighbors. You need a hammer, a pry bar or another stiff-bladed instrument, galvanized nails, butyl caulk, a caulk gun, and a drill. Here's what to do when shakes split:

1. **Drill pilot holes through one split edge of the shake and then the other.**

2. **Nail the sides down.**

3. **Cover the heads with roofing cement to seal them.**

If there's a hole:

1. **Place flashing — a sheet of metal used to waterproof the angle between the chimney and roof — under the shake and covering the hole.** You want to cover the area so water won't penetrate to the roof structure.

2. **Fill the hole with cement.**

If the shake can't be repaired:

1. **Take it out.**

2. **Drive the old nails as far down as you can.** If you have a pry bar, place the handle over the nails and hammer down on it.

3. **Put the new shingle down.**

4. **Place a thick piece of wood along the bottom edge of the shake.**

5. **Hammer on the bottom edge of the block to drive the shake until it's in as much as adjacent shakes.** Don't go too high or drive it in at an angle. It's supposed to look even with the remainder of the row.

6. **Place two nails at the top of the new shingle and drive them in at a 45-degree angle rather than straight down.** If you have a nail set, use it to make the nails flush.

7. **To seal out water, caulk the nail heads.**

## Finding and fixing water leaks

You know the roof is bad when water stains the ceiling or walls. But unless shingles are missing or obviously damaged, finding the leak may be difficult because water can enter the roof in one place and run down to another before it starts soaking in. You may be able to spot the leak if you have an attic and go up there on a rainy day. Then you can mark the area and on a nice day, have a helper tap on the mark while you're on the roof. After you pinpoint the location, apply roofing cement or new shingles as needed. Don't forget to inspect the rubber seals called boots around the electric service and plumbing vent pipes, air vents, and exhaust fan flashing. See Figure 14-7.

If you have a severe winter and your roof isn't insulated well enough to keep the snow from melting, it doesn't have to rain for the roof to leak. When a layer of snow on the roof melts, it first runs down and freezes over the eaves, which causes ice dams, and then the water backs up behind the dam and under the roofing shingles. Ultimately water will seep in through the ceilings and walls. Hardware and home improvement stores sell long-handled roof rakes. We've also seen neighbors on the roof in the middle of winter shoveling the snow off — if you do that, be careful not to cut into the shingles (or fall off the roof!). A thick layer of insulation in the attic or crawl space provides an effective barrier, trapping warm air in the house where it belongs and keeping the roof itself cooler so the snow doesn't melt quite as fast.

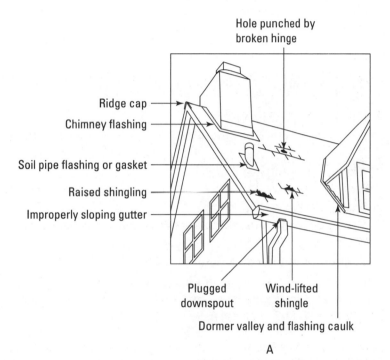

Hole punched by broken hinge

Ridge cap

Chimney flashing

Soil pipe flashing or gasket

Raised shingling

Improperly sloping gutter

Plugged downspout

Wind-lifted shingle

Dormer valley and flashing caulk

A

Actual leak location

Apparent leak location

Wet insulation

B

**Figure 14-7:** Looking for leaks outside your house (A) and inside (B).

## Adding flashing around chimneys and stink pots or plumbing vents

Many roof leaks occur around the chimneys and vents on roofs. Flashing is supposed to go under adjacent roof shingles and then up the chimney or pipe for a couple inches. The joints have to be sealed. If they aren't, the water runs right down through the roof and into the house, although it may travel a little down the roof and actually enter at a lower point. If the sealant leaks or the flashing rips, you should reseal joints. You need a putty knife, a wire brush, roofing cement, and medium-weight sandpaper. Here's what to do:

1. **Using the putty knife and wire brush, take out the old sealant.** You get a better bond if it's gone.

2. **Brush out all debris.**

3. **Apply roofing cement along all joints.**

4. **Using the putty knife, push the cement into all of the joints, leaving a layer on the surface.**

5. **Scrape the putty knife on top of the cement to make it smooth.**

6. **If you have any holes, fill them with roofing cement.** See Figure 14-8.

7. **If you see any ragged edges or areas that have the potential for going bad, smear roofing cement on top of them too.**

8. **If it's the rubber boot around the pipe that's cracked or broken, that can be replaced usually without replacing the whole flashing.**

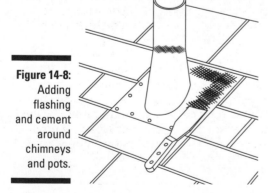

**Figure 14-8:**
Adding flashing and cement around chimneys and pots.

# Fixing flat roofs

Flat roofs are notorious for causing problems and giving owners headaches. Water and snow don't run off as readily as on a sloped roof. If the covering is made of overlapping tar paper with roofing cement spread on top, the edges may peel or rip and eventually standing water will find a way into the house. If you see puddles or pooling on the roof, you should reseal it to make sure it doesn't leak through to the ceiling and walls. You need a flat-edged spade, a utility knife, roofing cement, replacement patches, a trowel, and roofing or fiberglass mesh. If your roof was graveled, a load of fine gravel will be needed to protect the surface from further damage and hold down the tar paper. Here's what to do when the damage has already occurred:

1. **Shovel existing gravel off the roof.**

2. **Look for tears or holes in the tar-paper layer covering the roof, especially along the seams.**

3. **Cut away the bad sections with a utility knife.**

4. **Fill the areas that you intend to patch with roofing cement.**

5. **Put some mesh over each area.**

6. **Layer more roofing cement on top of the mesh on the patch.**

7. **Using a trowel, smooth the cement.**

8. **Put gravel on top of the roof as ballast to hold the tar paper down.**

Put down just enough gravel to cover the tar paper. Adding too much will add unnecessary weight and too many loose pebbles, and both can cause much worse problems. Also, adding gravel to a roof that didn't previously have it isn't a good idea. The roof may not support the additional weight because it probably wasn't designed to handle a lot of extra weight. If you want to do this, first consult with a structural engineer who can determine how much load your roof can take.

Keep an eye on new products being made for flat roofs. Commercial and institutional buildings now use a strong membrane roofing that minimizes seams and adheres to the structure at different points so that it doesn't need ballast. Gravel shifts around or blows off flat roofs when it's windy. And the wind can't get under and lift the membrane because it's anchored. This new product is more expensive than tar paper, cement, and gravel, but definitely worth considering for use on your home.

# Getting Those Gutters and Downspouts in Good Shape

Even though they're galvanized, metal gutters rust on the inside and should be inspected each year for damage. You can brush off the rust, repaint the interior, and even patch small and large holes. In the meantime, be sure to clean out gutters to remove leaves and debris that trap moisture.

To cut down on work, get a mesh cover for vinyl and metal gutters. You can find them in hardware and home improvement stores.

## Clearing clogs from gutters and downspouts

Gutters are especially prone to clogging in the autumn when leaves drop off trees. Falling leaves aren't the only things that clog gutters. Some trees pollinate in the spring, releasing an avalanche of seed pods and fuzz. Spring and summer rainstorms knock tiny twigs off trees; they're too small to be noticed, but large enough to make a dam in the gutters. And if you have youngsters in the house or neighborhood, don't be surprised to find tennis balls and everything else where they shouldn't be. Our kids loved to see who could toss a ball the farthest over the house. Needless to say, they didn't always succeed.

Gutters and downspouts keep rain and melting snow from puddling next to the foundation and causing water problems in and around a home. The water should collect in the gutters, run through the downspout, and drain out into the yard, as far away from the building as possible. But when the gutters and downspouts are clogged, rain just runs off the roof and drops straight down next to the foundation. That can make a wet basement wetter. And if a soggy mass sits in a metal gutter, eventually the metal rusts and holes develop.

You should check your gutters and downspouts at least twice a year — after the trees finish pollinating in the spring and after most of the leaves have fallen in autumn. If gutters are clogged, clear them on a warm, sunny day because standing on an extension ladder on a cold, windy day and scooping out handfuls of wet, decaying matter isn't a pleasant task. All you need is the ladder and a garbage can next to the ladder to catch the trash you scoop out. Or you can just drop the debris and shovel it up into the trash can when you're off the ladder. Next do the downspouts because if they stay blocked, water will back up into the gutter and overflow. To clear the downspout, have someone hand you a garden hose, put it into the top of the downspout, and flush it with water. A plumber's snake also does a good job. If the spout is plugged solid, the only way to clear it is from the bottom — you may even have to take the sections it apart to get at the plug.

When cleaning metal gutters and downspouts, look for rust. If you see any, set aside a day to repair them. We explain how to do it in the section "Repairing holes and leaks in gutters and downspouts."

If you want avoid cleaning out gutters in the future, wire mesh caps are now available. Get them from a home improvement store. Most come with installation instructions.

## Repairing holes and leaks in gutters and downspouts

Walk around the house several times a year looking for trouble spots. If you cleaned the gutters and downspouts recently, you know if and where you have rust. But also look for water leaks, holes, dents, and bent or sagging downspouts. Look at the hardware, too, to find out whether any brackets and hangers are loose or missing.

### Removing rust and patching small holes

If small holes have developed because of the rust, you can fix them. All you need is a wire brush, a garden hose, a putty knife, roofing cement or a gutter caulk, and a clean scouring pad. Here's what to do:

1. **After cleaning out the gutter use a wire brush to loosen rust.**

2. **Flush the gutter with the garden hose.** You can also use pails of water; just tie the pail to a rope and haul the pail up after you're on the ladder.

3. **Use a soap-free scouring pad to rough up the surfaces to be repaired.**

4. **On a dry day, spread roofing cement or gutter caulk with a putty knife onto the bad spots.** See Figure 14-9A.

5. **Run the edge of the putty knife over the patch, thinning the cement at both ends of the patch.**

6. **Repeat as often as necessary to do all the bad spots.**

**Figure 14-9:** Patching gutters.

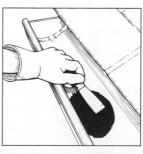

A                    B                    C

### Fixing large gutter holes

You can also repair large holes. You need asphalt-coated glass fabric (available in 4- and 6-inch rolls at home improvement center roof departments), roofing cement, and a putty knife. Here's what to do:

1. **Cut a piece of fabric large enough to cover the hole and extend beyond it on all sides.**

2. **Using a putty knife, apply roofing cement to the area to be patched.**

3. **Place the fabric patch on top of the cement.** See Figure 14-9B.

4. **Smooth the fabric and cement with the putty knife.**

5. **Put down one more layer of cement and let it dry.** See Figure 14-9C.

### Fixing leaks between the gutter and downspout

Instead of water going directly from the gutter to the downspout, it sometimes pours out of the drop outlet, a short connecter that attaches the gutter to the downspout. Refer to Figure 14-9C. That occurs when a metal connector rusts and develops holes. You can patch the holes with roofing cement or replace the drop outlet with a new section of gutter containing the outlet. Follow the patching and replacing instructions for gutters. If you decide to put in a new section, seal the opening of the drop outlet in the gutter with roofing cement around the edge of the hole, and spread it out to make the outlet last longer.

### Replacing a bad gutter section

Rather than tearing the whole gutter down, you can remove a bad section and replace it with a new piece. You need one length of gutter similar to yours (and sufficient to replace the section you want to remove), a hacksaw, roofing cement or a gutter repair compound, and hangers for the patch. Go to the roofing section of a hardware or home improvement store. Here's what to do:

1. **Cut out the bad section with the hacksaw.**

2. **Cut the new gutter so that it will overlap the old by 1 inch on each side.**

3. **Bend the gutter patch, if necessary, to fit inside the existing gutter.**

4. **Seal the ends with roofing cement.**

5. **Nail the new roof hangers in, one at each end.**

6. **Hang the patched section on the new hangers.**

# Replacing Rotted Soffits

If you have an overhang on the roof, it has flat boards underneath called the *soffit*. Sometimes water gets into the space between the bottom of the roof and the boards and when it does, the soffit gets wet and eventually rots. We had a run-in with this problem early in 2004, six months after roofers took off two layers of shingles and laid a new roof, complete with drip edge. We'd had a hard winter: The ice on roofs didn't start melting until early March. Before that, however, we noticed a section of soffit that looked damp. We figured the roofers had forgotten to seal the flashing around a chimney pot with roofing cement, so we cemented it on a day warm enough to work. About a month later, we noticed strips of paint hanging off the soffits — not everywhere, just certain sections. But other boards were also definitely damp.

We asked the supplier what was going on and learned something new. Although the roofers had mostly done a good job, they didn't start the bottom row of shingles low enough to overlap the edge of the roof. That meant that when water streamed off the roof, instead of hitting the gutters, it ran under the roof edge and into the space over the soffit. No wonder they were wet! Luckily we had extra shingles. We cut 4-inch-wide strips and tucked them underneath the bottom row of shingles, leaving ½ inch hanging off the roof. Then we cemented them in place. Now water runs directly into the gutters. We also put more air vents in the soffits to dry out moisture and repainted everything — soffits and house. (It needed it, anyway.)

Go outdoors when you have a light rain on a warm day. Check the gutters and downspouts to make sure water's running through them, not backing up and spilling over.

You can replace a damaged section of soffit, usually made of ¼-inch plywood on older homes; now they're usually aluminum or vinyl. To replace damaged wood, you need a screwdriver, a sawsall, a hammer, nails, screwdriver and screws, and a drill. You also need primer paint, and a brush to finish off wood soffits. Exterior-grade plywood comes in sheets which have to be cut to match the amount of damage, plus 1 foot on either end. Or you can take off the whole piece of soffit and replace it with a piece the same width and length. Here's what to do:

1. **If you think a board seems wet, poke a screwdriver into the wood.** If it goes in easily, you've got a problem.

2. **Figure out how much of the soffit is damaged, and then add 1 foot or so to either end of the damaged area and buy new boards.**

3. **With your saw, cut out the bad section.** Remember to go 1 foot longer at each end just in case the wood there is slightly damaged. You're better off putting in new, sound wood.

4. **If you want to put in vents, cut rectangles in the new board and existing soffits.** Space them out evenly where you want them to be.

5. **Nail the new board to the rafters.**

6. **Mount the vents into the holes you cut in the soffits.**

7. **Fasten them in place.**

You can replace wooden soffits with aluminum or vinyl soffits, and not worry about rotting.

# Chapter 15

# Improving Your Outdoor Leisure Areas

*In This Chapter*

▶ Repairing wood decks, fences, and porches

▶ Fixing chain link and vinyl fences

▶ Tuning up gas grills

▶ Ungumming fountains and sprinklers

▶ Giving new life to old outdoor furniture

*I*f your house has a patio, a porch, or a fenced-in yard, you may eventually discover boards and posts that are leaning or rotting. Even pressure-treated wood is susceptible to the elements. When a board or post gets bad you don't have to tear everything down and start over. You can repair or replace damaged wood and fix chain link and vinyl fences. In this chapter, we guide you through these easy repairs. And we also give you tips about how to prolong the life of your gas grills and tell you what you can do to revitalize outdoor furniture.

## *Working on Wood Decks, Fences, Gates, and Porches*

Homeowners build wood decks, porches, and fences with lumber because it looks good, especially when it first goes in. Quality boards that are pressure-treated and with a high rating — we explain the ratings in the sidebar "Wood and all that rot" — can last about 40 years. But you can't assume that all porches, decks, and fences were built with these boards, so you have to be vigilant and repair damage when you see it. In any case, you need to watch out for moisture, insects, and dry rot.

Most repairs that can be done to your wooden deck or porch are identical to those made to wooden floors. For additional useful information on these types of repairs, refer to Chapter 3.

When you need new wood for an outdoor project, you'll find that pressure-treated wood, which should look green throughout the board, costs more than other types of lumber. Wood rated .25 and .40, however, has a similar cost, so most stores stock only .40-rated lumber. You generally need to special order lumber with a higher or lower rating.

Look for boards with stamps or tags indicating the concentration of preservatives. The quality of pressure treatment can vary, so be careful. Don't buy boards that haven't been stamped or aren't consistently green throughout. Also, someone at the lumberyard or hardware store may advise you to purchase a preservative for coating trimmed edges. We don't think additional preservative is necessary, but it's your call.

## Spot-treating dry rot

Get rid of dry rot by scraping it out, and then fill the hole with epoxy wood filler. You need a chisel or large screwdriver, a dry-rot killer, wood preservative, epoxy wood filler, and a putty knife or trowel. Here's what to do:

1. **Scrape out all of the dry rot, using the chisel or screwdriver.** Test the wood in areas adjacent to the dry rot to make sure no soft spots are developing.

2. **Use the dry-rot chemical to kill the fungus.**

3. **Coat the joist and hollowed area with several coats of wood preservative.**

4. **Fill the hollow area with epoxy wood filler.** Press it down firmly so it spreads into every crevice.

5. **Let the epoxy dry, and then put the floorboards back on as described in the "Replacing rotted floorboards" section.**

Dry rot is a fungus that can decay any lumber that is subjected to the elements. The fungus consumes the cellulose or tissue in wood, leaving a soft skeleton. While not noticeable at first, dry rot eventually becomes powdery. You can test old wood boards by trying to push the tip of a screwdriver, by hand, into the wood. If it goes in easily, dry rot is present. If you find dry rot, the boards should be replaced before the fungus spreads and does more damage.

## Wood and all that rot

Untreated wood has to be refinished or repainted frequently to keep water from seeping into posts, joists, and floorboards. If the unprotected boards don't rot, wood-eating insects may attack and have a feast, or fungi may develop, causing dry rot. To help reduce these problems, people began coating wood with sap, then *creosote,* a tar-based substance, to retard damage. They next developed chemicals and treated lumber before it was sold. (Buyers can also treat the wood with these chemicals themselves )

Any time you're dealing with dry rot, no matter where, treat the wood and adjacent areas with a dry-rot killer first. Then apply a preservative.

Nowadays the best — and most expensive — lumber has chemicals forced into the boards.

Called *pressure-treated lumber,* this lumber contains preservatives that repel termites, fungi, and moisture, the precursors of most damage to wood. Currently the best preservative is chromate copper arsenate (CCA). It's rated .25, .40, or .60 pounds (of preservative) per cubic foot. Forced all the way through the wood, its numbers indicate where the lumber should be used, respectively: for above-ground, ground-contact, or below-ground purposes. The higher the rating, the better the lumber is at repelling termites and fungi. But you must exercise caution in buying pressure-treated wood because how well the lumber is treated can vary. Always get lumber from a reputable dealer.

# *Replacing rotted floorboards*

Instead of replacing a whole deck or ripping out a floorboard that has a section that's rotted, you can cut out the damaged portion and piece in a new section. When you remove the damaged board, cut 1 extra foot off on each side in case the adjacent piece has started to go bad. You need a circular saw, a hammer, nails and/or screws, preservative containing copper naphthenate or another fungicide for dry rot, and either a pry bar, wood chisel, or *cat's-paw*. See the sidebar "A cat's-paw for the dirty work" for an explanation about cat's-paws. Here's what to do:

1. **Cut off the damaged board plus 1 foot off each end.** Try to expose at least three *joists* (the boards or metal beams that support floors and ceilings), so you can anchor the replacement board securely and don't have to worry about it rocking.

2. **Remove all the old nails on the board.** Pound the cat's-paw under each head and raise it high enough to get the claw hammer under it.

3. **Pry the board out.**

4. **Remove the nails from each exposed joist.**

5. **Poke the joists with a screwdriver.** You're looking for *dry rot* — a soft, spongy area on the wood. Dry rot is caused by fungi and is usually found on boats, but it can develop anywhere when wood is untreated or poorly treated.

6. **If there is a spongy area, chisel out the soft wood and then treat the exposed areas with a fungicide.** If you don't treat the wood, the fungi will still be there to cause more dry rot.

7. **If a large area of the joists has to be removed, consult a structural engineer to find out whether the wood is still sound enough to use.** Another option is to purchase some pressure-treated lumber and use it to shore up or replace the damaged joists. We tell you how to do this in the "Adding a joist" section.

8. **If only a small part of the joist rotted, after treating it with fungicide, cover the bad spot with a flashing tin.** A *flashing tin* is a flat, square piece of metal that you can get in the roofing department of a home improvement or hardware store.

9. **Bend the excess metal down on each side of the joist and hammer or press the edges flat.**

10. **Trim a replacement floorboard the same size as the hole.**

11. **Coat the raw edge with preservative if you want to.** Remember, it's your decision. We don't believe it's necessary if you have quality pressure-treated wood.

12. **Nail the floorboard to the top of all three joists.**

Although joists aren't directly exposed to weather, if fungi forms on floorboards, it may also get into the joists. And in very humid climates, fungi can easily start forming on supposedly dry wood, especially if it isn't pressure treated. If you can get under the joists, poke them periodically with a screwdriver to find soft and spongy areas.

## A cat's-paw for the dirty work

A cat's-paw is a small, all-steel pry bar with an octagonal handle and curved, rounded claws. It looks similar to a small, all-steel claw hammer without a head. When you hold the handle upright and drive the claw under the head of a nail, it will raise the nail about ½ inch, enough for you to slide the claws of a hammer under the head and pull the nail out. A cat's-paw is especially useful where you can't remove a board by pounding on the back of it or if you don't want to damage adjacent boards by prying against them. Be aware that the cat's-paw will damage the board you're working on.

## Adding a joist

Adding a joist to a deck is easier than removing a joist and putting in a new one. You just put in the new joist parallel to the old and nail or screw them together. If you want to replace the joist, then follow the directions below. You need a hammer, nails and screws, screwdrivers, shims, and possibly a couple joist hangers. Here's what to do:

1. **Take off all the decking or porch boards that sit on the joist.**

2. **If existing joints are fastened to the house and post, put the new one in that way.** If they're nailed into joist hangers at either or both ends, get replacement hangers. If it's *toe-nailed* (angle-nailed) into the post and/or beam, you need long screws or nails to refasten it similarly.

3. **Fasten the new joist on both ends.**

4. **Replace the floorboards and nail them into place.**

If the joist moves or rocks after it's in, put wooden shims between the edges and the house or between the joist and post to stabilize it.

## Getting rid of mildew on porch and deck floors

If humid weather and rainstorms cause mildew or mold to form on decks and porches, get rid of the invaders as fast as you can. Use a mixture of bleach and water to scrub the area or purchase a commercial-grade product for getting rid of mildew. Otherwise, the area will spread, especially if the damp weather continues. This will work on a roof, too, or on anything that has mold or mildew on it.

If that area doesn't seem to dry out and mildew persists, try drying it with a fan. Or consider tearing out the damaged floorboards and putting in replacements. Follow the steps in the "Replacing rotted floorboards" section.

# Working on Columns and Posts

Peeling paint at the base of a porch column or deck post often indicates that the base has been and still is wet. You can find out how bad the problem is by peeling back a little more of the paint — you have to repaint the column anyway. Now push a screwdriver into the wood. If it feels soft and spongy, it's rotted. Repair it before it gets worse.

## Repairing decorative columns

You can remove the bad wood, seal the solid wood behind it, and camouflage the repair if the damage hasn't penetrated too far. If it has, then you have to replace the column or post. We explain how to do this in the "Replacing posts" section. You need a chisel, wood preservative, large nails, a hammer, and concrete or several graduated sizes of flat boards that can be fashioned into a decorative base. Of course, you have to repeat the repair several times so that all the columns or posts look the same. Here's what to do:

1. **Draw a line around the column about 2 inches above the rotted area and install a temporary brace under the deck, porch, or roof.**

2. **Using a chisel and hammer or a Saws-All (a power reciprocating saw with a long, skinny blade), chip out the damaged wood below that mark, taking out as much as necessary.**

3. **Use a brush or spray bottle to coat preservative on the exposed bare wood.** Get one that retards moisture, as well as termites and fungi. Work it into all the cracks and corners to prevent future rotting.

4. **Build up the new base so that it's high enough to conceal the repair.** You can pour concrete into a wood form you construct around the column and take out the form after the concrete sets (for more on working with concrete, see Chapter 16), or you can purchase a metal post base. For a more decorative base, stack several graduated pieces of lumber or figure out your own design by combining a couple of these ideas and coming up with something unique.

5. **Fasten the base to the column.** If you're using a wood base, angle long nails through the column and into the base. If using a concrete base, drill a hole into the concrete and put a cement anchor in it. If the base is metal, finish it off with a piece of wood on top and anchor it with nails.

   If you put in wood or concrete bases, slope the top slightly and round off the edges so water flows off the base instead of pooling. If you choose wood, alternate the grain as you stack each piece.

6. **Repeat Steps 1 through 5 so that all the columns look exactly the same and have the same dimensions.** Measure precisely.

## Replacing and stabilizing wood posts

Damaged posts eventually cause decks to sag and perhaps even collapse if the load on top of them is heavy. Fence posts lean and wobble, undermining the stability of the whole fence. In the following sections, we explain how to replace and/or stabilize posts.

### Removing old posts

Removing a post and replacing it is a lot of work. But sometimes you don't have an option because there are so many rotted areas on the wood. To remove a post you need a shovel, a hammer, a post-hole digger (rent or borrow it), a drill, wrenches, concrete, tools for working with concrete, and a helper if you can find one. Here's what to do to remove a post:

1. **Dig around the old posts.**

2. **Use a rented post puller and a shovel to dig around and under the post and concrete.** You have to get beneath the concrete base as much as possible and have a big enough hole so that you can rock the post and base out of the ground. (You can use a wrecking bar and 4-x-4 to give you extra leverage.)

3. **Rock the post back and forth, to work it loose.**

4. **When it's loose, pull the post and base out of the ground.**

To reduce the risk of rotting posts, keep grass and weeds around them well trimmed. Vegetation holds moisture and keeps exposed sections of wood wet.

To keep a deck from sagging or collapsing when a post is bad, put in a second post close to the original, while still giving yourself enough room to work.

Any time you want to remove a fence or deck post, get a helper because two people have more strength, and also provide stability and safety.

When a deck post is bad and space is tight, you can add a second post instead of taking out the bad one. Here's how:

1. **Brace the deck with temporary bracing — a stack of bricks or a piece of lumber.**

2. **Dig out the rotted areas of the original post and treat them with a preservative.**

3. **Dig a hole for the new post.**

4. **Following the directions in the following section for putting in replacement posts.** When putting in an additional post, get it as close as possible to the original post.

### *Putting in a replacement post*

Always use pressure-treated wood for replacement posts and set them in concrete, poured over a gravel base, to keep water away from the bottom and sides of the post. The gravel will drain the water away from the bottom of the post and the concrete will buffer it from water-soaked soil.

There are two ways to put concrete into a post hole; the traditional method is to use wet concrete — a combination of Redi-Mix and water. After you add the water to the Redi-Mix and work the water in, you haul it with a wheelbarrow to the post hole. Then you pour in the wet concrete. The second method, described below, is much easier because you'll be pouring dry Redi-Mix into the hole which is already filled with water. It's a lot faster than the old method and isn't such backbreaking work.

Whether you have several posts or just one, the easiest and cheapest concrete to get for the holes comes in bags of Redi-Mix concrete. The sacks, available in different-sized bags, have the sand, gravel, and cement already mixed together. You add water to the mix to make concrete, mixing it in a tub or child's swimming pool, and use a wheelbarrow to haul the wet concrete to the post hole. There's also a new way to setting posts in concrete with no mixing or hauling involved. We explain how to do it in Step 6. You can decide whether to use this new method or use concrete mixed in a wheelbarrow.

Here's how to set posts using the dry-mix method. You need gravel, one or more bags of premixed concrete — depending on how many posts you are replacing — water, and the posts. To set the posts:

1. **Pour at least 4 inches of gravel into the bottom quarter of each hole.** The gravel serves as a drainage area so the post doesn't sit in water when it rains.

2. **Set the post in the gravel in the hole.** Make sure the bottom of the post, at ground level, is in line with the other posts.

3. **Add dry premixed concrete until the hole is half full.**

4. **Add water up to the top of the hole.** Some water will soak in or run off, the rest will get the concrete wet. You won't have to add any more water.

5. **Level the post as you want it.** Don't worry; it will stay there if you let go.

6. **Add dry premixed concrete until the hole is full.** The concrete displaces excess water so you may see some more water running out of the hole.

7. **Using a trowel, smooth out the surface and slope the concrete down toward the ground.** That allows water to flow right off without standing against the wood.

8. **Repeat these steps for each post you replace.**

## Girdling wood posts with concrete

A post doesn't have to be damaged to wiggle from side-to-side or lean in one direction. If it's not damaged by rot, the fence was improperly put in or the post worked its way loose during winter freezes and thaws. A concrete girdle can stabilize posts forever — if they don't rot. You need a claw hammer, tapered surveyor stakes, premixed concrete, and water. Here's what to do:

1. **Take out adjacent fence construction.** You probably will have to go all the way back to the adjacent posts.

2. **Cut or buy a few tapered (top to bottom) surveyor stakes about 24 inches long.** You can get them at home improvement stores.

3. **Drive a stake into the ground next to the post or next to the concrete until the top is almost to ground level.**

4. **Pull the stake out by prying it up with the claw of your hammer.**

5. **Fill the hole with water.**

6. **Level the post.**

7. **Add dry premixed concrete to the top of the hole — excess water will spill out of the top.**

8. **Wait a half-hour or if you plan to do another post, work on it while you're waiting.**

9. **Go to the other side of the first post and repeat Steps 3 through 8.**

10. **After a half-hour, go back to the first post and if it's still not stable, repeat Steps 3 through 8 several times more, each time moving to a different position around the post.** After you encircle and stabilize the post with a concrete girdle, it will never lean again.

Don't rush the job. If you don't give the concrete a half-hour to set, you could end up doing more work than you have to. Be patient. Take a break or start working on another post.

11. **Reassemble the fence the next day.**

## Splinting wood posts

Another way to stabilize a post is to put a splint on it. You need scrap 2-x-4s, a .60 preservative that also protects against water damage, a hammer, and bolts. Here's what to do:

1. **Soak the 2-x-4 splints in preservative for a minimum of 12 hours.**

2. **Dig around the post so that you have room to fit a 2-x-4 splint beside it on two sides.** See Figure 15-1.

3. **Slope the edges of the splints so water runs off.**

4. **Put preservative on the edges.**

5. **Pound the splints into the ground.**

6. **Secure the splints to the pole with bolts.**

7. **Use dirt, pebbles, or gravel to refill the hole.**

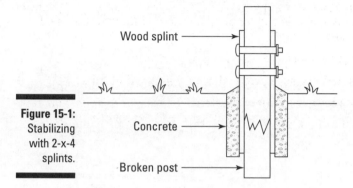

Wood splint

Concrete

Broken post

**Figure 15-1:**
Stabilizing
with 2-x-4
splints.

# Fixing bottom rails in wood fences

You can repair cracked wooden rails and replace those that are too rotted to repair.

### Replacing the rail

To replace a damaged or rotted rail, you need pressure-treated wood, a saw, a hammer, and screws. Here's what to do:

1. **Remove the pickets on the section to be replaced.**

2. **Take out the old rail and if there are nails or screws on either post, remove them as well.**

3. **Cut a new rail the same length as the old one.**

4. **Mount it to the posts on either side.**

5. **Finish it to match the rest of the fence.**

6. **Fasten the pickets to the top and bottom rails.**

### Repairing the rail

If you don't want to replace a rail that's only slightly damaged by rot, you can repair the rail. The rotted patches should not be deep or large. Extensively rotted rails should be replaced. To patch a rail, you need wood preservative, a 2-x-4 or T-brace, a drill, a chisel, and galvanized screws or short deck screws. Just follow these steps:

1. **Remove as many wood pickets as needed.**

2. **With a chisel, remove the rotted wood.**

3. **Kill the fungus that causes dry rot.** We like Get Rot, a product designed for boats, but you can find similar products sold at lumberyards and home improvement stores.

4. **Coat the rail with a moisture-retarding preservative.**

5. **Fill in the chiseled damaged area with an epoxy wood filler.**

6. **If the rail needs to be reinforced, fasten a T-brace to the post and rail or fasten a length of pressure-treated 2-x-4 as described in Steps 7 through 11.** If you use a T-brace, skip to Steps 10 and 11. See Figure 15-2.

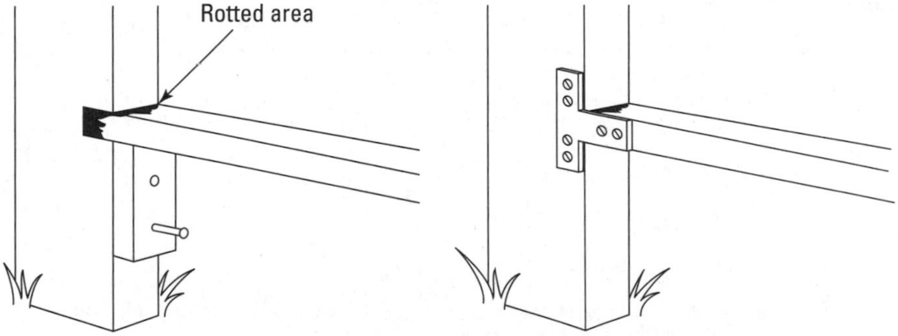

**Figure 15-2:** Bracing a weak rail with a steel brace and a wood 2-x-4.

Rotted area

7. **Cut the 2-x-4 to the size you need.**

8. **Apply preservative to the cut edge if you wish.**

9. **Wedge the 2-x-4 tightly under the rail and onto the post.**

10. **Nail the 2-x-4 (or T-brace if that's what you're using) to the post using galvanized nails.**

11. **Paint the 2-x-4 (or T-brace) to match the fence.**

Butyl caulk will not harden, so apply it to the joints between the rail and post. It will retard rot and also stays flexible if you use it to seal the joints between the rail and post.

# Shoring Up Wood Gates and Hinges

When your gate sags, check the posts on either side to find out what shape they're in. If they're rotted or wobbly, take a look at the "Replacing and stabilizing wood posts" section earlier in the chapter. If the posts look good and don't move, then you probably need to replace the hinges on the gate. They rust, bend, and wear down (sometimes they just weren't strong enough for the gate in the first place). Hinges have to withstand the ravages of weather and that can make them work loose, leaving the gate sticking or sagging.

## Tightening loose hinges

There are a few things you can do to repair loose hinges:

✔ When the hinges are loose, take them off. Fill the holes with waterproof glue, and then stuff in as many toothpicks or kitchen matchsticks — break the heads off — as you can. Hammer them in for a tight fit if necessary. Once the glue is dry, drill holes through the toothpicks/matches and screw the hinges back in.

✔ If the hinges have to be replaced, get replacements that are larger than the originals. They will last longer and need fewer repairs. If the hinge has a strap, bend it around the post because that will make it even stronger.

## Adding a brace

If the posts and hinges are all good and the gate still sags, purchase a wooden screen door brace. It has two metal rods with a turnbuckle in the center. Here's what to do:

1. **Pry up the gate to the height where you want it to be.**

2. **Put blocks under it to keep it there while you're working.**

3. **Attach the turnbuckle diagonally from the bottom corner where the gate swings open to the top on the hinge side.** See Figure 15-3.

4. **When it's secure, tighten the turnbuckle until it holds the gate straight.**

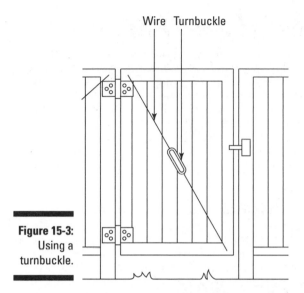

Wire  Turnbuckle

**Figure 15-3:**
Using a
turnbuckle.

# Repairing Chain Link and Vinyl Fences

Metal posts supporting chain link fences don't rot, but they often get rusted after they've been up for a number of years. The best way to prevent rust is to paint the fence and posts periodically. And whenever you see rust, use a stiff wire brush to scrape it off, and then paint over the spot.

## Covering rust with a metal sleeve

Another way to cover rusted areas on posts is to put on a metal sleeve, commonly found at hardware stores. We explain how to do it below. You need a wire brush, spray paint for metal, a sleeve, pliers, and bolts. Here's what to do:

1. **Remove the rust with a wire brush.**

2. **Cover the damaged area with paint formulated for metal to stop further rust damage.**

3. **Put a metal sleeve over the painted section.**

4. **Bolt the sleeve tightly to the post and paint it, if necessary.**

## Replacing sections of fence pipe

Badly damaged sections of metal posts can be cut out and patched with a new piece of pipe and a sleeve to hold the sections together. You need a metal saw, a length of galvanized pipe, a metal sleeve, bolts, and a wrench or pliers. Here's how to patch in a new pipe:

1. **Brace the chain link fencing to hold it up.**

2. **Use a metal saw and cut out the bad part.** Never trim it to ground level. You have to have room for the sleeve around the cut and new pipe.

3. **Fit a new piece of pipe into the space.**

4. **Put a metal sleeve around the ends of the existing and new pieces.**

5. **Bolt the sleeve on tightly.**

## Replacing sections of chain link

A damaged section of chain link fencing can be cut out and replaced. You should replace the whole section between two existing posts. You need to get more screening to match what's there, pliers, and someone willing to help you. It's a two-person job, so call a buddy to help you. Here's what to do:

1. **Rent a fence stretcher.**

2. **Anchor one end of the fence stretcher to each side of the section that's to be replaced.** Leave plenty of room to work.

3. **Straighten the bent wires or untwist them on the bottom and top edges of the damaged fencing.**

4. **Tighten the fence stretcher until the bad section of chain link becomes very loose.**

5. **Unscrew the two wires — one on either side of the bad section.** Save the screws. You'll need them again.

6. **Count the wires in the section you've removed.**

7. **Count off and mark just as many wires on the new piece of fence.**

8. **Straighten or untwist and unscrew the very next wire.** You should have a replacement section that exactly matches the length of the old fencing that's been removed.

9. **Hold the new section, same side up, to the fence.**

10. **Fasten each end wire with the screws you just removed.**

11. **Rebend the ends of wires on each side of the new section to match the rest of the fence.**

12. **Release the fence stretcher.**

# Adjusting Gas Grills

Summer grilling is a great American pastime. But eventually the starter gets balky, the lines get clogged with grease, or there's rust and corrosion. Unless the grill itself has rusted so badly that the bottom is about to fall out, try fixing it. Here are few quick fixes for some of the most common grill problems:

✔ When a gas grill won't light, first make sure the tank isn't empty.

✔ When the starter doesn't work, you can install a new one from stores that sell grills, accessories, and replacement parts.

✔ If you need to replace the gas lines, get out your instruction manual. Manufacturers who make quality grills probably have parts available that they'll mail to your home. Otherwise, there are generic grill parts at do-it-yourself or home improvement and hardware stores. They may not be up to par of the brand name, but you'll get a few years more on the grill. After you have the new line, follow the manufacturer's instructions for replacing it.

If you can't find your manufacturer's instructions, go to the company's Web site. Many companies provide online repair instructions for their products.

If the grill has flames shooting up in one spot, the burner might be rusted out. Here's what to do:

1. **Lift off the grate with the lava rocks on it.**

2. **Lift out the burner.** It may have a screw or two holding it in.

3. **Take the burner to the grill store and buy a replacement.**

Lava rocks and grates often get clogged or coated with grease. They're inexpensive to replace, but if you don't mind the job, you can also clean the old ones by boiling them in water on the stove. Dump off the grease and water and let the rocks cool down before you handle them. They'll be hot!

# Unclogging Fountains and Underground Sprinklers

As water evaporates, it leaves mineral deposits that clog up pipes. You can get rid of the deposits, as well as bacteria that can also build up by adding vinegar, a solvent for mineral deposits. Also add bleach to fountains that re-circulate water. You can also get calcium and lime remover from the grocery store. Just remember to remove all traces of bleach and cleaners before introducing live plants or fish.

You often can get replacement sprinkler heads and install them in minutes. But if you can't find replacements or just want to save a couple bucks, get the mineral deposits off sprinklers by following these steps:

1. **In a pail large enough to hold the sprinkler, mix a calcium and lime product according to the manufacturer's instructions.**

2. **Submerge the sprinkler in it for a few hours.** Be sure to wear safety glasses and gloves when working with any chemicals.

While your sprinkler is soaking you may want to put your showerhead and faucet screens in a cupful of the solution. When you're finished, don't throw the mix away. Use some on a brush on the rust stains on your sidewalk or driveway. And, yes, there's still more. If the rusted sprinkler has changed the color of your siding to brown, scrub some on the stain with a brush dipped in the solution.

Make sure you do this project in a well-ventilated area so no one is hurt by the fumes. If you work in the garage, open the doors.

Set aside some old containers for projects like this and store them in your garage or basement. It's safer to use special containers than to try cleaning them up and putting food in it — it's a potential health risk. Also, if you've used a tablespoon to measure gardening supplies, use that only in the garage. Better be safe than sorry.

# Rejuvenating Outdoor Furniture

Outdoor furnishings have to stand up to a lot of abuse: rain, wind, fat cousin Charlie. In this section, we give you a few pointers on how to keep your outdoor furniture looking young.

# Replacing plastic webbing

We've replaced woven webbing on inexpensive aluminum chairs, chucking them out only after the aluminum frame kinks or splits apart. You can also replace the whole-sheet plastic webbing often found on new aluminum furniture. Webbing is often sold in garden departments in hardware and home improvement stores and also at chain discount stores that sell everything from food to tools and other supplies. Sometimes, however, the product is too specialized to be carried, so you'll have to hunt for a source such as a patio shop or regular furniture store.

To fix plastic webbing, you'll need the new webbing; some scissors that are strong and sharp enough to cut it easily; a compatible screwdriver, nut driver, or socket driver (whatever is needed to remove the old fasteners — check with your local hardware supplier); pliers; a hammer; an awl; a small block of wood; and nuts, bolts, and washers that fit the holes left behind by the old webbing fasteners if they become destroyed. Here's how to replace bolted plastic webbing:

1. **First take out the old webbing by disassembling the chair itself, removing the screws from the frame.** To remove webbing secured by rivets, drill out the rivets or get some end-cutting pliers from your local hardware store. Make sure the old webbing is whole when you remove it — don't cut it apart.

2. **Once you've removed the old webbing, use it as a template for the new webbing.** Place it over the new webbing and cut around it to make your replacement piece.

3. **On the new webbing (and still using the old webbing as a template), fold the edges exactly where and how they were folded in the old webbing.**

4. **Use the hammer and awl (don't cut yourself!) to poke holes in the center of each new fold exactly in the same places that they appeared in the old webbing, so you can secure the new webbing to the furniture.** Put the block of wood behind each area that needs a hole before hammering in the awl, so you won't damage anything under your handiwork.

5. **Lay the new webbing on the furniture so the webbing and frame holes match up.** Reattach with the old fasteners if they're intact, or use the bolts. Insert a bolt and washer into the each hole. Use the pliers to hold the head of the bolt in place while you screw down and tighten the bolt at the other side.

For webbed furniture that uses woven plastic strips, be sure to install the new horizontal strips first, and then weave the new vertical strips into them.

## Looking for special furniture supplies

We recently ordered a large roll — about 25 feet — of rubber banding that supports the fabric cushions on our porch furniture. You might be using a similarly constructed set outdoors with waterproof cushions and bands that run from front of the frame to the back. They weren't in stock anywhere, but we got what we needed through a locally owned furniture store.

If you need bands or accessories for furniture, use the Yellow Pages to save on gas. Talk to a salesperson, explaining what you need. Ask if it can be special ordered. Then go to the store and order it, taking a sample with you to verify that you and the salesperson are talking about the same thing. When we ordered the roll, we discovered that we could also get the clips that hold the bands to the frame. The originals were worn.

Plastic web lining on cast aluminum furniture is often held in place with splines, similar to how screened windows and doors are constructed (see Chapter 4). Many patio furniture manufacturers contain information on their Web sites explaining how to replace the lining, and even sell replacement lining for that purpose. It's much cheaper than buying new!

## Wooden furniture fixes

Most repairs on outdoor wooden furniture are identical to those that can be done to indoor furniture (though, of course, don't bother with the indoor furniture repairs that involve glue!). See Chapter 13 for information on repairing wooden furniture.

## Dolling up metal furniture

Aluminum and cast-iron tables and chairs last forever. But cast iron gets shabby as it rusts and should be repainted periodically to seal the metal and keep it from oxidizing even more. Remove the rust with coarse sandpaper or a wire brush. Smooth the surface with fine-grain sandpaper. Buy one or more cans of spray paint at a paint, hardware, or home improvement store — read the directions while you're still there to find out whether the manufacturer recommends a primer. You can find products specifically formulated for metals in a wide variety of colors.

When you're ready to start spraying, put large pieces of cardboard behind and under the piece. Otherwise, you'll color the patio, grass, or garage as well as the table and chairs.

# Chapter 16

# Repairing, Patching, and Sealing Concrete and Asphalt

- - - - - - - - - - - - - - - - - - - - - - - - - - - - - - - - - - - - - - - - - - - - - - - -

*In This Chapter*

▶ Working on concrete

▶ Fixing asphalt

▶ Solving pavement problems

▶ Stopping up pools

- - - - - - - - - - - - - - - - - - - - - - - - - - - - - - - - - - - - - - - - - - - - - - - -

**W**ouldn't it be great if asphalt, concrete, and paving stones never caused you an instant of worry after they were installed in your driveway or basement (or wherever)? Sadly, even concrete and stone break down or crack. But you don't have to feel stuck with your unsightly asphalt and concrete. Although they may eventually need to be replaced, you can extend the life of the sidewalk, driveway, steps, and paved areas by patching cracks and holes. In this chapter we show you how to do these things. We also give you some tips on your in-ground swimming pool.

# Sealing, Patching, and Leveling Concrete

We take concrete for granted, until it chips, breaks, cracks, and heaves. Then we grumble because it's unsightly, we stumble on raised sidewalks, or it ruins our tires and suspension when we hit potholes in the road.

Blame the weather, especially in areas that experience cold winters. Concrete expands when it's hot outdoors and shrinks when it's cold — that's why road contractors separate sections of newly poured concrete with expansion joints. Ground frost — as much as 3 feet or more below the surface in some climates — causes some soils to expand, and heavy concrete slabs to lift and buckle. Add water to a small crack and if it freezes, you soon have a much larger crack or hole. The soft gravel (often sandstone) used to mix concrete absorbs water and when it freezes, the concrete explodes or *spalls* and as spalling continues, the holes get larger. Spalling also occurs if the concrete was poorly troweled when installed, the mix was weak, or the concrete was poorly cured. Inevitably the whole surface will break down and you'll have to redo the drive or walkway.

That's why it's best to seal and patch concrete driveways, sidewalks, and steps when you see small cracks and holes. Sealing helps prevent or delay the need for costly replacement. We explain how you can patch, seal, and fill cracks in the following sections.

Concrete — not a synonym for cement (which is actually one of the ingredients) — is composed of Portland cement, sand, gravel, and water.

## Filling small concrete cracks

To repair small cracks in a driveway, sidewalk, or basement wall (less than ⅜ inch wide), you need a 10-ounce tube of latex, epoxy, or vinyl concrete patch, a caulking gun, a wire brush, and a wet rag. Use this technique for cracks in the sidewalk, driveway, garage floor, basement, or steps. Here's what to do:

1. **Clean the crack of all debris — dirt, particles of concrete, or pebbles.** Use a vacuum cleaner or soft brush after you've cleaned out larger particles with a wire brush.

2. **If the crack is wet, let it dry or else use a hair dryer.**

3. **Put the concrete patch in a caulking gun.** You can put a tube of patching compound into a caulk gun, roughly shaped like a stubby machine gun. When you pull the trigger, a piston or washer moves, squeezing the tube from the bottom up. You also use caulk guns to seal windows and doors (see Chapter 4), and can use it when sealing the joint between a wall and a tub, shower, or sink (see Chapter 9).

4. **Squeeze the patch into the crack, following the manufacturer's directions.**

   If the crack is deeper than ⅜ inch, fill the crack in layers. Do ⅜ inch at a time, giving the product time to *cure* (dry) between applications.

5. **Wipe excess patch off the crack with a wet rag.**

6. **Let the patch cure.** You can paint the concrete surface if you want after a month, when you're sure the patch is completely dry and settled.

Some basements have concrete-block walls instead of poured concrete. Concrete blocks can crack and break too. If left unattended, these broken blocks may allow ground water to seep into the basement. Repairing the wall may be a little more work than sealing a crack or filling a hole, but you can do it if you're game. See the "Replacing a broken concrete block" section later in this chapter, and also Chapter 3 for more information on dealing with basement cracks and leaks.

## Patching concrete holes

After a crack gets larger and becomes a hole, repairing it takes a little more effort. At this point, patching in a tube is too expensive. Purchase a tub/bucket of premixed (ready-to-use) concrete or mix a small bag of Portland cement, gravel, sand, and water. You need concrete, a trowel, and an epoxy sealant. Here's what to do:

1. **Clean the patch of all broken concrete, pebbles, dirt, and any other debris.** Use a wire brush at the edges to get at loose pebbles under the adjacent concrete.

2. **Spread the patching compound into the hole with a trowel.**

3. **Smooth the patch with a flat mason's trowel or the straight edge of a board.** See Figure 16-1.

4. **Let your patch cure at least 24 hours before letting anyone walk or drive over it.**

5. **Seal the patch with commercial epoxy sealant.** For more about sealing concrete, see "Cleaning and sealing concrete" later in the chapter.

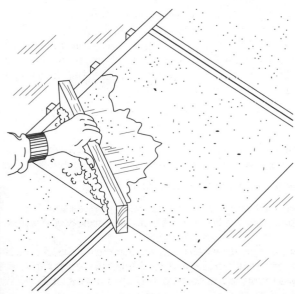

**Figure 16-1:** Sealing and patching concrete holes.

## *Repairing broken edges*

Concrete edges sometimes break off or crumble. If it came off in one piece and you still have it, you can refasten it with an epoxy cement. You need a wire brush, two-part epoxy adhesive, a board, and a concrete block or some other weight. Here's what to do:

1. **Clean the area.** Use a wire brush on the concrete and the edge you want to refasten to get rid of any particles that might impede bonding.

2. **Apply epoxy cement to both surfaces — the pavement or step, and the broken piece.**

3. **Hold it firmly in place for a couple minutes until the bond starts forming, according to package directions.**

4. **Place a board and a concrete block or a pile of bricks against the glued surfaces to hold them firmly until the adhesive cures.** If you glued the edge of a step, place one board against the riser and another board on the step. Put concrete blocks against one and on top of the other board. See Figure 16-2.

5. **Let the patch cure. Depending upon the patch material used you should let it cure overnight or for about a week.**

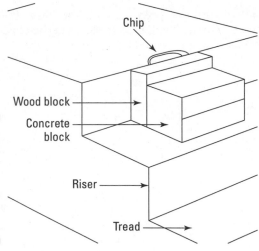

**Figure 16-2:**
Using concrete block and wood to hold glued edge.

Chip

Wood block

Concrete block

Riser

Tread

Epoxy cement seals-in spalls, too. Clean out the popped-out concrete and then follow the manufacturer's directions.

Old concrete that has crumbled, making dust and small bits of concrete, cannot be repaired. You have to hire a contractor to replace the old concrete. It's a big job. We explain why in Chapter 17.

## Repairing large broken concrete edges

If a big chunk of concrete broke off a step, you can repair it without having to spend money on taking out the old concrete and rebuilding the entire steps. If, however, the steps are generally in pretty bad shape — with crumbling concrete on the surface and deep cracks in other parts of the concrete — then the steps should be replaced.

Repairing a large broken edge is similar to repairing a small piece of concrete, but you need to put a rod into the sound portion and the new edge. You need a wire brush, a latex bonding product, concrete patching material, scrap boards, and some concrete blocks or adhesive tape to hold the boards in place while the patch cures. Here's what to do:

1. **With your masonry bit, drill a hole into the center of the break into which you can insert a steel dowel, called re-rod.** Get all loose pebbles and dirt off the step or the bonding agent won't adhere as tightly as it should. The rod will help reinforce the patch. See Figure 16-3.

2. **Clean the broken edge of the step.**

3. **Blow out the hole (a turkey baster works great), coat the rod and the hole with bonding material, and pound it in, leaving half its length sticking out.**

**Figure 16-3:**
Putting a
steel dowel
into the step
and bracing
the patch
with wood.

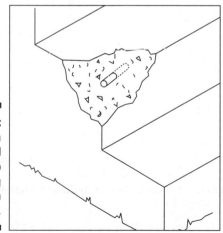

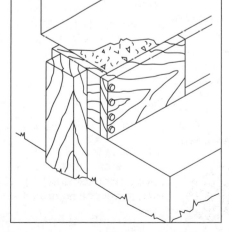

A                                    B

4. **Apply the latex bonding material to the broken edges of the step.** If you use a liquid, you can brush it on and make sure it reaches into all the crevasse.

5. **Mix the patching compound with water and the bonding agent that you used in Steps 3 and 4.** Read and follow the manufacturer's directions.

The mixture will be thick and look like wet concrete. Be careful not to get it too wet because then, even though it's easier to work with, it will not make a strong bond or hold up for long.

6. **Place the scrap lumber up against the step to make a form.** See Figure 16-3.

7. **Tape it on or use some cement blocks to hold it in place, or screw or nail the boards together at the corner.**

8. **Use a trowel to apply the thick mixture to the top and sides of the step, tamping it into place and smoothing out the top.** Experiment with matching the rest of the step. Stipple it with the tip of a dry brush or wash a little cement off the top to make it look old.

9. **Cover the patch with plastic if you expect it to rain within the next 24 hours.** It doesn't matter if the patch gets a little wet, but you don't want rain drumming into it because too much moisture will limit its strength.

10. **After 24 hours take off the plastic, but leave the boards in place for a week while the concrete cures.**

## Leveling concrete

When a sidewalk or any other small slab of concrete — no more than a 4-x-4-foot section — lifts, you can get it back in place if you don't mind hard work. And you might need a helper. It's hard to find professionals willing to do these small jobs, and if your first attempt doesn't work, so what? You'll be right back where you started. You need a couple thick pieces of wood or shims, a chisel or pry bar, a small bag of Portland cement, sand, and water, or a tub/bucket of premixed, ready-to-use concrete.

### Filling low spots

Here's what to do with low spots:

1. **Raise the slab with your pry bar high enough so that you or your helper can stuff wood or shims under one corner.** Put a brick or block of wood under the pry bar as a fulcrum (teeter-totter) so the slab lifts easily. See Figure 16-4.

Don't try lifting the slab or any other heavy weight with only a pry bar. It could cause serious back injuries that may never heal properly.

If you lift the concrete too high or you lift two edges at the same time, it might crack or break. Some concrete is not strong enough to hold its own weight.

2. **Mix some sand, water, and cement into a slightly wet mixture that can be moved easily.**

3. **Fill the low spot with the mixture.** You may have to shove it under the slab with a stick if you aren't able to lift the slab very high. Try to get as much of the mix into the low spots as you can.

4. **Take the shims from the front corners and set the slab in place.**

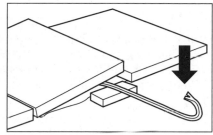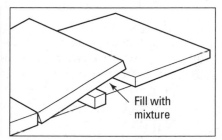

Figure 16-4: Using a brick as a fulcrum to lift slabs and fill low spots.

Fill with mixture

## Leveling heaved slabs

When a slab lifts, it's usually because ground frost or roots from a nearby tree heaved the pavement. You have to try to level the ground under the slab so it can lay flat. Here's what to do:

1. **Follow Step 1 in the preceding section.**

2. **Level the ground under the slab as much as possible by taking out soil that's built up or cutting off the tops of the roots.** If it looks like a primary root system, check with a nursery to find out whether it would destroy the tree or shrub.

Don't reach under the slab with your hand or arm. Use a long-handled shovel, a rake, or a hoe to move dirt around.

3. **After the ground is as level as you can get it, lower the slab back down and repeat these steps, if necessary, at another corner of the slab.** If you should happen to break it, go ahead and break up the rest of the slab and take it out.

4. **Build a new form.** If it's for a sidewalk, it has to match the thickness of the adjacent ones. Then you can easily level the dirt and pour a new section.

## Cleaning and sealing concrete

Cars don't have to be very old before they start leaving oil and grease stains on the garage floor and driveway. You can get rid of these unsightly markers fairly easily and without spending a lot of money either.

Buy a 5 percent solution of muriatic acid and/or a box of TSP (trisodium phosphate) powder. Both are available at hardware and home improvement stores. TSP is available as a liquid, too, but save some money and mix it with water yourself. It also helps if you have an old broom — one destined for the trash pickup — to scour the spot, and a garden hose to clean out the garage afterwards.

Muriatic acid and TSP both eat up oil and grease and both produce pungent odors that you don't want to inhale in tightly closed spaces. So do your work on a day when you can fling open garage doors and windows and leave them open until the floor is clean. If you have lung problems, get a helper so that you can cut down on the amount of time you're inhaling fumes, or have a family member do the job.

Wear safety glasses any time you're working with acids! Some acids will eat your skin, although muriatic acid is not one of them. Nevertheless protect yourself to avoid a skin irritation or rash by wearing old clothes with long sleeves, long pants, and gloves.

Here's how to clean your concrete:

1. **Pour muriatic acid or the TSP solution onto the grease and oil stains.**

2. **Use the old broom to scrub the stains.**

3. **Rinse the pavement with plenty of water from the garden hose.** (You may want to rent a high-pressure hose.) As the acidic water flushes out of the garage, it will clean up the rest of the floor.)

After the floor is clean, you can seal it. Sealing the floor will reduce the porosity of the concrete so that it won't absorb oil quite as quickly. Then you can go to an auto parts supplier and get a commercial product that will chew up surface oil and grease.

Apply a commercial concrete sealer with a paint roller; attach a long handle to it so you can stand up while working.

You can make your own sealant for concrete, using boiled linseed oil and turpentine. Use equal portions, the amounts depending on the size of the surface that has to be sealed. Or take a look at the commercial sealers. They come in various colors, which is a nice bonus for people wanting a new look.

Each fall, seal the surface, especially if you live in the Northern states. It will protect the concrete from the salt used to de-ice streets and from absorbing water that causes spalling.

## Replacing a broken concrete block

Replacing one broken block is tricky because while chipping out the old one, you might inadvertently chip or damage an adjacent block. It's also tedious, time-consuming work to take out a block. But it's even more difficult to find someone willing to come in and replace one block, so you might as well try. You need a power drill, a masonry bit, chisel, hammer, a tub of premixed mortar, a new concrete block, and safety glasses. Here's what to do:

1. **With the drill or a chisel, break out or crack the block into pieces.** Start at the center and work toward the edges. There's less likelihood, then, of damaging other blocks.

2. **Chip off all the old mortar.** The mortar is softer than the block, but again go slowly and be careful not to damage adjacent blocks.

   Always wear safety goggles when you hammer or chip out anything. Pieces fly in all directions and you want to protect your eyes.

3. **Using the trowel, apply mortar to the top of the block below the one you're replacing.** Most beginners tend to spread it too thinly. Apply it liberally, matching the thickness of the existing mortar, and fill the joints fully. See Figure 16-5.

4. **After the bottom edge has mortar, apply mortar to the sides and top of the hole.** A few bits of mortar may drop, but most will stay in place.

5. **Set the new block into the hole.** Be sure it's flush on all edges with the adjacent blocks.

6. **Push mortar in all the spots that it's missing (tuck pointing), and then when it sets a little, smooth a recess in the joints with a trowel or screwdriver handle.** If mortar oozes out, take off the excess with your trowel.

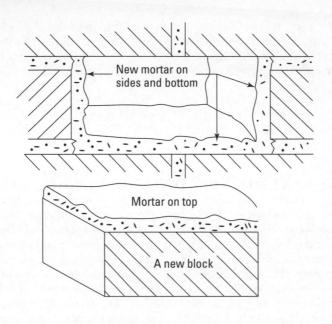

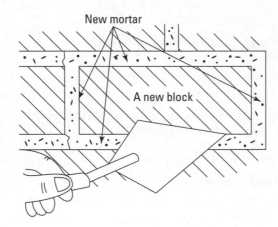

**Figure 16-5:**
Applying mortar to replacement block.

# Sealing and Patching Asphalt

Asphalt is softer and less durable than concrete, but quite a bit cheaper to install. That's why cities and towns use it when roads get bad. But asphalt becomes pliant in the sun and brittle in the cold and tends to develop a myriad of tiny cracks. You can avert some of the damage by sealing an asphalt driveway every two years with a commercial sealant. And you can patch small cracks and holes to make the surface last longer.

Asphalt is composed of aggregate and a petroleum-based, tar-like binder. Try to schedule the work while the outside temperature is a minimum of 50 degrees Fahrenheit since asphalt — workable when it's hot — will quickly cool down and lose its pliancy. If that's impossible, store the mix where it's warm, not outdoors.

Patching compounds composed of vinyl or other products are also available and they are not affected by temperature. If it's late fall and you really need to work on the asphalt, get one of them.

To seal asphalt, buy a 5-gallon bucket of commercial sealant at your hardware or home improvement store. Pour some out onto the driveway, and then brush it around using an asphalt sealer broom. When the area is coated, pour out a little more and work that onto the surface. Repeat these steps as many times as it takes to complete the driveway. Sorry — it takes two complete coats to do a good job. So after the first application dries, start all over again.

Don't get involved with questionable contractors who may ring the doorbell when they see an asphalt driveway, especially one that's deteriorating. Whenever you want to hire some work out, ask friends who they recommend. For more information, see Chapter 18 and the Cheat Sheet in this book.

## Sealing asphalt cracks

If cracks develop in your asphalt, buy a liquid asphalt sealer and a small bag of sand. You also need a putty knife or trowel, and a brush or asphalt broom. Here's what to do:

1. **Clean out the crack with a brush or putty knife.**

2. **Make a paste by mixing sand and a sealant.**

3. **Push the mixture into the crack, using a putty knife or trowel.**

## Filling asphalt holes

When faced with asphalt that has a big hole in it, you've got a bigger job on your hands, requiring more time and effort. It's doable, however, if you don't mind the work. You need a shovel, stones or pebbles, asphalt mix, sand, and a tamper — a weight that will compress the soil and eliminate air pockets. Then the soil won't settle under the patch and eventually cause a collapse.

You can make a tamper yourself. Screw a 2-x-2 piece of wood on end, about 2 to 3 feet long, to a sturdy plank or piece of plywood that is smaller than the hole. This is your tamper. You can also buy one with a flat-steel plate.

(Or, if you're fit, jump up and down or stomp on the patch repeatedly.) Here's what to do:

1. **With a flat-bottom shovel, make vertical cuts all the way around the hole.** You want the sides of the patch to have vertical edges.

2. **Take all loose dirt and debris out of the area you want to patch.**

3. **Use the tamper to compress the surface.**

4. **If the hole is deep, fill it with pebbles or small stones, like pea gravel.** Then you can reduce the amount of asphalt needed for the patch.

5. **When the hole is no more than 4 inches deep, add the asphalt mix.**

6. **Chop into the asphalt with the edge of your shovel. That will help eliminate** air bubbles or pockets and compress the patch so it doesn't collapse later.

7. **Use the tamper now to further compress the asphalt. Pound it down hard all over the patch.**

8. **Add more asphalt mix and repeat Steps 6 and 7.**

9. **When the surface of the patch is no more than an inch lower than the driveway, add more patching material.** This time mound it up on the patch.

10. **Tamp the patch again with force until it's as flat as the asphalt around it.**

# Repairing and Replacing Paving Stones and Blocks

Patio blocks and pavers are just as susceptible to the effects of weather and tree roots as concrete and asphalt — not surprising considering most are made of concrete. You can fix them by taking out the ones that have heaved or settled and then filling the area beneath if it has settled, or leveling the ground if it's no longer flat. Getting under the first paver or patio stone is the biggest job. To realign the patio or walk, you need a crowbar or screwdriver, a level, a cement trowel and, perhaps, a small bag of sand and a shovel. Here's what to do:

1. **Raise a paver or patio block from the center of the sunken or heaved area.** Slide the crowbar or screwdriver under one edge of the block and lift it. Don't try lifting two edges because you might crack the block.

2. **Grab hold of the block and wiggle or pull it up out of place.**

3. **Set the block aside.**

4. **Continue working on adjacent blocks or pavers until you remove all those affected.** Also take out the row of blocks immediately adjacent to the area so that when you put the blocks back in, everything will be flat.

5. **Look at the ground underneath the blocks.** If part of it is raised, remove the excess dirt, clay, sand, or roots. (If it's clay, remove all of it to a depth of three or four inches, then fill that area with sand.).

6. **When you've finished, make sure all of the base is level.**

7. **Reset the pavers or patio blocks and tamp them down carefully with a rubber mallet.**

8. **Fill the joints (between blocks and pavers) with sand.**

Patio blocks or pavers should have a good base — a minimum of 3 inches of gravel and at least 1½ inches of sand. Compact the gravel before topping it with sand; when working on large areas, you can rent a gas-operated compactor at rental centers. Compacting reduces movement caused by weather and settlement. If you put the pavers or blocks directly onto the ground, expect to level them again several times.

If you find clay under the paving blocks, remove it to a depth of 3 or 4 inches. Then fill the area with a layer of gravel and then a layer of sand before you put the block in place. Clay retains water for a long time and may increase buckling and heaving.

# Correcting Minor Pool Cracks

In-ground swimming pools that develop small cracks in the concrete and loose tiles should be fixed before leaks develop. If you have a leak, water may get behind the pool, causing much larger problems later if the water freezes. Plus, you're paying for water you're not using. Here's what you can do to fix the problem:

✔ Before starting the repair, you must drain water from the pool so that it's lower than the area you want to work on.

✔ Always clean the surface that needs to be fixed first. Then scrape out any loose particles or debris. Let it dry thoroughly. Then apply the patching or bonding mixture to the crack or tile.

✔ Fill larger cracks and holes in the concrete with concrete patch compound. It's available in small bags at hardware and home improvement stores, but make sure that the manufacturer recommends its usage specifically for swimming pools. If you can't find any, try a pool supply shop. Mix it according to package directions, and then apply it to the clean, dry areas that need restoring.

✔ Fill small cracks in concrete pools as quickly as you notice them with a caulk tube of mortar repair, following package instructions.

✔ If pool tiles fall off and crack, clean the area behind them and put on more adhesive.

If your attempts to make the repair fail, and you find a leak, call in an expert immediately. The cost of hiring professional help is much lower than paying for gallons and gallons of water running through your meter. See Chapter 18 for tips on hiring a professional.

# Part VI
# The Part of Tens

The 5th Wave                    By Rich Tennant

"Rebecca shuddered with anticipation as she
and Drake approached the broken flush valve.
Drake smiled, and gently reached for his
3/8" wrench and plumbers tape..."

# In this part . . .

The Part of Tens is a popular feature in all *Dummies* books. In this section, we provide you with lists telling you when to get professional help for difficult jobs and how to find the people best suited to work for you. Each Part of Tens chapter is short, concise, and full of good information — just what you need when you're taking care of your home.

# Chapter 17

# Ten Repairs You Should Leave to the Professionals

*In This Chapter*

▶ Recognizing jobs that you should hire someone else to do

▶ Looking at things you shouldn't try by yourself

**S**ure, you can rent, borrow, or buy special equipment and do just about everything around the house yourself. But the questions is, "Do you really want to?" Some jobs require specialized skills or are clearly a pain in the back for the average householder. Others need multiple hands — and backs — and you can't work fast enough on your own to do a good job. And then there's work that local codes specifically say should be performed by a licensed contractor. In this chapter, we talk about the kinds of things you should think about hiring out and why.

## Repairing and Replacing Gas Lines and Fittings

Fixing gas leaks and hooking up gas appliances can be extremely dangerous. Natural gas is as explosive as gasoline and propane is even more so. These gases are heavier than air and sink to the lowest area, lying in wait for a spark to set them off.

Any time you smell gas, leave the house immediately and call the gas company from your cellphone or a neighbor's house.

# Opening Up Microwaves

Electronic circuit boards, *magnetrons* (generators), transformers, and capacitors are what you'll find in a microwave. And the capacitor stores high levels of voltage. So unless you have training in electronics and have specialized equipment, avoid opening up a microwave and poking anything inside it. It's dangerous.

# Rewiring Old Houses

Although frayed wires aren't dangerous in and of themselves, they get that way when the two wires in each line begin to touch and cause a short. Signs of a problem may be that lights mysteriously flicker on and off or there's erratic power to an appliance. It's a job for professionals. They spend five years as apprentices learning the trade. They know what's dangerous and how to pull lines through existing walls and rewire buildings safely. So even though your state and city may not care if householders work on their own electrical systems, get electricians who know what they're doing. Stick to rewiring lamps and other appliances you can unplug.

# Handling Septic Tanks and Fields

Practically speaking, installing or replacing a septic field and tank is no simple task. You need a backhoe to dig the hole, a crane to lift the septic tanks — and dump trucks to haul away displaced soil. And you need to truck in sufficient sand and gravel to make a drainfield bed, and then finish it off with layers of soil and topsoil. Determining where septic fields should be and putting in two 8,000-pound, concrete septic tanks should be done by professionals. You should also call them regularly to vacuum the tanks (usually once every two to three years) and cart the waste away to government-approved dump sites. And it may be smart to have someone from the county health department test the purity of your water and topsoil periodically to make sure you and your family are safe. You have to pay a small fee, but it's worth it to avoid health risks.

One last thought: Don't bother buying those cans of enzymes that claim they'll eat waste in a septic tank. There's no way a small can of anything can handle all the sewage that's in there. Save your money so you can have your septic tank vacuumed, or pay to test for water and soil purity.

# Repairing Cold Furnaces

Other than changing the filter, there's not much an average householder can do to fix a malfunctioning furnace. Like so much today, furnace manufacturers embraced electronics and electronic ignition burners. So it's probably best if you restrain yourself to changing the filters every month to six weeks during the cold-weather months. And don't forget, before you call repair, check the circuit box. You can't come close to guessing how many times people call for service only to find that all it took to get the furnace working again was resetting the circuit breaker. Then to add insult to embarrassment they're still liable for the house call — paying the minimum fee charged by service companies.

Be sure to have the furnace serviced annually by a professional technician, and ask whether they'll do central air at the same time. Many companies have packages for annual inspection and cleaning of both, which can save you a lot of money in the long run. They can also clean out the central air vents.

# Evicting Termites and Other Stubborn Beasties

You may bait a trap with cheese and catch a couple field mice. Or use a bug bomb to get rid of flying insects. But if you have a serious problem with termites, carpenter ants, or other critters, call in a professional extermination service. You may have to stay out of your house for 8 to 12 hours to avoid the fumes, but with a professional to do the job, at least you won't be inhaling it while it's being sprayed. Termites travel underground to their next source of food and they burrow into your floor joists, columns, and beams unseen, behind walls and under floor coverings. Sometimes it takes drilling into concrete and soil to make holes into which the pesticide is poured. And for serious infestations, the company very likely will come back several times to retest and retreat the premises. There's no way the average householder can be as effective as a good exterminator.

Some "exterminators" offer humane trapping and "relocation services" for raccoons and other critters if you want the animals out of your property but don't want them hurt. This is highly recommended for furry animals that escape your best efforts and won't leave your home alone!

# Doing Complex Carpentry

You may be able to put up studs and replace rotted boards, but if you want to decorate ceilings and walls with intricate moldings and trim that's not available at the home improvement centers, a carpenter or professional woodworker may be needed. You need specialized cutting and sanding tools to carve intricate trim. And you won't get the job done quickly if you're just a novice. And if you're not sure you want to replace studs and floor joists, a carpenter can help there too. See the "Tearing Out Interior Walls" section in this chapter for more information. Carpenters can also make short work of hanging doors and installing new and replacement windows. Yes, it will cost more than if you do it yourself. But what's more important — time or money? You have to decide.

# Removing Old Roof Shingles

If you have two layers of shabby shingles on your house and want to replace them, think twice about doing the job yourself. Even though you can purchase a roofing shovel to get under the old shingles and tar paper, it's backbreaking work to lift and scrape them off. It can be dangerous too, depending on the height and slope of your roof and your age. Professionals take safety into account, and no doubt they aren't bothered by heights. Forget about being macho. This isn't a task for a novice.

# Tearing Out Interior Walls

You may know how to tear down a wall and rebuild it. But unless you can identify load-bearing walls and know how to keep the house from collapsing in on itself, don't take anything out without getting advice from a structural engineer. Work on load-bearing walls only after you put in columns and beams to shore up the weight. An engineer can tell you exactly where and how to do this so that you don't risk taking out the house itself.

# Pouring New Concrete and Asphalt

It's much more difficult than you think to spread wet concrete around and create a smooth new surface on a driveway, patio, or sidewalk. But you can patch the old, as we explain in Chapter 16. You have to hire an asphalt contractor to lay or replace an asphalt driveway.

# Chapter 18

# Ten (Okay, Twelve) Tips for Hiring a Repair Specialist (When All Else Fails)

### In This Chapter

▶ Knowing what you need

▶ Finding out who to call

▶ Specifying the work

▶ Looking at quotes

▶ Knowing what's in the contract

*N*o matter how handy you are, some jobs require skilled, licensed contractors with specialized training and equipment. Sure, you can find long lists of electricians, plumbers, builders, and carpenters in the Yellow Pages: But what should you be looking for? How can you tell one established company from another? What can you believe? If you feel that picking a company blind is a lot like playing "Pin the Tail on the Donkey," you're right. Get a pin, close your eyes, stick it into the page, and call whichever number you've selected. Then hope that you haven't made a mistake.

It doesn't have to be that way. In this chapter, we give you some suggestions that will launch you on your way to getting good service from an established, professional company. There are also excellent "independent contractors" available. They're more difficult to check out and you'll need to rely mostly on references. Just be sure they're insured.

# Recognize How Urgently Your Home Needs Help

Before picking up the phone, figure out whether you have a routine service call, a nuisance that you can live with until Monday, or an emergency that needs immediate attention. What do you want the service company to do? Are you willing to pay weekend or night prices or can you buy two bags of ice cubes — one for the freezer, the other for the refrigerator — and wait until Monday to make the call?

There's a big difference between a plugged-up toilet and a drain that's pumping sewage back into the house. If the furnace conked out, what's the weather like? Will extra sweaters and blankets help you get through the weekend or is it so cold and blustery outside that waiting for service could jeopardize your health and the water pipes?

Do you smell gas? That's an emergency you should act on right away. Call the gas company immediately, not furnace repair.

# Get Names, Names, and More Names

You may not know a contractor, but a friend, neighbor, or someone in the family might. Ask them who they recommend and why. Were the plumber's charges reasonable? Did the furnace repair service respond quickly? Did the roofers clean up after themselves? And, most telling of all, would your friend call the same company again to do more work?

Don't settle for just one name unless you have a simple repair — something that will take about an hour to fix. If you have a big project, such as reroofing the house, get the names of at least three companies and plan to talk to all of them.

Many cities have companies or consumer advocacy groups that rate service providers, such as "Angie's List" (www.angieslist.com). They often have annual subscriptions for homeowners and businesses who often hire service providers.

# Use Licensed Professionals

Everybody knows a plumber, carpenter, or friend who does side jobs for some extra income. These folks usually do the work for less money than an established service company. Going with Uncle Joe is okay if you want someone to unplug the toilet. But if you're looking for a contractor to put in a new bathroom or rewire the house, ask yourself whether a moonlighter, who might not be licensed, is really a good idea. Unlicensed workers might not know or follow local and state building codes.

If the work you have done isn't up to par, you may have to pay the piper when you want to sell your property. Inspections are now a routine part of the selling process, giving prospective buyers assurance that a house is in good shape and up to code. So, if the inspector deems something to be shoddy, inadequate, or unsafe, your home probably won't be approved for sale until the deficiencies are corrected. Then you'll have to pay someone else to do the work again.

Professionals cost more for a reason: Along with their professional training and background, they know local and state codes, when it's necessary to get permits, what they can't do because of environmental or other legislation, and how to do things right. See the "Asking for Credentials" section for more information on how to select a contractor.

# Check for Bad Apples

Okay, you've got a few names. Now what? Start out by calling the Better Business Bureau (BBB). They won't tell you who to hire, but they will let you know whether a specific contractor has any unresolved complaints made by customers. For more information about BBB criteria for accepting complaints and the kinds of complaints they do not accept, contact your local Better Business Bureau or visit their Web site at www.bbb.org.

In most communities, there are professional organizations for specific trades, as well as umbrella organizations, such as a homebuilders association. Reputable companies and/or professionals usually belong to one or two of these professional organizations because it adds to their credentials.

Pay attention to work being done on houses in your neighborhood. If you see work that you like, whether on a driveway, windows, roof, and so on, get information and feedback about the person doing the job from your neighbor. Then keep the info in a file just in case you later need help on a similar project.

# Avoid Companies That Ring Your Doorbell

Think twice about doing business with any company that rings your doorbell. They canvass neighborhoods, looking for older roofs and windows, or unsealed asphalt driveways. Perhaps some do a good job; others disappear as soon as they have their money and if the workmanship or materials used are shoddy, you have no recourse. You may find that the phone number is out of service or the address may not exist. Or even if the company operates in the city, they might not return your calls. Be careful!

# Make the Initial Contact

Now you're ready to phone the contractors still on your list. You want to get some general information and if you like what you hear, ask each to come out to your house to give you a quote. Let everyone know upfront that you will be getting quotes from a couple others.

Here are some things you should ask about:

✔ **Before you make the call, have a good idea of exactly what work you want done.** Explain what's wrong and ask whether they do that kind of work. (Some contractors only do commercial or industrial projects. Don't expect them to come out to your home.)

✔ **Take notes throughout the entire process.** That way, you won't lose information or be confused later about who said what, especially when you're comparing estimates.

✔ **Ask what's included in their fees.** Is there a walk-in-the-door minimum? How much? Ask about warranties and guarantees. Will they clean up after themselves? Who cleans up? Do they haul the trash away? If it's important to you, ask if they take checks and/or credit card payments.

✔ **Ask how long the work usually takes.** Will the time fit into your schedule? If not, then you may have to adapt your own schedule to compensate for the work time.

---

## Calling those references

Don't be apprehensive about calling your contractor's references. Most people are happy to praise or complain about the service and workmanship a company provided for them. Ask whether the contractor did a satisfactory job.

Did they finish on time? Did they clean up afterwards? And most telling of all — would the reference call the contractor again? You can ask if they'd mind if you go to their house to look at the work.

---

✔ **Ask if they provide a free estimate for their work.** Most contractors do, so be suspicious of anyone who won't.

✔ **Ask for references for work done on similar projects.** The Better Business Bureau highly recommends contacting contractor references before hiring one.

✔ **Wrap up your phone call by saying you're seeking information and will call back when you're ready to make appointments.** Or you can get an appointment immediately. You're not obligated to the contractor either way.

Be sure to ask a contractor to come to your home to talk about the project and give you a verbal estimate. It does not cost anything, nor does it commit you to hiring anyone. The contractor knows you're getting bids from several others. The home visit is also important because it's an opportunity for you to judge whether or not you'd like that person to work on your home. It's not quite like choosing a partner for life, but if the chemistry is wrong, back off! Calling someone to your home does not mean you're committed to hiring that person.

You may hear the words *estimate*, *bid*, and *quote* used interchangeably, but there's a difference between them. A contractor will give you a verbal estimate, or price range, for a job. It can't be exact because he or she has to check out the prices for materials, and so on. Then you'll get a bid — a written quotation — detailing the job and costs for labor, materials, and any add-ons, such as a dumpster. The written bid is usually good for the next 30 days.

# Ask to See Credentials

The person or company you hire should be bonded, registered with the city or county, and licensed by the state. (Licenses are generally renewed every year or two, depending on what state you're in.) While those credentials are no guarantee that you'll like the contractor's work, at least you'll know that he is licensed and it does give leverage with them if you have to take them to court, call the BBB, or contact the agency that issued the license. If the contractor wants to stay in business, he needs licensing. And your contractor should be insured for workers' compensation, property damage, and personal liability insurance. Independent contractors might not have workers' comp, but they should have proof of medical, disability, and liability insurance, and up-to-date registration. Call the insurer to verify insurance coverage. Then call the state, city, and county housing authorities to verify the licensing and bonding.

# Communicate Exactly What You Want Up Front

During the contractor's visit, give the contractor a clear picture of what work you want done and don't change it midstream. Think the project through before they walk in the door or give you a quote or contract. It's okay to ask for suggestions, say on a remodeling job, or for professional advice on which furnace is best. But after you accept their quotes and sign a contract, don't make any changes. So if you signed your contractor to install a new high-efficiency furnace *only*, don't start thinking about adding on new or rerouted duct work while they're in the middle of working on your home. That sort of thing can be contracted and done after the current project is finished.

If the contractor knows exactly what you want upfront, it helps him to ensure that the work done is top-notch. Being indecisive with a contractor creates frustration and will only give you headaches and work that's delayed or not as good as it could have been.

# Compare Bids

Now that you've talked to several companies and they've been out to see your project, you should ask for and receive several detailed bids in writing from each one. (If you don't hear from a contractor, it means they're too busy to take on another job or not interested in doing the project. Rarely will they communicate — they just drop out of sight.)

If you convey a clear picture of what work you wanted to each contractor, comparing the bids should be easy. You'll see what each contractor includes in services. You should also have an itemized list of materials that will be used and how much they cost and what you have to pay for labor.

The bid should say what work will be done, for instance, tearing off the old roofing materials, and then laying tar paper and putting down new asphalt shingles. That allows you to compare one bid to another. You don't want to end up having one contractor talking about apples while the other mentions oranges.

The bid should include an agreed-upon payment plan, say 10 percent down, and the rest upon completion of the job. Look for the extras, clean-up included, a warranty on parts and labor, start and completion dates — although they might change if the job before takes a little longer or the weather interferes with completion of your job. And be sure the bid gives a name, phone number, and address, in case you want to contact them afterwards.

The low bid looks attractive, but before you settle on it, make sure you're not getting a better deal from another bidder, perhaps a two-year guarantee on parts or labor instead of one. Or clean-up after the job that's not on the other bids. And here's where your intuition comes in. Would you prefer working with one or the other? Do you have any reservations about one company more than the others? Don't sign a contract if you sense a potential for a personality clash or differences of opinion. Then make your decision.

## Find Ways to Save Money

Be sure the contractor knows that you're getting quotes from others. If one needs work to keep employees busy, that may tip the quote to be lower than the one from a company swamped with jobs. Conversely, if all contractors are swamped at the moment, you can expect bids to be high. If you can, then, delay the project for a while.

Wait for an "off" season. If you want a new driveway, call early in the spring or late winter. Most homeowners don't put in replacement windows in late fall or early spring. If you can put up with heat loss for a day or two, you may get a lower bid from the installer.

## Spell Out What the Contract Covers

After you've made a decision, you'll get a contract from the provider. It should be detailed, including the company's name, address, and telephone number in the letterhead. It should state exactly what services are provided, what work will be performed, start and completion dates, and exact prices for materials and labor. Make sure there's a sentence or clause that says the contractor is responsible for cleaning up and hauling away old materials. The warranty or guarantee should be in writing right on the contract. It should include the payment schedule and it should be signed by both you and the contractor.

# Make Payments

The contractor probably will want an initial payment before work begins. But never, *under any circumstances,* agree to pay everything upfront. Your only recourse for shoddy work, unfinished work, or a messy job site is to withhold payment. It's the only way you'll get satisfaction. After the money is in their pocket, you'll rarely, if ever, get them back to do the work to your satisfaction.

A friend of ours gave the go-ahead for an expensive replacement roof. The contractor wanted its money upfront because the materials were expensive — and got it. For months afterward, we heard numerous complaints from our friends because they were still cleaning up roofing materials and nails left in the yard. Sure, they called the contractor back and he promised to come back. Then he just ignored their calls. The roofer had what he wanted — all his money. Making more on another job was his only concern.

Here are several rules of thumb you can follow to make sure the same thing doesn't happen to you:

- ✔ Give the contractor a deposit of 1 percent of the total cost, or $100.

- ✔ You can pay for materials once they've been delivered — generally about 50 percent of the total job. The rationale is if your contractor doesn't show up, you can always hire someone else to do the job.

- ✔ You shouldn't pay the last 40 to 60 percent — the labor costs — until the work is completed and cleaned up to your satisfaction.

Don't even agree to pay all but 10 percent of the bill up front. Some contractors deliberately tack an extra 10 percent onto their bid so they can walk away from that extra cash if they choose. Withhold all of the cost of labor until the project is done!

# Index

• *N* •

• *O* •

• *P* •

## BUSINESS, CAREERS & PERSONAL FINANCE

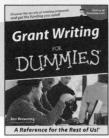

0-7645-5307-0

0-7645-5331-3 *†

**Also available:**

- Accounting For Dummies †
  0-7645-5314-3
- Business Plans Kit For Dummies †
  0-7645-5365-8
- Cover Letters For Dummies
  0-7645-5224-4
- Frugal Living For Dummies
  0-7645-5403-4
- Leadership For Dummies
  0-7645-5176-0
- Managing For Dummies
  0-7645-1771-6

- Marketing For Dummies
  0-7645-5600-2
- Personal Finance For Dummies *
  0-7645-2590-5
- Project Management For Dummies
  0-7645-5283-X
- Resumes For Dummies †
  0-7645-5471-9
- Selling For Dummies
  0-7645-5363-1
- Small Business Kit For Dummies *†
  0-7645-5093-4

## HOME & BUSINESS COMPUTER BASICS

0-7645-4074-2

0-7645-3758-X

**Also available:**

- ACT! 6 For Dummies
  0-7645-2645-6
- iLife '04 All-in-One Desk Reference
  For Dummies
  0-7645-7347-0
- iPAQ For Dummies
  0-7645-6769-1
- Mac OS X Panther Timesaving
  Techniques For Dummies
  0-7645-5812-9
- Macs For Dummies
  0-7645-5656-8

- Microsoft Money 2004 For Dummies
  0-7645-4195-1
- Office 2003 All-in-One Desk Reference
  For Dummies
  0-7645-3883-7
- Outlook 2003 For Dummies
  0-7645-3759-8
- PCs For Dummies
  0-7645-4074-2
- TiVo For Dummies
  0-7645-6923-6
- Upgrading and Fixing PCs For Dummies
  0-7645-1665-5
- Windows XP Timesaving Techniques
  For Dummies
  0-7645-3748-2

## FOOD, HOME, GARDEN, HOBBIES, MUSIC & PETS

0-7645-5295-3

0-7645-5232-5

**Also available:**

- Bass Guitar For Dummies
  0-7645-2487-9
- Diabetes Cookbook For Dummies
  0-7645-5230-9
- Gardening For Dummies *
  0-7645-5130-2
- Guitar For Dummies
  0-7645-5106-X
- Holiday Decorating For Dummies
  0-7645-2570-0
- Home Improvement All-in-One
  For Dummies
  0-7645-5680-0

- Knitting For Dummies
  0-7645-5395-X
- Piano For Dummies
  0-7645-5105-1
- Puppies For Dummies
  0-7645-5255-4
- Scrapbooking For Dummies
  0-7645-7208-3
- Senior Dogs For Dummies
  0-7645-5818-8
- Singing For Dummies
  0-7645-2475-5
- 30-Minute Meals For Dummies
  0-7645-2589-1

## INTERNET & DIGITAL MEDIA

0-7645-1664-7

0-7645-6924-4

**Also available:**

- 2005 Online Shopping Directory
  For Dummies
  0-7645-7495-7
- CD & DVD Recording For Dummies
  0-7645-5956-7
- eBay For Dummies
  0-7645-5654-1
- Fighting Spam For Dummies
  0-7645-5965-6
- Genealogy Online For Dummies
  0-7645-5964-8
- Google For Dummies
  0-7645-4420-9

- Home Recording For Musicians
  For Dummies
  0-7645-1634-5
- The Internet For Dummies
  0-7645-4173-0
- iPod & iTunes For Dummies
  0-7645-7772-7
- Preventing Identity Theft For Dummies
  0-7645-7336-5
- Pro Tools All-in-One Desk Reference
  For Dummies
  0-7645-5714-9
- Roxio Easy Media Creator For Dummies
  0-7645-7131-1

\* Separate Canadian edition also available

† Separate U.K. edition also available

Available wherever books are sold. For more information or to order direct: U.S. customers visit www.dummies.com or call 1-877-762-2974.
U.K. customers visit www.wileyeurope.com or call 0800 243407. Canadian customers visit www.wiley.ca or call 1-800-567-4797.

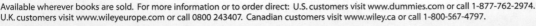

0-7645-5146-9

0-7645-5418-2

**Also available:**

- Adoption For Dummies
  0-7645-5488-3
- Basketball For Dummies
  0-7645-5248-1
- The Bible For Dummies
  0-7645-5296-1
- Buddhism For Dummies
  0-7645-5359-3
- Catholicism For Dummies
  0-7645-5391-7
- Hockey For Dummies
  0-7645-5228-7

- Judaism For Dummies
  0-7645-5299-6
- Martial Arts For Dummies
  0-7645-5358-5
- Pilates For Dummies
  0-7645-5397-6
- Religion For Dummies
  0-7645-5264-3
- Teaching Kids to Read For Dummies
  0-7645-4043-2
- Weight Training For Dummies
  0-7645-5168-X
- Yoga For Dummies
  0-7645-5117-5

## TRAVEL

0-7645-5438-7

0-7645-5453-0

**Also available:**

- Alaska For Dummies
  0-7645-1761-9
- Arizona For Dummies
  0-7645-6938-4
- Cancún and the Yucatán For Dummies
  0-7645-2437-2
- Cruise Vacations For Dummies
  0-7645-6941-4
- Europe For Dummies
  0-7645-5456-5
- Ireland For Dummies
  0-7645-5455-7

- Las Vegas For Dummies
  0-7645-5448-4
- London For Dummies
  0-7645-4277-X
- New York City For Dummies
  0-7645-6945-7
- Paris For Dummies
  0-7645-5494-8
- RV Vacations For Dummies
  0-7645-5443-3
- Walt Disney World & Orlando For Dummies
  0-7645-6943-0

## GRAPHICS, DESIGN & WEB DEVELOPMENT

0-7645-4345-8

0-7645-5589-8

**Also available:**

- Adobe Acrobat 6 PDF For Dummies
  0-7645-3760-1
- Building a Web Site For Dummies
  0-7645-7144-3
- Dreamweaver MX 2004 For Dummies
  0-7645-4342-3
- FrontPage 2003 For Dummies
  0-7645-3882-9
- HTML 4 For Dummies
  0-7645-1995-6
- Illustrator CS For Dummies
  0-7645-4084-X

- Macromedia Flash MX 2004 For Dummies
  0-7645-4358-X
- Photoshop 7 All-in-One Desk
  Reference For Dummies
  0-7645-1667-1
- Photoshop CS Timesaving Techniques
  For Dummies
  0-7645-6782-9
- PHP 5 For Dummies
  0-7645-4166-8
- PowerPoint 2003 For Dummies
  0-7645-3908-6
- QuarkXPress 6 For Dummies
  0-7645-2593-X

## NETWORKING, SECURITY, PROGRAMMING & DATABASES

0-7645-6852-3

0-7645-5784-X

**Also available:**

- A+ Certification For Dummies
  0-7645-4187-0
- Access 2003 All-in-One Desk
  Reference For Dummies
  0-7645-3988-4
- Beginning Programming For Dummies
  0-7645-4997-9
- C For Dummies
  0-7645-7068-4
- Firewalls For Dummies
  0-7645-4048-3
- Home Networking For Dummies
  0-7645-42796

- Network Security For Dummies
  0-7645-1679-5
- Networking For Dummies
  0-7645-1677-9
- TCP/IP For Dummies
  0-7645-1760-0
- VBA For Dummies
  0-7645-3989-2
- Wireless All In-One Desk Reference
  For Dummies
  0-7645-7496-5
- Wireless Home Networking For Dummies
  0-7645-3910-8

# Do More with Dummies

## Products for the Rest of Us!

**From hobbies to health, discover a wide variety of fun products**

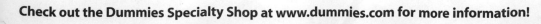

**DVDs/Videos • Music CDs • Games
Consumer Electronics • Software
Craft Kits • Culinary Kits • and More!**

Check out the Dummies Specialty Shop at www.dummies.com for more information!  **WILEY**

## HEALTH & SELF-HELP

0-7645-6820-5 *†

0-7645-2566-2

**Also available:**

- Alzheimer's For Dummies
0-7645-3899-3
- Asthma For Dummies
0-7645-4233-8
- Controlling Cholesterol For Dummies
0-7645-5440-9
- Depression For Dummies
0-7645-3900-0
- Dieting For Dummies
0-7645-4149-8
- Fertility For Dummies
0-7645-2549-2

- Fibromyalgia For Dummies
0-7645-5441-7
- Improving Your Memory For Dummies
0-7645-5435-2
- Pregnancy For Dummies †
0-7645-4483-7
- Quitting Smoking For Dummies
0-7645-2629-4
- Relationships For Dummies
0-7645-5384-4
- Thyroid For Dummies
0-7645-5385-2

## EDUCATION, HISTORY, REFERENCE & TEST PREPARATION

0-7645-5194-9

0-7645-4186-2

**Also available:**

- Algebra For Dummies
0-7645-5325-9
- British History For Dummies
0-7645-7021-8
- Calculus For Dummies
0-7645-2498-4
- English Grammar For Dummies
0-7645-5322-4
- Forensics For Dummies
0-7645-5580-4
- The GMAT For Dummies
0-7645-5251-1
- Inglés Para Dummies
0-7645-5427-1

- Italian For Dummies
0-7645-5196-5
- Latin For Dummies
0-7645-5431-X
- Lewis & Clark For Dummies
0-7645-2545-X
- Research Papers For Dummies
0-7645-5426-3
- The SAT I For Dummies
0-7645-7193-1
- Science Fair Projects For Dummies
0-7645-5460-3
- U.S. History For Dummies
0-7645-5249-X

# Get smart @ dummies.com®

- **Find a full list of Dummies titles**
- **Look into loads of FREE on-site articles**
- **Sign up for FREE eTips e-mailed to you weekly**
- **See what other products carry the Dummies name**
- **Shop directly from the Dummies bookstore**
- **Enter to win new prizes every month!**

**\* Separate Canadian edition also available**

**† Separate U.K. edition also available**

Available wherever books are sold. For more information or to order direct: U.S. customers visit www.dummies.com or call 1-877-762-2974.
U.K. customers visit www.wileyeurope.com or call 0800 243407. Canadian customers visit www.wiley.ca or call 1-800-567-4797.